The Disabled State

HEALTH, SOCIETY, AND POLICY
A SERIES EDITED BY
SHERYL RUZEK AND IRVING KENNETH ZOLA

THE DISABLED STATE

Deborah A. Stone

TEMPLE UNIVERSITY PRESS
PHILADELPHIA

Portions of Chapter 5 originally appeared in Deborah Stone's "Physicians as Gatekeepers," *Public Policy* 27, no. 2 (Spring 1979): 227–254. Copyright © 1979 by the President and Fellows of Harvard College. Used by permission of John Wiley & Sons, Inc.

Tables 1 and 2 on page 8 are excerpted from Robert H. Haveman, Victor Halberstadt, and Richard V. Burkhauser, *Public Policy Toward Disabled Workers: Gross-National Analyses of Economic Impacts.* Copyright © 1984 by Cornell University. Used by permission of the publisher.

The Epilogue is excerpted from *Cross Creek*, by Marjorie Kinnan Rawlings; copyright renewed 1970 Norton Baskin. Reprinted with the permission of Charles Scribner's Sons.

Temple University Press, Philadelphia 19122

Published 1984
Printed in the United States of America

Library of Congress Cataloging in Publication Data

Stone, Deborah A.
The disabled state.

(Health, society, and policy)
Includes index.
1. Insurance, Disability.
2. Disability evaluation.
3. Handicapped—Government policy.
I. Title. II. Series.
HD7105.2.S86 1984 362.4′0456 84-8760
ISBN 0-87722-359-9
ISBN 0-87722-362-9 (pbk.)

TO SYBIL AND STEVE

Nothing is so difficult to distinguish as the nuances which separate unmerited misfortune from an adversity produced by vice. . . . What profound knowledge must be presumed about the character of each man and of the circumstances in which he has lived, what knowledge, what sharp discernment, what cold and inexorable reason!

Alexis De Tocqueville, "Memoir on Pauperism"

Contents

Preface

As a graduate student studying national health insurance in West Germany, I thought I had come upon a strange native practice of having doctors certify workers for short term wage-replacement benefits. That doctors should diagnose illness, prescribe treatment, and get paid by public health insurance agencies seemed only natural to me; that they should also preside over an enormous income transfer program astonished me.

When I returned to the United States with my reports of how the natives behave, I quickly learned that medical certification for non-medical benefits is a red-blooded American custom. But I probably wouldn't have found the phenomenon strange and puzzling if I had first discovered it in my homeland. Living abroad turns out to be an excellent way of getting oneself hopelessly lost, and there's nothing like being lost to make one see the exotic monsters in ordinary forests.

In the first draft of the first chapter of my Ph.D. thesis, I included a few pages about physicians as gatekeepers to non-medical benefits. Suzanne Berger, the chair of my thesis committee, matter-of-factly suggested that the idea was worth saving for my second book. Until then, it had never occurred to me that I could just decide to write a book (I somehow thought books happened to people), or that I could write a book to explore something fascinating, much as one signs up for a tour to find out what a place is all about. And if my first discovery hinged on my being out of context, the second surely depended on Suzanne's putting things out of order. From the perspective of the next book, the one in the typewriter looks more like a stepping stone than a mountain.

The idea for this book became a constant companion. I read about it, spoke about it, clipped articles, and collected anecdotes. Two years ago, Suzanne and I had lunch in a Chinese restaurant. We talked about my book, still unwritten. Suzanne was enthusiastic, but my fortune cookie was somewhat skeptical: "A good memory does not equal good black ink."

I followed the cookie's advice and retreated to my house in New Hampshire with Aunt Emma, my new word processor. I had brought her home on sheer faith (having not the slightest experience with her kind) and a promise from my colleague Larry Bacow that he would get me out of any jam. Larry kept his promise a thousand times over, starting with my first call to ask "Does the cable plug go in with the colored side up or down?" Aunt Emma, for her part, gave me everything I asked for in good black ink.

Computers give you only what you ask for, though, so I am grateful to my friends and family, who gave me what I needed as well. Beverly Bader gave me courage to unplug the phone. Martin Krieger sent jokes and certificates-of-merit. My sister sent ten pounds of chocolate bits. Dave and Judy Brenner, with some trepidation about having a schoolmarm nextdoor, adopted me as a neighbor and taught me lots I needed to know without ever making me feel like a pupil.

An author can decide to write a book, but shaping and polishing it is decidedly a collegial affair. Alex Merton virtually took over my job at MIT, demonstrating all too well that professors aren't really needed to run a first-class university. Later, Alex made friends with Aunt Emma and coaxed her to yield up hundreds of scattered footnotes into a single file—no small task. My research assistants, Vicky Hattam and Lee Perlman, made friends with numerous librarians (at least, that's their version) in order to keep me plied with materials I requested. Lee wrote some insightful memos on particular research questions, and Vicky helped me think through the structure of the general argument. The students in my seminar on The Welfare State gave my manuscript such a thoughtful reading and me so much good advice that I should have paid *them* tuition. To John Coleman, Lois Olinger, Jean Schroedel, Steve Smith, Boaz Tamir, Andy Tager, and Mark Templer I give my warm thanks.

There were plenty of people to whom I wished I could assign my manuscript, and one of the things I treasure most about academia is how generous people are with their intellectual efforts. Several people took time to read all or part of the manuscript and give me careful comments: Larry Bacow, Suzanne Berger, Henry Brehm, Joshua Cohen, Martha Derthick, Robert Fogelson, Martin Krieger, Keith Lind, Michael Lipsky, Dan Metlay, Lucian Pye, Stanley Reiser, Harvey Sapolsky, William Simon, Paul Starr, Irving Zola, and, as always, my father. Only they and I know how much unnecessary text you have been spared by the intelligent copy-editing of Pat Sterling. And perhaps only other authors will understand my appreciation of Michael Ames and David Bartlett, who run the kind of publishing house all of us dream of finding. To these people, I offer special thanks and my standard absolution: no blame for the errors that remain, but should any come to light, I hope someone will console me with a collegial ice cream sundae. I'll provide the chocolate bits.

Goshen, New Hampshire
April, 1984

The Disabled State

Introduction: Disability in the Welfare State

Medical certification of disability has become one of the major paths to public aid in the modern welfare state. Various forms of disability insurance—such as disability retirement pensions and industrial accident compensation—are familiar examples of this phenomenon, but there are numerous other medically contingent benefit programs as well; in both Europe and the United States, they are growing so rapidly that media and policymakers in many countries have proclaimed a new "crisis" of disability insurance. At the same time, more and more handicapped and disabled citizens are organizing as active interest groups to seek equal access to public and private facilities, equal educational and employment opportunities, monetary compensation, and various special privileges, all on the basis of some medically certified disability.

There are, of course, many ways one might choose to examine the phenomenon of disability. Psychological analyses tend to regard it as an individual experience, with an eye to understanding how physical and mental limitations interact with personality development. Economic analyses treat disability as a social position with its own income stream, much like a job, and seek to explain the extent to which individual choice determines the assumption of the disabled role. Sociological analyses focus on the institutions that treat, house, and manage disabled people—including families, schools, hospitals, and rehabilitation clinics—and above all, they examine disability as a stigmatized social status, exploring the means by which stigma is created, maintained, and resisted.

The analysis presented here adopts a political approach. Its basic goal is to explore the meaning of disability for the state—the formal institutions of government, and the intellectual justifications that give coherence to their activities. Thus, this book focuses on disability as an administrative category in the welfare state, a category that entitles its members to particular privileges in the form of social aid and exemptions from certain obligations of citizenship. Why does the state create a category of disability in the first place, and how does it design a workable administrative definition?

The focus on political privilege is meant to be a conceptual lens, not an exclusive vision. The argument that disability functions as a privileged category is meant in a very precise sense: the state accords special treatment to some people who are disabled. Disability accounts for a substantial proportion of income redistribution and, in much smaller measure, for the distribution of some fundamental privileges and duties of citizenship—the obligation to serve in national defense, to obey the laws of the state, and to honor financial agreements. The reverse side of the "privilege" of being disabled is the harshness of social treatment of those who are not officially categorized as disabled but are nonetheless unable to achieve a decent standard of living. The very act of defining a disability category determines what is expected of the nondisabled—what injuries, diseases, incapacities, and problems they will be expected to tolerate in their normal working lives.

To argue that disability creates political privilege is not to deny that it also entails handicap, social stigma, dependence, isolation, and economic disadvantage. The fact that the state creates a formal category for the disabled within its distributive policies and accords this category privileged status does not obviate the myriad ways in which the disabled suffer in both private relationships and treatment by public institutions.

Medical certification has become the core administrative mechanism for a variety of redistributive policies. A simple catalogue of the direct monetary transfer programs based on illness or disability is impressive. In the United States, a host of pension programs provide for early retirement due to disability. These include the Social Security Disability Insurance program, the separate Civil Service Retirement system for federal employees, service-connected and general pensions for veterans, military disability retirement plans for members of the armed services, the Railroad Retirement system, and hundreds of state and municipal employee plans. European countries, too, have retirement systems for the permanently disabled. As in the United States, there tends to be a major system of social security covering most workers, supplemented by a series of occupationally based schemes for workers who historically have been well organized—railroad employees, miners, farmers, and civil servants, to name the most common groups.

Unlike the United States, European governments generally provide cash benefits in lieu of wages to people with temporary disabilities and illnesses, as well as the long-term or permanent disability pensions described above. These "sickness benefits" operate in Europe as part of a national health insurance scheme. The insured person draws sickness benefits for a period of one or two years, and if his disability has not been eliminated within the specified time, he is switched into a permanent pension program. In the United States, public programs for short-term income replacement are relatively rare. Most government employees at all levels have these benefits, and there are five states with compulsory temporary disability insurance programs. Otherwise, such benefits are provided primarily through voluntary sick leave plans in private industry and through commercial insurance policies.[1]

Another whole set of programs in both Europe and the United States is based on disabilities caused by work. Most European countries have industrial accident insurance, and in the United States, all states operate workers' compensation programs. Federal government employees are covered under the Federal Employees Compensation Act, and state and municipal employees are usually covered under special state laws. Still other income maintenance programs base eligibility on a combination of financial need (or "means test") and disability. The federal Supplemental Security Income program and several state general relief programs are examples. There is even one disease with its own federal cash assistance program—black lung disease.

Not only does disability provide the basis for many cash transfer programs; it also provides exemptions from some important obligations of citizenship. Military service is perhaps the most important and probably the first area where disability-based exemptions were introduced. In the United States, medically certified disability has provided release from military service during times of compulsory draft. During the Vietnam War, in particular, many other forms of military disqualification were curtailed or discontinued (e.g., occupational, student, fatherhood, and hardship deferments), leaving medical disqualification as the major vehicle by which men could escape the draft.[2] It is significant that medical disqualifications survive when a government decides to tighten its military exemptions policy. Exemptions based on disability have an enormous intuitive appeal because the requirements for physical fitness among soldiers are so obvious. The other deferments can simply be eliminated; medical deferments may be altered but must be preserved.

The criminal justice system is another area where medically certified disability can provide exemption from normal obligations and sanctions. The insanity defense is the most important example. Because conviction for a criminal act requires a demonstration that the defendant was capable of understanding and controlling his actions at the time of the crime, certification of certain mental illnesses can provide immunity from the normal sanctions of criminal law. More recently, other medically certified conditions, too, are being considered as defenses in criminal trials.[3] As the connection between organic changes and behavior or mental capacity becomes clearer, there will be even more pressure on courts to expand the use of medically certified disability as a defense. Severe illnesses and dependence on medical aid may also be used to mitigate sentencing or to avoid court related duties such as answering subpoenas and testifying.

Further, to a still small extent, disability can provide an exemption from the normal civic obligation to honor one's debts. Public utilities (telephone, electricity, gas) in many states may not terminate service to a sick or disabled person who cannot pay his or her debts if the person provides some kind of certification from a doctor—usually a simple letter.[4] Essentially, this policy amounts to the automatic extension of credit to certain consumers based on medically certifiable conditions. In 1971, Congress almost enacted an income tax exemption for the disabled[5]—a move that would certainly have raised the stakes in disability certification. A somewhat ludicrous example of disability-based tax exemption comes from Belgium, where blind citizens are not required to pay the normal television tax.[6]

Several other important legal entitlements are also pegged to medical certification of disability. Special education is based at least in part on clinical evaluation of the child.[7] Before the Supreme Court decision in 1972, a "legal" abortion in the United States was always contingent on certification of medical need, and since then, the medical requirement has been a feature of many proposals to limit abortions. Nursing-home care is provided at public expense only to those elderly people who have a demonstrable medical need (usually evidenced by a prior hospital admission), even though most such care is custodial rather than medical. Finally, special access to public housing is often given to the disabled. In the United States, this special access is relatively informal; it includes shortened waiting periods or allocation of larger apartments to people with medically certified special needs. In Sweden, which has an income-tested municipal housing subsidy program, part of a disability pension is not counted as income, permitting the disabled to qualify more easily for the housing subsidy.[8]

The Crisis of Disability Pension Programs

As disability entitlements proliferate, there is at the same time a widespread sense in both the United States and western Europe that disability pension programs are somehow in crisis. As with other so-called crises in social policy, this view derives primarily from concern over the rapid growth of the programs and the expenditures they entail, and only secondarily from a concern with program adequacy or efficacy. One can now find a wealth of published material about the size of disability pension programs in several countries, along with various explanations about why they have been growing so rapidly, particularly during the late 1960s and early 1970s.[9]

Of course, there are great differences in specifics of national programs—eligibility criteria, benefit levels and duration, and monitoring procedures—and in the growth rates of programs for particular subgroups of the population. Yet when one looks at the figures for several countries in cross-national perspective, some remarkable similarities stand out.

First, many programs seem to have grown rapidly during the late 1960s and early 1970s. This growth is reflected in both the number of beneficiaries of the programs (see Table 1), and the level of expenditures for the disabled (see Table 2). In the United States, the number of beneficiaries of long-term disability programs (*excluding* those for work-caused injuries) nearly doubled between 1960 and 1970, from about 3.7 million to about 6.7 million.[10] In 1977, public expenditures for the disabled through public income assistance, service, and health care programs amounted to over $47 billion. Smaller programs for particular groups of disabled citizens (such as the blind, or blind veterans) and general welfare programs for which the disabled are only a small part of the clientele (such as Aid to Families with

Table 1 Growth in Beneficiaries of Disability Programs

Country	*Beneficiaries as Percentage of Employed* 1968	1978	*Annual Rate of Growth (%) 1968–1978*
Federal Republic of Germany	11.3	15.1	2.5
France	8.4	8.8	2.6
Italy	9.0	18.0	8.1
Netherlands	4.4	13.0	11.3
Sweden	5.3	8.7	5.2
United Kingdom	6.3	7.8	1.8
United States	9.3	14.7	7.0

Source: Robert Haveman, Victor Halberstadt, and Richard Burkhauser, *Public Policy Toward Disabled Workers: Cross-national Analyses of Economic Impacts* (Ithaca, NY: Cornell Univ. Press, 1984), Table 5.1. Figures include social security, industrial accident, health, farmers', civil servants', employers' and veterans' insurance, as well as public assistance, tax savings and other in-kind transfers.

Table 2 Growth of Expenditures for Disability Income Support Programs

Country	*Expenditures as Percent of National Government Spending* 1968	1978	*Annual Rate of Real Growth (%) 1968–1978*
Federal Republic of Germany	12.9	15.7	5.3
France	12.3	6.6	6.7
Italy	10.4	25.6	12.7
Netherlands	5.8	13.6	18.6
Sweden	2.6	4.3	11.7
United Kingdom	3.8	2.9	.5
United States	5.8	8.0	6.3

Source: Robert Haveman, Victor Halberstadt, and Richard Burkhauser, *Public Policy Toward Disabled Workers: Cross-national Analyses of Economic Impacts* (Ithaca, NY: Cornell Univ. Press, 1984), Table 5.1. Figures include social security, industrial accident, health, farmers', civil servants', employers' and veterans' insurance, as well as public assistance, tax savings and other in-kind transfers.

Dependent Children) account for another $23 billion.[11] Even estimated very conservatively, disability expenditures account for at least 17 percent of all social welfare expenditures in the United States.[12]

The issue that concerns analysts in most of these countries is simply growth, however measured. The time periods for the data may vary slightly,[13] but the point is always the same: that there has been an alarming increase in the expenditures for and number of beneficiaries of disability pension programs and, consequently, that these programs are requiring ever higher taxes and consuming ever more of the GNP.

A second trend common in all countries experiencing a "disability crisis" is that the growth of programs seems to have peaked in the mid-1970s. A decline in growth rates beginning about 1972 has been noted for Finland, Sweden, and Denmark and about 1975 for the United States, the Netherlands, and West Germany.[14] The flurry of policy proposals to stem the growth of programs occurred after growth rates had begun to slow down.

Third, disability benefits are increasingly awarded for those disorders that are hardest to assess. There has been a growth in the proportion of all awards granted on the basis of mental as opposed to physical conditions. And, at least in some programs in the United States and the Netherlands, there has been an increase in the frequency of awards based on muskoloskeletal disorders, which include lower back pain.[15]

Fourth, there has been an increase in the value of disability benefits relative to those of other transfer programs (such as old age, unemployment, and welfare) and relative to the value of the average earnings in society. In most countries, the level of disability benefits is indexed to wages or prices, and adjustments are made annually or semiannually. Observers in several countries have speculated that people are using disability programs as a source of income because, in comparison with other possible sources, the benefits are more attractive.[16]

Fifth, there has been a decrease in the rate of terminations of disability pensions, either by death or by recovery.[17] Thus, where disability programs have experienced high growth rates, there has been not only an increase in the number of applicants and the number of claims awarded but also a decrease in the number of people leaving the rolls. The meaning of this trend is unclear, but harbingers of crisis often take it to indicate that the programs are ineffective because they are rehabilitating fewer people.

A sixth common trend is that in all the countries with substantial disability program growth, there have been significant statutory and judicial changes in the program eligibility criteria. The most important of these is the redefinition of "disability" to include or give greater weight to the availability of suitable jobs. The Netherlands, West Germany, and Sweden have all expanded the definition from a rather more narrow medical and vocational concept to a broader concept tied to a standard of living and the state of the labor market.[18] Outside the United States, the definition of disability is usually tied to some notion of capacity to earn a living; early standards pegged this level to some fixed minimum, but more recent changes have pegged it to an individual's earnings prior to the onset of disability. A variation on this theme is the use of local labor markets, rather than the entire national economy, as the standard for judging an applicant's possible employment. For example, under Social Security Disability Insurance in the United States, an applicant must be found unable to do any job in the entire national economy; in the Netherlands, however, the applicant must be unable to earn what a healthy person could earn in his own job, in a former job, or in a similar place of employment.[19] Moreover, benefits are now being adjusted dynamically through indexing to collective bargaining contracts or other wage indices. It is worth noting that in those countries where disability programs are thought to be in crisis, the crisis was preceded by legislative and judicial expansions of the programs.

There is one more cross-national similarity to be noted. The incidence of disability pension awards is clearly related to the performance of the economy—specifically, to the unemployment rate. When unemployment goes up, so do disability pensions.[20]

The Standard Explanations

If the phenomena observed in the various welfare states are similar, so too are the reigning explanations. Policymakers and analysts look to the same set of factors in explaining increased program size and growth rates.

At the top of the list come the "natural" or "background" factors. Population growth is assumed to explain some of the increase in the sheer number of program beneficiaries. Changes in the demographic composition of the population are also adduced: because mortality rates have declined over the last several decades, the proportion of elderly in the population has increased, thereby increasing the proportion of people who are likely to be disabled.[21] But this explanation is not terribly convincing. For one thing, the growth rates of programs hold even when standardized for age.[22]

Another standard explanation is that popular attitudes toward disability and social insurance programs have changed. This argument holds that even if there is no higher rate of actual disability in society, the *willingness to use disability benefits* is growing. For various reasons, usually only vaguely specified, people are alleged to feel less restrained about making application for benefits. One version says there is a decline in the "work ethic";[23] another, that there is merely increased awareness of the programs;[24] still another, that people are more likely to *think* of themselves as disabled than they were in earlier times, given the same disability, because being handicapped is less stigmatizing now. There is precious little evidence for any of these attitudinal changes, nor does it seem plausible that the same attitudinal change is happening the world over.

A third common explanation is that the incidence of disability is actually increasing. Two reasons are often given. One is that advances in medical technology have allowed people to remain alive with debilitating conditions that would formerly have been fatal. The other is that industrialization, particularly certain new technologies, have made work more hazardous, so that more and more people are in fact disabled in the workplace. Both are variations on the theme of the ills of modernity: economic development and industrialization cause a deterioration in human welfare, even as they enhance productivity and material well-being in other ways.

The fourth explanation uses one of the observations noted above to explain program growth: legislative liberalization of eligibility criteria and expansion of benefits. This explanation implicitly relies on a rational-actor model of individual behavior, in that potential applicants are thought to be "attracted" by the increased opportunities offered through disability benefit programs. A variant focuses on the increases in the value of disability benefits relative to other income sources and sees increased applications as the direct result of enhanced economic attractiveness.[25] Of course, this explanation begs the question of why so many countries saw fit to expand or liberalize their disability benefit programs during the 1960s and 1970s.

Finally, the most recent theory holds that disability pensions are sometimes used to regulate the labor market by selectively absorbing older people from the labor force and thus easing unemployment.[26]

Some Unanswered Questions

Some of these theories can plausibly explain short-term fluctuations in program statistics, and they provide appealing descriptions of mechanisms through which programs expand. Others, particularly those that attempt to explain why disability programs in most welfare states should be experiencing similar rapid growth, are more vague and less satisfying. Many puzzling questions remain.

Why should the expansion of disability programs be such a pervasive phenomenon? It seems implausible that more people are actually physically disabled now than at some earlier period (except for times of war), given advances in preventive, therapeutic, and rehabilitative medicine. Are we really to believe that, on balance, life in the 1980s is more disabling than life in the 1930s or even the 1950s?

If disability is a medical phenomenon, why should there be so much variety in the definition of disability in public programs, both from country to country and from program to program within the same country? Can't physicians agree on what conditions are truly disabling, as they can on how to diagnose measles or treat pneumonia? And why is an American government employee considered disabled when he can no longer perform his previous job, but an ordinary wage-earning citizen not considered disabled unless he can no longer do *any* job in the entire national economy?

Why is there a trend toward the medicalization of social problems? Why are educational problems such as reading difficulties now labeled as "learning disabilities" and diagnosed by clinical teams? Why do returning Vietnam soldiers want their difficulties to be recognized as a medical syndrome linked to a chemical defoliant (Agent Orange)?

And finally, how can we explain the political backlash against the disabled (in the form of wholesale cuts in the disability rolls) when benefits for the handicapped would seem to be a classic "motherhood issue," one that no politician could afford to oppose? What could be lower than picking on a group of people unable to defend themselves? Why is the Reagan administration treating many disabled citizens as cheaters and subjecting them to much the same treatment as that given to AFDC mothers in the seventies?

The answer to these questions is to be found neither in the details of program administration nor in population characteristics, but rather in the underlying concept of disability-based benefit programs. The very notion of disability is fundamental to the architecture of the welfare state; it is something like a keystone that allows the other supporting structures of the welfare system and, in some sense, the economy at large to remain in place. At the same time, the notion of disability is highly problematic. The problem, in brief, is that we are asking the concept of disability to perform a function it cannot possibly perform. We ask it to resolve the issue of distributive justice.

The critical distributive problem for all societies is how to decide when people are so poorly off that the normal rules of distribution should be suspended and some form of social aid—be it from kin, neighbors, church, or state—should take over. In the modern societies with which we are familiar, this problem appears, crudely drawn, as a conflict between work and need as the basis of claims on resources. The essence of the modern welfare state's approach has been to establish *categories* of need in order to determine who should be allowed to make need-based claims, and to provide for people in these categories out of public monies administered by state agencies. Thus childhood, old age, sickness, and disability became legally recognized as conditions entitling individuals to social aid.

If categories create entitlements to social aid, then a study of disability must examine how it became, first, an administrative category that creates automatic entitlements, and second, a clinical concept that defines the nature of those entitlements. Chapter 1 expands on the notion of work versus need as the fundamental distributive dilemma and explains how the concept of disability is an important part of the categorical resolution. Chapter 2 traces the origins of disability as an administrative category for social policy in three countries at three particular times by examining English Poor Law, German Social Insurance, and American Social Security Disability Insurance. In all three cases, disability was fashioned into an administrative device to place boundaries around need-based distribution, but these three countries illustrate the importance of national politics and historical development in shaping the particular definition of the category and its uses. Chapter 3 examines how disability as recognized by the state—as a legal entitlement to some form of aid—came to be dominated by clinical concepts.

Chapters 4 and 5 consider how the disability concept functions as a boundary device. Chapter 4 concentrates on aspects of the disability category designed to be restrictive and to provide a tight boundary around the need-based system; Chapter 5 focuses on the pressures for expansion and the interaction between these pressures and the boundary-maintaining mechanisms. In these two chapters, American Social Security Disability Insurance is used as the major example, not only to give the discussion some coherence but also because, as the most recent program, it embodies the clinical concept of disability *in extremis* and so presents a magnified version of the central definitional problem of all disability programs. Chapter 6 shows how the intellectual underpinnings of the concept of disability combine with institutional incentives to produce a powerful dynamic of definitional expansion.

1

The Distributive Dilemma

All societies have at least two distributive systems, one based on work and one on need, whose coexistence is a thorny problem in social policy and political theory. On the one hand, societies depend on their members to perform work of some kind; in varying degrees, people are expected to be self-sufficient and to produce a little bit extra to trade, sell, or give to others in order to improve the condition of society as a whole. On the other hand, in any society, not everyone can meet all of his or her own needs all of the time, and the very essence of society is providing help to those in need.

There are many possible responses to need, however need is defined or perceived. A society may not recognize real needs or may deny that they exist. It may recognize needs in some groups but not in others. It may recognize needs but be willing to let people suffer anyway. But if it decides to undertake any sort of humanitarian aid, it faces the problem of how to help people in need without undermining the basic principle of distribution according to work.

One reason for the tension between the two distributive systems has to do with the "logic of collective action."[1] In order for need-based distribution to be possible, some people must not only produce more than is necessary for their own subsistence but must also refrain from consuming the surplus. If surplus product is available for redistribution, however, what incentive is there for individuals to produce surplus, either for their own use or for possible redistribution to others? The need-based system is a classic example of a public good, and "the logic of collective action" leads individuals to withhold contribution—in this case, extra work.

The other major reason for the tension has to do with the motivation for work in market societies. The hallmark of market societies is that labor is treated as a commodity, and people receive wages or salaries as compensation for their work. They can then convert their income into goods and services, also through the mechanism of market exchange. A critical assumption of theories of the market economy is that people work only for instrumental reasons, not for the inherent satisfaction or reward derived from work. In this view, if people could attain all the goods and services they needed and desired without working, no one would work.

This assumption about human motivation is at the core of Malthus's eighteenth century analysis of English welfare policy and, for that matter, most contemporary analyses of the welfare state:

> It seems perfectly visionary to suppose that any stimulus short of that which is excited in man by the desire of providing for himself and family, and of bettering his condition in life, should operate on the mass of society with sufficient force and constancy to overcome the natural indolence of mankind.[2]

Malthus attributed the alleged aversion to work to "natural" human traits. Contemporary Marxists would attribute the instrumental or materialist attitude toward work to socialization under capitalism: because capitalism forces the laborer to sell his labor power as a commodity, people learn to think of work only in instrumental terms.[3] But both analyses lead to the conclusion that there must be some coercive element to induce people to work, and that element is the denial of satisfaction of material needs.

Given this view of the nature of work, the work-based distributive system will be most effective—inspire the most productivity—when it is the only distributive system. Its incentives function best when they are not undercut and weakened by nonwork opportunities to fulfill one's needs. Yet paradoxically, the work system can never meet even the most minimal needs of many people. Some are incapable of working at all, or working enough to fulfill even basic material necessity. Labor markets never function perfectly; there are lag times and transition periods when markets have to "adjust," and disruptions in local or national economies, so that jobs are simply not available. And working itself creates new needs or perceived needs, so that even when people do work, they are in a sense always "behind" in meeting their needs and wants.

The conflict between work- and need-based systems obtains in both capitalist and socialist societies. Both are market societies, but with the difference that in one, accumulated capital is controlled privately while in the other, it is controlled publicly. It is the accumulation of capital per se, not the locus of control over capital, that creates the distributive dilemma. Private control over investment certainly makes persons without capital less secure than owners of capital; their future well-being depends on continued employment, and therefore on the investment decisions of those who have capital. But even under socialism, where capital is collectively owned, the individual is at the mercy of investment decisions over which he or she has very little control; the lone voice of the average citizen is but a whisper in any large group, whatever its ideological persuasion. Thus, both capitalism and socialism contribute to the insecurity of individuals and their need for need-based redistribution.

But neither capitalism nor socialism *creates* the distributive dilemma. The clash between work- and need-based distribution does not derive from the individual's lack of control over capital, however that lack occurs.[4] The clash comes ultimately from the fundamental tension between consumption and saving. How can people be given an incentive to save and economic security at the same time? Saving requires restraint from immediate consumption and, therefore, some restraint on what sorts of consumption people define as necesary—their concept of need. But need-based distribution, by definition, gives expression to need; by its very existence, it encourages people to think more expansively about what they define as necessary.

The tension between the two systems based on work and need is the fundamental distributive dilemma. To resolve it, society must develop a set of rules to determine the boundaries of the two systems, rules that specify who is subject to each distributive principle and what is to be distributed within each system. There is no natural boundary between the two systems, no inherent definition of what constitutes need or who "belongs" in one system or the other. Rather, the boundary is something that each society has to invent, to redesign in the face of changing social conditions, and to enforce. Different societies will resolve the dilemma differently, and any one society will find different resolutions at different periods of its history. A successful resolution of the dilemma will have certain general characteristics, but every particular resolution is designed by politics, not by some universal logic.

The distributive dilemma has been portrayed here in a particularly stark version, assuming societies to have only two distributive principles—work and need. In fact, several distributive principles may operate simultaneously in a given society, though it is probably fair to say that in all modern societies work remains the *primary* distributive criterion in the dominant political ideology. (In actual practice, property or wealth would seem to be the dominant criterion.) In addition to distribution according to labor, certain goods, services, opportunities, and privileges may be distributed on the basis of ascriptive characteristics (such as age, birth order, gender, or religion); blood relationships (as in special tax treatment of family gifts, or college admission preference to children of alumni); property ownership (as in tithes, rents, and stock dividends); or special kinds of achievement (such as military service, fame, and extraordinary talent). But the existence of multiple distributive principles does not eliminate the distributive dilemma.

Instead of viewing the dilemma as a tension between the work and need systems, we can view it as a tension between *all* rule-based systems on the one hand, and the need-based system on the other. Rule-based systems are those that use some principle other than need to allocate goods and services. Ascriptive characteristics, religious affiliation, blood relationships, ownership, and special achievement are all principles for rule-based systems. The question is, then, *when should need be allowed to supersede other rules* as a principle for distribution?

Need-based distribution is understood to be extraordinary, outside the normal rules. The need system is different in character from the others because it is regarded as a system of last resort, to be invoked only when all other systems have failed. The need-based system might usefully be viewed as society's "rescue" method; it is the distributive system that allows society to save people who cannot survive in the normal distributive regimes. Thus, even where there are multiple rule-based systems, a society still has the problem of determining when people should be allowed to receive social aid through a need-based system.

In societies where sheer subsistence is the overriding concern, there are elaborate, if usually unwritten, social arrangements for aiding people in dire need. E. P. Thompson's classic study of food riots in eighteenth century England[5] shows that English towns had a well organized emergency system for dealing with grain shortages, codified in a "Book of Orders." When local officials failed to implement an emergency distribution system, popular protests in effect reproduced the system specified in the Book of Orders and signaled the town magistrates to initiate emergency measures and public relief. Food riots, far from being random acts of violence, were highly organized, consistently patterned crowd behavior, shaped by very specific notions of political and moral obligation. James Scott has shown similarly that peasant societies of southeast Asia have definite social arrangements for guaranteeing subsistence to their members; communal land, regional granaries, reciprocal aid among kinsmen and friends, charity from the better off, and famine relief arranged by local governments are all part of a need-based distributive system that provides a measure of social security.[6]

The subsistence ethic characteristic of peasant societies is part of what has been called the "moral economy." In these societies, there is a shared belief that all members of a community are entitled to a living out of local resources, and that those with surplus have an obligation to give aid to those who might otherwise starve. The moral economy of a society is its set of beliefs about what constitutes just exchange: not only about how economic exchange is to be conducted in normal times but also, as Scott and Thompson have emphasized, when poor individuals are entitled to social aid, when better-off people are obligated to provide aid, and what kinds of claims anyone—landowners, employers, governments—can legitimately make on the surplus product of anyone else.

The concept of moral economy can be applied not only to peasant societies but equally well to modern societies. The moral economy is about nothing if not the boundary between work and need. That boundary may be "thinner" in peasant societies than in modern ones; the difference between what a person can comfortably provide for himself in the best of times and near starvation in the worst of times may not be very large. But the boundary's dimensions are not given by nature; rather, they derive from a set of ideas about need and justice, and a set of social arrangements that carry out those ideas. Although its substance may be different, the moral economy of modern societies still must provide legitimating answers to the same question about distributive justice: when should need-based supersede work-based distribution?

Further questions then arise: why are some kinds of needs thought to be appropriate objects of social policy while others are ignored? Where does a societal concept of need at any particular moment come from? There is no fixed quantity of needs, or even a fixed definition of what constitutes a need. Rather, needs are a complicated mixture of social resources and individual striving, of public expectations and private imagination.

Need systems, if they are established at all, are set up to meet needs not satisfied in the work system. In a very important sense, a society's concept of need mirrors its concept of work. People are thought to be in need when they do not have whatever it is that most people in the society obtain through their work. In subsistence economies, where the primary derivative of work is food, welfare systems (or more accurately, charity and norms of reciprocity) tend to provide aid in kind. In market economies, where wages are considered the primary benefit of work, welfare systems tend to provide aid in the form of cash.

Of course, work provides much more than subsistence in either case: it can be a source of social status, friendship, information, frustration, and pride; it gives opportunities for creativity, self-expression, learning, protest, and political organization; and it establishes many of the routines and rituals that structure our lives. Still, not all of these needs are satisfied for everyone in the work system, yet public and private programs single out a few of them as legitimate.

In peasant societies, dire need is commonly understood as *global but temporary*—an act of God or nature that affects the whole of society (or its crops) but clearly a seasonal, temporary event. Droughts, pestilence, bad harvests, and famine are the reigning images here. In ordinary circumstances, the economic norm may be self-sufficiency through independent farming and petty trade, but the moral economy recognizes that even in ordinary times, most peasants live close to the margin of survival. Thus, in subsistence societies, need-based distributive systems are always in the wings, and the interesting political question is how these systems are called into operation and allowed to override the prevailing distributive system based on self-sufficiency and reciprocal aid.

In modern welfare states, poverty is more likely to be understood as *partial and continuous*—a condition that affects only some individuals, localities, or categories of people within a society but one likely to last indefinitely for those segments. Need-based distributive systems are no longer in the background, to be implemented only in emergencies, but rather exist alongside work- and property-based distributive systems. The central political question is then how need systems are turned *off* or, more precisely, how they are constantly monitored and limited. In place of the triggering mechanisms of peasant societies, modern societies try to establish a regulating mechanism that continuously controls the boundary between need and other distributive systems.

The Categorical Resolution

A successful resolution of the distributive dilemma must perform certain functions. First, it must provide a rationale for assigning people to either the work-based or the need-based distributive system. Each system has its own set of rules about how allocations are to be made *within* it, but there must also be rules to determine who will belong to each one. Under what conditions should the needs of an individual be allowed to take precedence over his obligations to participate in the primary work-based system? The rationales for allowing individuals to participate in the need-based system must accord with the basic assumptions about human nature and justice that underlie the work-based system.

A successful resolution must also provide a validating device—a test for determining exactly when each distributive system should be operative. The validating device is in a sense a means of applying the rationale to individual cases. Two kinds of information are required. One pertains to the needs of the individual: are the person's needs in fact not being met under the primary, work-based system? The other pertains to the rationales for separating the two distributive systems: does the person have a valid excuse for being in need or for not participating in the work-based system? The validating device is the mechanism by which society obtains knowledge about individuals for the purpose of deciding whether to give social aid.

A good resolution must also perform one other function: it must maintain the dominance of the primary distributive system. It must allow for the possibility of rescuing people in dire straits (however that condition is defined), but it must also ensure that the work-based distributive system remains primary. The definition of boundaries between the work and need systems must maintain need-based distribution as an extraordinary phenomenon, not the norm.

The system we have come to call the "welfare state" is characterized by one particular resolution of the distributive dilemma: categorical exemptions from the labor market. Under this resolution, people will be given social aid when they belong to a category that has been granted social exemption from participation in the work-based distributive system. Welfare states have adopted the principle that certain characteristics—youth, old age, widowhood, and sickness—render people automatically incapable of participating in the wage-labor system. An important feature of this resolution is that the *categories* have a legitimate claim to social aid, not the individuals. Individuals are given social aid only if they meet the test of belonging to one of the formally defined categories.

The categories thus act as boundaries between the primary, work-based distributive system and the secondary, need-based system. They are the devices that determine which people will belong to each system and under what conditions people will move from one to the other. The categories might be likened to membranes or filters designed to let only certain elements pass through.

As with any general resolution of the distributive dilemma, the categorical resolution must perform certain basic functions in order to be successful. Since the categories serve to define the boundaries, they must themselves be defined in ways that contribute to a stable resolution of the tension between the work-based and need-based systems.

Each category must be based on a culturally legitimate rationale for nonparticipation in the labor system. Since the dominant ideology in a market society holds that each individual is responsible for fulfilling his or her needs by working and earning, categories will define conditions under which people cannot be held responsible for working. The traditional categories have been childhood, old age, sickness, and sometimes widowhood. The rationale behind these categories is that something inherent in the conditions they describe *prevents* people from working, no matter how strong the will to work in individual cases. The categories are meant to describe circumstances under which individuals cannot be held at fault for not working.

The definitions of categories are thus tied to concepts of control and responsibility. They are meant to describe general circumstances when individuals should be exempt from the duty to work and when *not* working can be unequivocally interpreted as beyond the conscious control of the individual. The definitions are also tied to underlying cultural notions about work. For example, if work is conceived as a physical process requiring certain kinds of strength and stamina, then the categories for exemption will be defined in terms of some lack of these abilities. If, however, work is defined as a mental process, requiring certain kinds of intelligence, imagination, and perception, then the categories might be defined very differently.

Each category must also be defined in terms of a validating device that determines whether the generally recognized, culturally legitimate excuses apply in particular cases. An effective validating device should enable a fairly speedy determination, since the applicants in question are presumably in dire straits and in need of immediate aid. Therefore, it must make use of information about individuals that is readily available or easily obtainable.

The validating device must also be based on objective rather than subjective information. This requirement is important because of the assumption in market societies that individuals do not desire to work, that they work only because labor is instrumental in acquiring things they do desire. Since individuals are assumed to be motivated to escape from the work-based distributive system, they are presumed to have incentives to misrepresent information about themselves in order to meet the categorical tests of the need-based system. Therefore, the validating device must rely on information that cannot be manipulated by the individual claimants.

The necessary information for some traditional categories of welfare policy is easily obtained and interpreted by distinterested individuals. Childhood and old-age require only evidence of a birth date (if not simply visual observation), and birth records were one of the first elements of public statistics. Similarly, proof of status as a widow requires only proof of a husband's death, and again, death records tend to be among the most accurately kept of social statistics. Disability, however, has always been more problematic, both because no single condition of "disability" is universally recognized, and because physical and mental incapacity are conditions that can be feigned for secondary gain. Hence, the concept of disability has always been based on a perceived need to detect deception. The problem of a validating device—a means to define and determine disability—is central to the current crisis of disability benefit programs.

The validating device must also provide information about the individual's needs. It should tell not only whether the person has a culturally legitimate excuse for not working but also whether he is in fact needy. If a person belongs to one of the socially defined categories, then he or she is by definition needy. The categorical resolution is so appealing precisely because it eliminates the necessity of a "means test," or information about an individual's financial resources and needs.

Finally, since any resolution of the distributive dilemma must maintain the dominance of the primary work-based system, each category must be highly restrictive, defined in such a way that the number of people who can possibly belong to it is very small relative to the number who do not. The question of what determines the relative sizes of a society's work- and need-based distributive systems has occupied many scholars of the welfare state. What is important to this discussion is that the tolerance of different societies for need-based distribution may vary, but the need-based system will be labeled as "in crisis" at precisely those moments when the *restrictiveness* of a category is felt to be too loose or ineffective. The definition of a category is essential to its restrictiveness, because the definition *is* the boundary; every definition is a mechanism for allocating people to the category.

Categorical exemptions are not the only possible solution to the distributive dilemma. Another possibility is a system of multiple citizenship statuses, with different sets of rights and privileges: typically, those who participate in (and are successful) in the work-based system (and perhaps all rule-based systems) have something like full citizenship, while those participating in the need-based system have only partial citizenship. In exchange for social aid, the recipients of need-based distribution give up some of the rights they would otherwise have. Under the old Poor Laws in Britain, virtually anyone could enter the need-based system, becoming a pauper, but in lieu of restrictions on entry, there were penalties meant to act as deterrents. Paupers lost some of their citizenship rights, such as the right to travel out of the parish, the right to live with their families (in the workhouse), and—notably—the right to vote. The categorical resolution allows for the provision of welfare to categories of citizens without having to define them as lesser citizens. The innovation of the modern welfare state was the invention of categories of *faultlessness* in which a person could be both a citizen and in need.[7]

Not all systems of dual citizenship are established as solutions to the distributive problem. For example, slaves are not given the opportunity to prove themselves first in the full-citizenship domain; they are assigned to slavery status on the basis of some criterion other than their personal achievement. When dual citizenship is used as a device to make rescue possible, however, personal achievement becomes relevant in determining citizenship status. People are given a chance to participate in the rule-based distributive system first, and only if they fail do they enter the need based system.

Another possible resolution of the distributive dilemma is the use of organizations other than the state to provide aid on the basis of need. In feudal society, the guilds had systems of social aid primarily for their own members, but they also provided charity for some poor people outside their membership. The church was, of course, the major institution for charity, and charitable foundations were also part of the feudal era's social landscape. Later on, in the eighteenth and nineteenth centuries, various mutual aid societies, friendly societies, and eventually trade unions took on the function of providing social aid to members in need. Indeed, these institutions coexisted with state programs for quite a while during the development of the welfare state, and many private organizations for social welfare based on need continue to exist.[8]

Relegating charity to the realm of private organizations does not in itself solve the problem of delineating the boundaries between work and need systems. If these organizations are allowed to set their own policies on entitlement (that is, on who will be allowed into their need-based systems), their policies may conflict with or undermine the work-based system. In fact, welfare policy in Europe evolved partly out of legislation designed to restrict the availability of private charity, and thus drew the state into one important aspect of conflict with the church.[9]

Another way that a society provides aid on the basis of need is through *unorganized* private charity. In all societies a certain amount of voluntary, informal charity exists alongside the primary distributive system. Goods and services may be provided to people in need through kinship networks and informal community ties, and the obligations to repay may be very strict, even if never formally stated.[10] Even less formal is the institution of begging, whereby people in need solicit aid from strangers. Begging and informal networks are in one sense good solutions to the distributive dilemma: because they are relatively invisible, they do not undermine the work-based system as much as public and more visible need-based distribution might. Aid received through these channels appears as an isolated, random, and infrequent phenomenon, rather than a stable institution upon which people might rely. The donors of charity are free to decide whether to give, how much to give, when to give, and to whom. However, as we will see in the next chapter, when private, unorganized systems of need-based distribution are thought to be undermining the primary system, even they will be subject to regulation.

The Disability Category

That old age, childhood, and disability should be conditions automatically entitling people to social aid seems entirely natural to us in the present day. But for social historians, what a society takes for granted is often much more interesting than its overt controversies. If one removes the contemporary cultural lenses through which disability is normally viewed, the obvious becomes very perplexing indeed.

In his study of the social treatment of children, Phillippe Aries found that for much of Western history, people did not perceive childhood as a distinct period in individual development or as a state of being requiring any special treatment.[11] The emergence in our culture of the idea of childhood as a distinct phase is a modern phenomenon. The same must be said of disability. What seems to us so obvious now—that there is a state of being called "disabled" which is clearly different from the normal state of being and which requires special treatment—is a fairly modern perception.

To understand the concept of disability and how it both resolves and complicates the distributive dilemma, we need to know how and when it became an administrative category of the welfare state. In very early descriptions of welfare programs in European towns, there was no category of disability as such, but only reference to special treatment for the aged and infirm, for lunatics and defectives, invalids and the lying-in, ablebodied and impotent beggars, and orphans. How did some of these originally distinct classes come to be lumped together in one unified category? How did disability come to be recognized as a single phenomenon, with enough shared cultural meaning to serve as a defining characteristic for public welfare programs?

This book takes the view that disability is a socially created category rather than an attribute of individuals. This perspective is not the same as the claim, common among disability advocacy groups, that the disabled are handicapped only because they live in a world dominated by the ablebodied and therefore not adapted to the needs of the minority: "It is not the fact that [a person] cannot walk that is disabling but that society is organized for walking and not wheel-chair-using individuals. [A person's] disability is not paraplegia but steps, pavement kerbs, buses and prejudiced shopkeepers."[12] In that view, disability, like other forms of discrimination, is created by the "ablist" biases of mainstream society: the disabled are like fish out of water, and if physical and social barriers to integration were removed, they would cease to be a distinct group. Such a perspective on disability has its merits, particularly as it reveals ways that society can make changes to enable the disabled to participate more fully. Without dismissing this view, I want to emphasize that it is not the sense in which I argue that disability is a socially created category.

Disability is a *formal administrative category* that determines the rights and privileges of a large number of people. The idea of blindness can serve as a good illustration. It might seem on first thought that blindness is a straightforward case of disability where everyone could agree that a person who "can't see" is blind and that the inability to see is purely an individual characteristic. Now consider these three instances. The first is a man who is "legally blind" but who sight-reads Bach at the harpsichord, up to tempo with nary a mistake; he has tunnel vision and can see only a small field, but enough to perform a musical feat. The second is a customer at a car dealership, who, after carefully examining the color charts in selecting the color of her new purchase, informs the salesman that she is going to pay for her car partly with a government check she receives by virtue of being legally blind. The last is a photograph in a university newspaper showing students from a nearby school for the blind visiting a laser sculpture exhibition in the university art gallery; the caption says that some of the students, who are "legally blind but partially sighted," are describing the exhibit to their blind classmates—truly a case of the blind leading the blind.[13]

Thus, there is blindness and there is "legal blindness." The claim here is that legal blindness is a socially created category, established for specific policy purposes as part of the general categorical resolution of the distributive dilemma. Along with the other categories, it is part of a search for a means of objectively determining who is deserving of social aid. The concept of disability embodied in the administrative category represents a politically fashioned compromise at any given time and place about the legitimacy of claims to social aid.

The argument that disability is a socially created category does not deny that certain characteristics of individuals significantly limit their ability to function. But to view disability as as a socially constructed phenomenon is to focus on a different set of questions: one asks not what is "wrong" with some individuals, but why social institutions respond to some individuals differently than to others. The phenomenon under examination is interactive, to be sure. Social institutions respond to some individual characteristics that people perceive, but they also engage in selective perception and actively shape the way people are treated.

Another historical problem is how the concept of disability came to be associated with clinical medicine and clinical reasoning. In earlier times, people could receive social aid on the grounds of conditions we still consider disability, but they could do so without ever going near a physician or hospital. If we do not take for granted what is true in our own society, it is not obvious why judgments about inability to work, or about the legitimacy of an individual choice not to work, should be made by physicians rather than by priests, judges, juries, teachers, or public officials. That the concept of disability is so connected to medical definition in contemporary society is an artifact of history.

The link between the formation of disability as an administrative category and its definition as a medical phenomenon is the concept of deception. The other two major categories of modern social welfare policy, old age and childhood, were always assumed to represent authentic states of being, totally independent of the will of individuals. Disability, on the other hand, even in its early incarnations as more specific conditions, was seen to exist in both genuine and artificial forms. People could either be truly injured or feign injury. In the modern understanding of disability, deception has become part and parcel of the concept itself, and the nature of this deception is tied to the particular form of validation used to detect it. The definition of disability and the means to determine it became critically linked.

Finally, a social observer cannot fail to notice that disability entails (or may entail) at least as much political privilege as it does social stigma. It is a political privilege because, as an administrative category, it carries with it permission to enter the need-based system and to be exempt from the work-based system. It can also provide exemption from other things people normally consider worth avoiding: military service, debt, and criminal liability. Disability programs are political precisely because they allocate these privileges. The evolution of contemporary programs must be seen in this context, and the intense political interest in disability benefit programs in recent years can only be understood if we see that the fight is about privilege rather than handicap or stigma.

2

The Origins of the Disability Category

English Poor Law Policy

To understand how the disability category evolved, we must go back to early English poor relief, which itself grew out of a series of fourteenth-century laws for the regulation of vagrancy. The relationship between vagrancy and disability would seem to be very remote, but an examination of poor relief policy shows important connections. Both vagrancy and disability are understood in the culture of their times as social roles that might be adopted either legitimately or illegitimately. A genuine vagrant or "honest beggar," as the phrase usually went, and a genuinely disabled person are those who occupy the roles involuntarily, forced by circumstances to enter the need system. Both disability and vagrancy are unstable states. Vagrants are literally on the move, and may at any time shift back and forth between steady employment and wandering. Disabled people are metaphorically on the move: their handicapping conditions may be improving or deteriorating, and their ability to move in and out of normal or nondisabled roles may be constantly changing. In poor-relief policy, the two conditions of vagrancy and disability intersect in the question of how to detect the genuinely needy beggar from the one who feigns disability.

The question of legitimacy pervaded all discussions of vagrancy from the fourteenth to the nineteenth century, and it is certainly true that vagrants have a bad name in English social history. Statutes, treatises on welfare and poverty, and proposals for reform of relief all portray vagrants as a major social problem.[1] Contemporary descriptions were unanimous on two points: that the number of vagrants was growing rapidly, and that all manner of social problems were caused by vagrancy. (In many ways, vagrancy played a role in early social thought akin to that played by the "middle class" and "urbanization" in twentieth-century social thought: both are always portrayed as increasing, and almost always invoked as causes of whatever social problem is under discussion.)

There are many theories about the causes of vagrancy and particularly about the sharp increase in England beginning around 1500.[2] Between 1500 and 1700, England experienced a dramatic growth of population, following on a century and a half of slow growth if not actual depletion from various plagues.[3] At the same time, employment opportunities in the countryside were diminishing as more and more land was converted from labor-intensive farming to sheep-raising, and as the cultivation of corn was made more efficient.[4] Periodic spells of bad harvests were often blamed for increases in vagrancy: as food prices went up, people had less money to spend on other goods: therefore jobs in the textile and manufacturing industries decreased.[5] In general, the transition from a feudal social order to a system of capitalist agriculture and industry based on wage labor left enormous numbers of people temporarily stranded.

Wars, too, were blamed for the vagrancy problem, though curiously, both too much and too little war have been seen as the culprits. In one theory, the decline of private wars by feudal lords eliminated a social mechanism for absorbing "restless men."[6] In other theories, too much war led to vagrancy through complex mechanisms. Henry VII and Edward VI paid for expensive wars in the mid-sixteenth century by debasing the currency, which led to inflation, which caused unemployment.[7] The Thirty Years War in central Europe and the Civil War in England were blamed because, when they were over, they released "swarms" of injured and jobless soldiers back into cities that could not absorb them.[8] Finally, vagrancy was at various times pinned to immigration of the Welsh, the Scots, and the Irish, just as some recent theories of unemployment in the United States locate the problem in illegal aliens.[9]

The phenomenon of vagrancy was virtually an obsession with social theorists and lawmakers all over Europe in the sixteenth, seventeenth, and eighteenth centuries. It is unlikely, therefore, that the specific causal theories elaborated for the English case tell the whole story. (Enclosure, or the conversion of public grazing land to private property, was probably the one phenomenon unique to England, at least in scope.) Bad harvests, currency debasement, price inflation, and the conclusion of wars may have temporarily exacerbated an existing situation, but the problem was clearly fundamental and pervasive. And whatever its actual magnitude in terms of numbers of vagrants, it was serious enough to command enormous intellectual, economic, and political effort. The nature of those efforts is what is important here.

The phenomenon of begging produced a host of theories locating the cause in the personality of the beggar. Many treatises, taking for granted that beggars had special personality traits, set about developing elaborate portraits. Begging was so ingrained into their character, it was said, that they would rather starve to death than work. As one officer of a benevolent society wrote, "Idleness and hypocrisy are so wrought into their natures that they are incurable. Living by hourly deception, *they have less character than even thieves*, and are more hopeless as to moral reformation: they are known to be *too idle even to beg when they have a shilling left to spend*, or can find a public house or a chandler's house that will trust them."[10] The phenomenon of begging also gave rise to a wonderful sociological genre in the sixteenth and seventeenth centuries—the description and classification of beggars, their methods of deception, and their special slang, called "canting." Thomas Harman in England, Martin Luther in Germany, and Giacinto Nobili in Italy each produced a major treatise in which beggars were divided into some twenty-five to thirty-five classes and their tricks of deception exposed. In France, beggars were actually organized into corporations with highly specialized subdivisions whose titles and activities were recognized in vagrancy laws.[11]

From these assessments of the character of beggars, it is not surprising that descriptions of their activities were essentially catalogues of horrible deeds. Vagrants were assumed to be idle, irresponsible, often criminal, and disrepectful of authority. They were often portrayed as roaming the countryside in gangs, extorting large sums from innocent passersby, and generally committing acts of thievery, pillage, and destruction.[12] They were even accused of destroying the king's forests. The "Act for the better Preservation of timber trees, and of Woods and Underwoods; and for the further Preservation of Roots, Shrubs, and Plants" was not George III's precursor of the Environmental Protection Act; rather, it was a law to prevent vagrants from cutting down trees, stealing wood, uprooting young shrubs, and conducting chases "to the great prejudice of his Majesty's deer."[13]

Understanding the character and behavior of vagrants was all the more complicated by their proclivity to deception. Conventional wisdom held that vagrants had all kinds of ruses to obtain alms and lodging. Some of them went about "using divers and subtle crafty and unlawful games and plays, and . . . feigning themselves to have knowledge of . . . crafty sciences."[14]

One method vagrants were commonly alleged to have used to elicit alms was feigning illness or disability. In fact, there are published stories from as far back as the fifth century B.C. to the effect that people feigned madness to avoid military service or other obligations.[15] In English reports and laws of the fifteenth through nineteenth centuries, there are innumerable descriptions of beggars' schemes for pretending to be crippled and blind, artfully producing counterfeit sores, lacerating themselves, and feigning epileptic fits, pregnancy, dropsy, or leprosy. In France, one particular order of beggars, the *mitoux*, were allegedly trained in medicine so that they could "produce the appearance of every kind of malady and even deceive doctors themselves."[16] Women were reported to "borrow" blind children or attach themselves as "aids" to blind men, all the while exploiting them mercilessly. Gangs of beggars bought children from orphanages and deliberately maimed and deformed them, and other gangs specialized in "teratological surgery," all for the purpose of inducing a flow of alms from sympathetic observers.[17] Regardless of the truth of these reports or the actual extent of such practices, they convey a certain "social truth" in the sense that officials believed that feigned disability posed a significant problem for the administration of relief.

This popular conception of beggars and their activities indicates the strength of the association between disability and deception, even before disability had come to be recognized as a distinct category for the purposes of welfare administration. By the time classifications of disability came into being in the nineteenth century, and by the time these recognized conditions were applied as specific eligibility criteria, the conditions were already firmly linked in the public consciousness with the possibility of deception. The connection between disability and deception meant that the very category of disability was developed to incorporate a mechanism for distinguishing the genuine from the artificial.

A recent reinterpretation of vagrancy in Elizabethan England gives good reason to be skeptical of contemporary images of vagrants. The descriptions were always written by members of the educated elite, who were both contemptuous and fearful of the vagrant. There is little evidence in official records to show that vagrants actually traveled in large groups, for example; moreover, it is likely that the majority of vagrants had legitimate occupations and legitimate reasons for traveling, such as searching for work, visiting relatives, or seeking medical cures.[18] Nevertheless, because local officials clearly *believed* them to be dangerous and probably dishonest, vagrants received increasingly harsh treatment both in law and in fact.

If in reality beggars were less numerous than reports would have us believe; if they did not usually travel in gangs; and if thievery, destruction, and idleness were not the norm, why was the popular and official image of beggars so negative? One reason is that they represented a threat to the social order simply by virtue of their mobility. As Beier says, "The life of the vagrant was about nothing if not movement,"[19] and personal mobility controlled only by individual will appeared highly threatening in a society where virtually every aspect of life was regulated. The vagrants' mobility was not only geographic but occupational; the most commonly stated reasons for travel found in their arrest records are searching for work and running errands as part of their occupation.[20] And although vagrancy probably presented very little opportunity for actual change in occupation, the idea of the laborer moving about in search of an employer and deciding for himself whether to undertake any particular job contrasted sharply with the feudal organization of work in which the laborer was bound to the master and had no choice about what tasks to perform. The very existence of vagrants thus appeared to challenge authority.

Given its connection to deception, at least in the common understanding, the phenomenon of begging must have been a threat to the social order in another very profound way. It challenged people's confidence that they could know the truth. That a concern with deception should accompany a social transformation characterized by sudden increases in geographic and social mobility should not be surprising; constant confrontation with strangers must have undermined people's sense that they could understand one another. And nothing could be more threatening to a sense of social order than the perception that the boundaries between the real and the fake are suddenly blurred.

Vagrants were also a challenge because they embodied the essential problems of an economic system in transition. If we understand the transition from feudalism to capitalism as incorporating a transformation not only in the system of production but also in the rules of distribution, then certain features of the evolution of poor-law policy begin to make sense. Under feudalism, there were elaborate distributive rules based primarily on ascriptive characteristics (one's "station" in life) and personal ties (hierarchical relationships and loyalty, most notably between masters and servants). Capitalism introduced a new distributive principle—labor—according to which people would receive wages determined by the value and amount of work they performed.

Periods of transition are by definition unstable, and in any period of transformation of primary distributive rules, there will be needs that cannot be met under either the old system or the new one. There will be people who fall betwixt and between, being neither firmly embedded in the old system nor fully incorporated into the new. At the same time, the secondary distributive system will also be undergoing transformation, and elements of the old secondary system will continue to persist along with the new primary and secondary systems. But the old secondary system of helping people in need, because it is derived from the old primary system, may in fact undermine the new primary system.

This formulation makes it possible to understand why begging, vagrancy, mobility, and labor shortage were seen as parts of the same problem by the architects of early welfare policy. If there was a labor shortage in some locality, that was because laborers were free to move about in search of higher wages, and they were free to move about in part because of the possibility of begging as a means of support between jobs. Vagrancy was possible because peasants were no longer firmly tied to their lords.

The possibility of begging and the existence of vagrancy were seen as draining people from the emerging wage labor system and allowing laborers to demand higher wages. Begging, which had been a humanitarian rescue system under feudalism, came to be seen as undermining the newly emerging system of wage labor. Thus, the early laws in the evolution of English welfare policy had two purposes: they sought to control the old need-based system of begging and vagrancy so that it would not inhibit development of the wage labor system, and they sought to establish a new need system based on new rationales and validating devices. Each act in the emerging Poor Law can be understood as serving one or both of these purposes.

The first law for the control of vagrancy, the Statute of Laborers of 1349, was passed on the heels of the Black Plague (1347–49) and was clearly a response to the labor shortage caused by the plague. The authors of the statute began by noting that since a large number of laborers and servants had recently died, those remaining were prone to demand "excessive wages." The law went on to forbid the donation of alms to beggars who could work:

> Because that many valiant beggars, as long as they may live of begging, do refuse to labor, giving themselves to idleness and vice, and sometime to theft and other abominations; none upon the said pain of imprisonment, shall under the color of pity or alms, give anything to such, which may labor, or presume to favor them towards their desires, so that thereby they may be compelled to labor for their necessary living.[21]

This statute makes clear the connection between the withholding of aid and the compulsion to work, and the underlying assumption that many men would refuse to work if other means of satisfying their needs were available. The purpose of this statute is clearly to limit the old secondary distributive system, by restraining impulses based on "pity," in order to shore up the emerging wage labor system. A companion statute in 1351 attempted to restrict begging further by forbidding most laborers from leaving their town of residence in search of summer work if summer work existed in the hometown.[22]

The problem of labor shortage and, more important, the ability of laborers to refuse work, to organize, and to demand high wages led to even more stringent restrictions on begging. In the statute of 1388 known as 12 Richard 2, we see the notion of deception connected with vagrancy. While earlier laws had attempted to remedy the problem by placing a prohibition on alms *givers*, the new statute mandated an inquiry into the motives of the alms *seekers*. Henceforth, local officials were to distinguish between beggars "impotent to serve and those able to serve or labor." The distinction was introduced to close a loophole in earlier laws that had enabled vagrants to leave their towns by *pretending* to be crippled or sick. Henceforth, those unable to work were allowed to travel to other towns if their own could not support them, but they now needed official letters to do so. The ablebodied were not allowed to leave town unless they had a good reason—going on a pilgrimage, moving to a new dwelling, or fulfilling an engagement with a new master. Local officials were to issue letters to each person with a valid reason, stating "the cause of his going and the time of his return." Any ablebodied person found outside his own town without such a letter was subject to a period of confinement in the stocks.[23]

Although these letters were actually permission to travel rather than permission to beg, they established the mechanism that would later be used to control begging per se. In fact, these letters devised in the fourteenth century bear a striking resemblance to the "sick leave certificates" required of people in most current systems of temporary disability insurance. Both the letters and the certificates consist of a diagnosis (a cause for the inability to work) and an estimated duration (the expected time of return to work). The importance of the statute of 1388 is thus that it established the elements of the categorical system, albeit in very crude form. It specified "ability to work" as the criterion by which people would be separated into the primary and secondary distributive systems, and it created a validating device in the form of certification by local officials.[24]

The later laws about vagrancy and poor relief, which were eventually codified into the statute of 1601 that is commonly known as the Poor Law, were all elaborations and refinements of the basic principles established in 1388. In 1495, the penalty for vagrancy without cause was redefined, and certain exemptions were specified: "women great with child" and "men and women in extreme sickness" were to receive a lesser penalty. In 1504, yet another category was added: "persons being impotent and above the age of sixty."[25] The articulation of these categories constituted the beginning of a new secondary system of distribution, one based on culturally acceptable reasons for nonparticipation in the labor market. The categories were in fact used to determine the exemption from punishment for begging, and they were grafted onto the old system of vagrancy control, but they would become the fundamental feature of the new system of social welfare.

A little more than twenty-five years later, under Henry VIII, Parliament expressed its frustration with the tremendous increases in vagrancy (and the alleged associated crime) that had occurred despite all its previous "good laws, strict statutes and ordinances." It then proceeded to establish yet another program, this time aimed at certifying legitimate beggars rather than ablebodied workers with legitimate reasons to travel. In a statute of 1531, Parliament directed local officials to search out the aged and impotent poor, assign them territorial boundaries for their begging, register their names, and provide each of them with a letter indicating authorization to beg within certain territorial limits.[26] The validating device in this new program continued to be the simple discretionary judgment of individual local officials, but prior laws had indicated the range of reasons Parliament found valid.

Even this program proved ineffective, and in 1536, a new statute created stronger penalties, a new method of enforcing the territorial limits for begging, and a program for public organization of private charity. The territorial limits were to be enforced by an elaborate system of deportation in ten-mile segments, with explicit instructions to local officials on how to feed unauthorized vagabonds and send them on their way. "Lepers and bedridden creatures," however, were not to be expelled. Local officials were to coordinate the collection and use of funds from voluntary almsgiving, and parishes with surplus funds were to share them with needier parishes. Individual almsgiving was generally forbidden; instead, people were supposed to put their money into a common box to be dispensed by the local officers. But the law made exceptions; notably, individuals were still allowed to give alms to blind and lame people on the streets.[27]

The problem of "idle beggars" of course persisted, and eventually, a system of licensure and "badging" was added to the armamentarium of the local guardians. In 1563, parishes were authorized to license their poor to go begging in the county, and to provide identifying badges to be worn "on the shoulder or on the breast."[28] In a variation on the same theme over a hundred years later, Parliament directed that *all* people legitimately on relief

> shall upon the shoulder of the right sleeve of the uppermost garment . . . in an open and visible manner, wear such badge or mark as is herein-after mentioned and expressed, that is to say, a large Roman P, together with the first letter of the name of the parish or place whereof such poor person is an inhabitant, cut either in red or blue cloth.[29]

The technique of issuing badges for legitimate beggars was paralleled by an even harsher system of branding offenders of the vagrancy statutes. In laws of 1530, 1547, and 1571, vagabonds without valid excuses were to be "marked with a hot iron in the breast with letter V," and upon a second conviction, branded with the letter S and declared slaves. Badging and branding did not add anything further to the development of categorization, but they did add another instrument of control to the existing system of discriminating between legitimate and illegitimate beggars.[30]

The next significant development of the categorical system came in 1834, with the Poor Law Amendment Act and the Poor Law Commission Report that preceded it. Other legal developments during this period established major principles of welfare policy in general, but these had to do with the treatment of people on relief rather than the principles for assigning people to the need-based distributive system.[31] The reform of 1834 is considered a watershed in the development of welfare policy because it introduced three new principles: national uniformity in welfare administration, denial of assistance outside the workhouse, and deterrence as the basis for setting benefit levels. Even though these principles were not implemented immediately and never fully, the amendment of 1834 serves as a *statement* of new policy principles and a goal toward which later reforms were aimed.

The Poor Law Amendment Act of 1834 attempted to impose national standards of welfare eligibility and benefits on the various parishes. The intent of this centralization was to restrict labor mobility by eliminating the incentives for beggars or laborers to move around in search of higher wages or better treatment by the poor-law guardians. As the Poor Law Commission put it, national uniformity would reduce the "perpetual shifting" from parish to parish. But Parliament actually set only the most general guidelines and left matters of implementation to a central authority, variously called the Poor Law Commission, the Poor Law Board, or the Local Government Board. The board worked by "negotiating" with the individual parishes or unions (combinations of parishes created as new administrative districts for the Poor Law), and through the next seventy years, policy was handed down to local authorities in the form of "orders" and "circulars." These regulations indicate that the central authority allowed the parishes to run their relief systems under at least three different formal principles and an untold variety of informal systems.[32]

Workhouses for paupers had existed long before the reform of 1834, but the new amendment established the principle that relief would be granted only to people willing to enter the workhouse, where they would live according to its rules and perform work provided by the parish. As early as 1722, Parliament had given parishes the right to deny alms to anyone refusing to enter a workhouse,[33] but the amendment of 1834 went further by expressly prohibiting so-called "outdoor relief," or relief outside a workhouse. This prohibition was never strictly enforced, however. Until the 1870s, fewer than a fifth of adult ablebodied male paupers and less than 15 percent of all paupers were on indoor relief (that is, confined to a workhouse). Even after 1870, when the central authority tried to crack down on local parishes and enforce the basic principles, fewer than a third of adult ablebodied paupers were forced to accept indoor relief.[34] The elaboration of categories of paupers in Poor Law administration after 1834 was precisely an exercise in defining exemptions to the policy of "no outdoor relief."

Deterrence was embodied in the oft-quoted "principle of least eligibility," which stated that the pauper's situation "on the whole shall not be made really or apparently so eligible as the situation of the independent laborer of the lowest class."[35] The workhouse was to be so unpleasant and unattractive that no one who could possibly work would choose to enter it instead. Husbands, wives, and children would be separated. Inmates would wear special uniforms instead of their own clothes. There would be no recreation and no socializing with others during working hours. The schedule would be rigid, and the diet limited to the bare minimum necessary to provide energy for work.

The principle of least eligibility was no more strictly enforced than the other principles. However accurate the literary and journalistic depictions of workhouses as places of uniformly dreary and harsh confinement, these conditions must have been somewhat mitigated for certain categories. Regulations of the several decades following 1834 manifest a deliberate policy of exempting certain categories of paupers from the principle of least eligibility.

Laws usually express a society's aspirations rather than its behavior, and nowhere is this maxim more pertinent than in English Poor Law history. The Poor Law Amendment Act of 1834 was a great deal more coherent than its actual administration. The method of implementing the program consisted primarily in defining categories of paupers who would be exempt from the principles of "no outdoor relief" and "least eligibility." Insofar as "uniformity" was a goal of the Poor Law Commission or the administrators of the Poor Law, it meant similarity of policy in different local districts, not uniform treatment of all paupers.

The most striking aspect of nineteenth-century Poor Law is that through it, a formerly undifferentiated mass of paupers came to be understood as comprising several distinct elements. The articulation of categories was in a sense an exercise in mapmaking. The vast unknown territory of paupers was explored and described with increasing detail, so that internal boundaries between types of paupers seemed to appear.

From the very beginning, the Poor Law Commission suggested that workhouses should separate their inmates into four groups: ablebodied males, ablebodied females, children, and the "aged and infirm." It clearly contemplated different treatment for the various groups, recommending that they be housed in separate buildings where they could be accorded appropriate care: "The old might enjoy their indulgences without torment from the boisterous; the children be educated; and the ablebodied subjected to such courses of labor and discipline as will repel the indolent and vicious."[36] Through the next several decades, the categories were refined and applied in two ways: first, to determine who would be exempt from the proscription of outdoor relief; second, to establish separate standards of treatment for different types of paupers once they became workhouse inmates, or, in effect, to determine who would be exempt from the principle of least eligibility.

The authors of the report of 1834 emphatically did not think they were establishing categories based on individual worth or merit. They knew that "any attempt to discriminate according to merit, in the award of outdoor relief, is dangerous and likely to lead to fraud."[37] They apparently thought of the original categories as describing universal human conditions, or at least immutable conditions of large groups, rather than characteristics of particular individuals. In this conception, the task of local officials should be relatively simple, because they would not have to inquire into the particular circumstances of individuals but could rely on assessing "obvious" traits. A modern analogue of this view of pauper categories might be twentieth-century notions of gender or race—something one can "tell by looking." (Perhaps one should say "early twentieth century," for even gender and race are problematic categories now.)

In the regulations of Poor Law administration and thus in the eyes of Poor Law administrators, five categories were important in defining the internal universe of paupers: children, the sick, the insane, "defectives," and the "aged and infirm." Of these, all but the first are part of today's concept of disability.[38] The five groups were the means of defining who was ablebodied; if a person didn't fall into one of them, he was ablebodied by default. This strategy of definition by default remains at the core of current disability programs. None provides a positive definition of "ablebodied"; instead, "able to work" is a residual category whose meaning can be known only after all the "unable to work" categories have been precisely defined.

What, then, did it mean for "disabled" (or "sick," "defective," or anything else) to become an administrative category in social welfare policy? If these categories were to function as a means of defining the ablebodied population by default, they needed to be shaped as administrative mechanisms. Three questions can serve as guides to discerning the shape of the categories. First, how was each one formally defined? Second, what kind of special treatment, if any, was accorded to the people within it? And third, what kind of validation device was associated with each category?

The Sick

The term "sick" was not defined in early regulations, though it was used often. Its meaning, like that of the other labels, was considered obvious and beyond need of definition. Some idea of what "sickness" meant can be gleaned from the types of sick wards set up in workhouses and Poor Law infirmaries. There were wards for fever cases, smallpox, and venereal disease; "itch cases," ophthalmic cases, and "dirty and offensive cases"; lying-in wards, sick nurseries, boys' and girls' "sore head wards," lunatic wards, and "lock wards." If these classes were the constituent elements of sickness in the mental map of the time, "sickness" must have been understood as primarily acute, temporary, and infectious disease.[39]

The notion of chronic sickness was more problematic. At times, people with long-lasting or permanent ailments seemed to be subsumed in the category "aged and infirm." But occasionally there are special provisions in Poor Law regulations for people we would now designate as chronically ill or disabled. For example, the General Medical Order of 1842, which established the first outlines of Poor Law medical service, directed local officials to prepare a "permanent list" every six months. The list would identify those aged, infirm, sick, and disabled who were constantly on relief, and these people would then be entitled to visits from the local medical officers without prior certification from the parish relief officer.[40] But the Poor Law struggled with the concept of chronic ailments and the problem of distinguishing those able to work from those unable to work. A major summary regulation of 1844 asserted that "poor persons who have frequent ailments, who are ruptured and are generally of weak constitutions" but who are "in receipt of wages," however low, must be considered for the purposes of outdoor relief as being ablebodied.[41]

Although the position of the chronically ill with respect to outdoor relief was ambiguous and changing, the rights of the acutely ill were clear, at least in formal policy. The Poor Law Commission Report of 1832, the Poor Law Amendment Act of 1834, and subsequent regulations all expressly exempted the sick from the prohibition against outdoor relief. Nevertheless, there was a great deal of local variation in the treatment of the acutely ill and in the harshness of the means test to which they were subjected. In many parishes, the sick poor were required to sell all their furniture and possessions before they could become eligible for Poor Law medical relief.[42] And one hard-line member of the central authority recommended, unsuccessfully, that even the aged and sick should be denied outdoor relief.[43] But official policy on the exemption never changed,[44] although the central authority did try to pressure local officials into tightening up on outdoor relief to the sick.

During the early years of Poor Law reform, no special treatment was accorded the sick; but in later years, especially after 1847, the central authority encouraged local parishes and unions to provide better medical care for the sick in their homes and to set up separate wards for them in the workhouses. The Poor Law Board mandated in 1865 that medical care for those on outdoor relief be of good quality, and that the guardians should supply medicines free of charge to the poor.[45] Actual conditions for the sick in workhouses varied from parish to parish, of course, but in general they were entitled to special provisions: they might be allowed visitors, whereas others were not; and they could visit with outsiders in privacy, rather than in the presence of the workhouse master. They might get larger food rations, and their diets were generally under the control of the doctor rather than the workhouse authority. Sick people could not be punished in some of the usual ways, such as confinement, heavy labor, or the withholding of tea, sugar, and other food.[46]

The question of whether the sick poor should be subject to the principle of least eligibility was never really resolved. Some people held that the sick were not "the proper objects for such a system [of deterrence]."[47] Others believed that the deterrence principle embodied in the 1834 Amendment "causes the lame to walk, the blind to see, and the dumb to speak."[48] Official policy took stances on both sides of the fence. The Poor Law Commission's annual report of 1841 came down strongly on the side of deterrence. If the pauper is always attended by a skillful doctor and provided with all the medicines necessary for his recovery, it said, then his condition is undeniably better than that of the "industrious ratepayer":

> The superiority of the condition of the pauper . . . as regards medical aid will, on the one hand, encourage a resort to the poor rates for medical relief, so far as it is given out of the workhouse, and will thus tempt the industrious labourer into pauperism; and on the other hand, it will discourage sick clubs and friendly societies and other similar institutions, which are not only valuable in reference to the contingencies against which they provide, but as creating and fostering a spirit of frugality and forethought amongst the labouring classes.[49]

This was the argument against establishing separate institutions for medical relief. But on the other side, the Poor Law central authority gradually introduced more and more special provisions for the sick, which indeed rendered their treatment more favorable and undermined the principle of least eligibility.

Because policy vacillated, there was—and still is—a running debate about whether the sick received good care or bad care. Was the workhouse a "pauper prison" or a "pauper palace?"[50] The question can be answered only relatively. While conditions inside workhouses were no doubt loathsome, conditions for the sick poor were probably better than those for the nonsick poor and often better than those for the nonpoor sick.

Who actually determined whether a sick person should be eligible for poor relief? In a few parishes, responsibility lay with the medical officer, but certification was most often the province of the Poor Law "relieving officer." Once a pauper had been accepted into the workhouse, the doctor could decide whether he or she belonged in a medical ward; and usually, once a pauper was considered sick, the doctor had control over his diet and his release back into the general workhouse.[51]

Doctors were generally perceived by both Poor Law officials and the paupers themselves to be more lenient than relieving officers. Not surprisingly, there was a struggle over which group should determine eligibility for medical relief. The debate has a contemporary ring. Doctors complained of "inconvenience and unnecessary trouble" caused by irresponsible paupers. They said relieving officers were not qualified to judge who was sick, and that they often delayed so long in certifying the sick that their diseases only got worse. Poor Law officers for their part complained that the doctors were too lenient and that their humanitarian instincts needed checking.[52]

The Insane

The insane were singled out from the mass of paupers earlier than any other group. Unlike the others, they were the object of special Parliamentary inquiries in 1807, 1815–16, and 1827; separate legislation in 1828 and 1845; a separate regulatory agency (the Lunacy Commission); and eventually a vast network of separate institutions maintained by the counties at the behest of national authorities. Thus, the Poor Law itself was not the major vehicle through which the insane were defined as a category; in fact, the Poor Law had less to say about this category precisely because it was already being dealt with separately.[53]

There is a certain irony in the fact that mental illness, the type of disease we now consider hardest to define, should have been separated conceptually and practically in welfare policy *before* physical illness. The intellectual controversies over the definition of insanity in the nineteenth century are peculiarly similar to controversies over the definition of disability in the twentieth. In both cases, the inability of the medical profession to present an objective definition did not stop policymakers from constructing a vast array of policy measures predicated on being able to identify a separate class of people.

Despite the volume of public policy for the insane in nineteenth century England, the category was rarely defined formally in policy documents, and definition of the boundaries between sane and insane remained an elusive hope. One indication of the confusion is the lack of standard terminology even within the Poor Law; the insane were variously labeled "lunatics," "idiots," "persons of unsound mind," "persons of weak intellect," "the mentally infirm," or "persons suffering from diseases of the mind."[54] But Poor Law documents never defined the terms, as though some common understanding made definition unncessary.

Meanwhile, there was a vigorous discussion of definitions within the emerging psychiatric profession. Numerous treatises elaborated lengthy, high-sounding criteria, full of medical terminology, as a segment of the medical profession tried to lay claim to a large population of clients.[55] Insanity was defined as "a loss of nervous tone"; "inordinate, irregular or impaired action of the mind, instincts, sentiments, intellectual or perceptive powers . . . produced by organic change in the brain"; or "a morbid state that influences our reflective, observant and imaginative faculties." As sociologist Andrew Scull says, "the arbitrariness of the whole business is suggested by the need most writers felt to coin a definition of their own." And for every writer who invented a definition, there could be found another who rejected the possibility of "a precise definition of madness" or dismissed all the attempts as involving "a subtlety more easily accomplished in books than in practice."[56]

Given the recognition of insanity as a problem, there were two major means of coping with it. Until the nineteenth century, public authorities generally left care of the insane to their families unless the person caused public disturbances, became dangerous to the public, or was uncontrollable by his relatives. Some institutions for the insane had been established in England, as well as the rest of Europe, as early as the seventeenth century, but a system of public asylums maintained by county governments was a reform of mid-nineteenth-century England. The enormous increase in public asylums was preceded by the growth of private "madhouses" and a system of boarding-out the insane on contract to willing families.

Public or charity asylums, as distinct from the private institutions for self-paying clients, often grouped together the insane, the criminal, the poor, the sick, the senile, the aged, and sometimes the orphaned as well. Lunatic asylums "functioned as museums for the collection of the unwanted,"[57] and their horrible conditions formed the leitmotif of nineteenth-century investigations. Inmates were crammed together in crowded rooms, sometimes in "crib wards" where they were chained inside small boxes, on straw mattresses. But the treatment afforded the insane by institutions was probably no worse than that provided for them at home. The family might confine the person to a hut (say, six by eight feet) or small outbuilding, or chain him or her to a tree or a wall.[58]

All the regulations of the Poor Law reform included a special exemption for the insane from the prohibition against outdoor relief, and these regulations continued in force throughout the administration of the Poor Law.[59] But recognizing the insane as a special category applied only to the question of admission to a workhouse and the granting of outdoor relief. Once inside the workhouse, they were not considered a special category; until the last quarter of the nineteenth century, regulations for internal operation of workhouses make no provision for segregating lunatics.[60]

Nevertheless, the category differed from others in some important ways. The insane were the only group among the "exempt" categories who were also subject to the jurisdiction of a second authority: the Lunacy Commission. The Lunacy Commission, particularly after 1848, took a strong stand in favor of segregating lunatics from other paupers and providing minimum standards of care; thus, lunatics had a separate agency acting as an advocate on their behalf. In their analysis of the Poor Law, Sidney and Beatrice Webb suggest that the advocacy wasn't of much use, however. The Poor Law authorities knew that if they required local officials to build separate facilities for the insane, the facilities would have to meet the standards of the Lunacy Commission—which were considered extravagant by the Poor Law authorities and economically unfeasible by local officials. To avoid the problem, then, the Poor Law officials maintained a virtual silence on the question of treatment of the insane.[61]

Another important difference between the insane and other categories was their civic rights. Until 1871, the guardians of workhouses had no authority to detain a pauper in a workhouse against his will, even if the person were suffering from a contagious disease.[62] But those who were certified as insane (not merely feebleminded or of defective intellect) were always subject to detention against their will.[63] The 1845 lunacy legislation (or Ashley's Act) required certification by both a lay magistrate and a medical doctor.[64]

The history of the definition and treatment of lunacy is largely a story of struggle between the medical profession and the magistrates. During the nineteenth century in England, when the county asylum system was established, the medical profession won control over these institutions, largely on the basis of successful claims that insanity was a physiological disease best treated by medical methods.[65] During the seventeenth and eighteenth centuries, when insanity was often perceived as a "lack of reason," a state of emptiness or nonhumanness, the judgment of lay authorities had usually been considered appropriate as a certifying device.[66] But as physicians gained control over the treatment of insanity, particularly over the management of asylums, they too were asked to make judgments of insanity for official purposes, including detention of the insane in workhouses.

By the end of the nineteenth century, the Poor Law had articulated fairly elaborate provisions for certification. The Lunacy Act of 1890 allowed for nondangerous lunatics to be transferred from asylums to workhouses if the manager of the workhouse (*not* the medical officer) thought the transfer appropriate. Civil officials were also allowed, at their own discretion, to detain a lunatic for up to fourteen days in a workhouse if they considered the person dangerous to him- or herself or the public. If an uncured lunatic was discharged from an asylum and the medical officer of the local workhouse certified that he could safely and appropriately be kept there, he could be detained against his will. And finally, medical officers of workhouses were allowed to certify that under certain conditions, lunatics could remain in workhouses instead of being sent to asylums.[67]

Defectives

The term "defectives" was originally used in Poor Law administration to designate the blind, deaf, and dumb: that is, persons having a deficiency of the senses. Later, the terms "lame" and "deformed" were added to the list, and in 1899, epileptics were included in the category for the first time. In 1903, the term "mental defectives" appeared: a Special Order of 1903 distinguished a class of children who were not certified as being of "unsound mind" but were nonetheless mentally defective.[68]

Defectives were always exempted from the prohibition against outdoor relief, and discussions about their treatment centered on their special educational needs. They were the focus of a variety of special exemptions from other policies as well. For example, the deaf and dumb were not required to learn to read and write before being eligible for an apprenticeship, and relief to defective wives and children was not counted as relief to the husband or father.[69]

Defectives were increasingly recognized by Parliament as a special category for whom local officials would be justified in providing special treatment, but there is little evidence to indicate that Poor Law guardians in fact provided such care. A spate of educational laws under Queen Victoria is the first indication of special provision for defectives, and after 1871, there seems to have been emphasis on vocational training.

The question of validation did not arise for this category until the very end of the century, when the concept was extended to include mental as well as physical defects. As long as only physical defects were at issue, the defects were assumed by definition visible and obvious. But the Special Order of 1903 makes reference to the need for physicians to distinguish between "children of unsound mind" and "mental defectives." Apparently this was a distinction between insanity and retardation, because the term "imbeciles" is also used in connection with mental defectives.

The Aged and Infirm

The phrase "aged and infirm" was always used as a single term denoting people with a permanent incapacity, regardless of age. (Before 1834, and occasionally thereafter, the category was called "aged and impotent.") According to the Webbs, it meant

> the class of persons permanently incapacitated, whether from old age, physical defect, or chronic debility, from obtaining any paid employment. The essential characteristic of the "aged and infirm" (like that of "children") was indeed the precise opposite of that of "the ablebodied." . . . The "aged and infirm" were those (not being children) who could not possibly get employment for any hire, however small.[70]

Although the aged and infirm were expressly exempted from the prohibition against outdoor relief from the very beginning, their treatment within the workhouse was more problematic, and fear of possible fraud and deception among this class was evident. In 1839, the Poor Law Commission expressed concern about the policy of separate and better facilities for the aged "so that they might enjoy their indulgences." The commissioners argued that if the workhouse were made attractive and pleasant on behalf of the aged, "it would immediately be useless as a test between indigence and indolence and fraud, it would no longer operate as an inducement to the young and healthy to provide support for their later years."[71] The report also said that young independent laborers would have no incentive to practice frugality and plan for their old age if they could not possibly hope to provide for themselves as well as the workhouse provided for its aged residents.

As with the sick, the appropriateness of applying "least eligibility" to the aged was a matter of debate throughout the nineteenth century. The aged and infirm clearly constituted a troublesome category. In part, the problem stemmed from the "exemplary effect" of attractive workhouse conditions and the possible effect on the motivation of young adults. But in some measure, the problem was also one of distinguishing between genuine and fraudulent infirmity.

Thus, the aged and infirm were a prime target when, in 1871, a major shift toward stringency occurred in the administration of the

Poor Law. In that year, Parliament abolished the Poor Law Board, which had existed only under temporary grants of authority, and transferred its authority to a newly created Board of Local Government with the status of a cabinet department. The new board began a campaign against outdoor relief, in which it tried for the first time to implement the principles of 1834. The turn toward stringency followed a period of economic downturn. The severe winter of 1860–61, followed by a rise in unemployment that resulted from the cotton shortage after the Civil War in the United States, led to a series of sharp increases in local relief expenditures. It was a reaction to these increases that brought about the new policy of 1871.[72]

In its mission to eliminate outdoor relief and reduce the relief rolls, the Local Government Board was led by the inspectorate, a regulatory staff that had served the Poor Law Board all along. The inspectorate's suggestions are all too familiar to anyone who has followed the cycles of twentieth-century American welfare crises. The rise in rolls was blamed on officials who granted relief "too readily and without sufficient inquiry."[73] The remedy was to be a more uniform application of the workhouse requirement, even to the sick and aged and infirm.

However zealous its inspectors were in the campaign against outdoor relief, the central authority did not take much heed of their recommendations or ever issue any regulations for their implementation. A circular of 1871 did direct the guardians to conduct "a more vigilant inquiry into circumstances" of all applicants for relief; and Mr. Longley, the hard-line inspector of London, took a firm stand in his own reports that the workhouse should be offered to the sick and aged as well as to the ablebodied. But the official policy on exempting the sick and the aged from the outdoor relief prohibition still did not change.[74]

The Local Government Board did have ways of tightening up relief to the aged and sick without actually prohibiting outdoor relief, however. One of these was to develop measures of "efficiency" and use them to pressure parishes and unions to reduce their rolls. These measures, the ratio of paupers to general population, and the ratio of people on outdoor relief to those on indoor relief, were published and circulated to embarrass the officials of parishes with high numbers. And since the measures took no account of the proportion of paupers who were children, sick, or aged, they placed an implicit pressure on local officials to reduce outdoor relief to these categories.[75]

Another method for tightening up relief was to conduct closer investigations into individual circumstances in order to distinguish true infirmity from fraud. In the period from 1834 to 1871, there was scarcely any mention of a need for a validation device for this category; the infirmities that rendered an adult incapable of working were thought to be obvious. From 1871 on, however, there were more references to using the "workhouse test" to separate the legitimate needy aged and infirm from the merely indolent. And in the period after 1885, when the tide had turned back toward a more humanitarian administration of relief, the Local Government Board still found it useful to recommend that local officials perform careful inquiries into the background of people "whose physical faculties have failed by reason of age and infirmity," and that relief should be given only to those "who are shown to have been of good character, thrifty according to their opportunities, and generally independent in early life."[76]

To what extent was the new policy of stringency actually implemented? Were thorough investigations of the aged and infirm actually conducted? Were more aged and infirm actually forced into the workhouses? It is difficult to answer these questions, because the records left to historians are the official documents of the assistance agencies, not the field notes of the local guardians or inspectors. Statistics show that the workhouses were indeed emptying, and that the proportion of paupers on outdoor relief dropped steadily until the end of the century.[77] There is substantial evidence that the number of recipients of both indoor and outdoor relief dropped from the late 1870s on. Despite an economic slump and high unemployment in the period from 1873 to 1879, the number of people on relief in 1878–79 was actually lower than at any other time after 1841.[78] However, since the Poor Law officials made a practice of lumping together the figures on all paupers, it is impossible to tell how much of the reduction was borne by each of the various categories, particularly by the nonablebodied.

An important feature of Poor Law policy during the period of stringency was the increase in separate facilities for children, the sick, and the aged. A series of scandals about conditions in the workhouses, followed by formal government inquiries, created pressure on local governments to establish separate schools for pauper children or to board them out to local families. Similarly, separate infirmaries for the sick and separate sick pavilions attached to workhouses became more common. One possible interpretation of the decline in outdoor relief, then, is that more and more nonablebodied paupers were housed and cared for in institutions rather than the workhouse. Local officials could be more stringent in applying "no outdoor relief" and "least eligibility," because the availability of separate institutions for the aged, the sick, and children meant that they didn't need to apply the harsh tests to these groups.

The essence of welfare policy during the Poor Law reform period, from 1834 to the turn of the century, was the increasing specification of special categories. Poor Law officials confronted the dilemma of believing that only harsh disincentives would stem the tide of relief, yet knowing that many people were "not proper objects" for harsh treatment. Categorization helped resolve the dilemma by giving reason to the distinction and specifying recognizable characteristics for sorting the poor and locating them in their proper place. The categories of welfare policy restored the illusion of order to a disintegrating social world.

The Significance of the Disability Category in English Poor Law

The analysis of the evolution of categories in English welfare policy yields some interesting insights about the meaning of the disability category, insights that are obscured by the current fixation on disability as a clinical concept. The most important conclusion is that the system of categorical exemptions created by the end of the nineteenth century was a response to a long-standing policy dilemma: how to reconcile the distributive principles of work and need without undermining the productive side of the economy.

English policymakers were ambivalent and confused about what kind of economic policies to follow and how strictly to implement the principles of a market society. Relief policies swung back and forth between programs based strictly on work and those based on need. By the time the statute of 1601 had consolidated earlier antivagrancy statutes into the Poor Law, the basic principle of distribution according to work was already in place. The Poor Law included a system of categorical exemption from punishment for vagrancy and a primitive validation device in the form of certification by local officials. The underlying assumption was that distribution would be strictly on the basis of labor, with a very few exceptions for people absolutely unable to work.

If this categorical work-based system had been a successful solution to the economic problems of the nation, it should have persisted once established. Why, then, in 1795, did England retreat from its categorical welfare system and set up instead the "Speenhamland System," whereby ablebodied laborers were guaranteed a minimum wage pegged to the price of bread? Why a sudden shift to need-based distribution? The old system was not working, and policy-makers were groping for another solution.

One classic interpretation of the Speenhamland phenomenon is that it represented the last gasp of a communal agrarian society attempting to protect itself from the destructive forces of capitalism. The system of wage supplements pegged to basic human nutritional requirements was a humanitarian gesture. But this gesture was a disaster, however noble its intentions. Instead of making economic conditions better for the average laborer, it drove down wages, reduced productivity, increased the birthrate, and generally made peasants and laborers worse off. Distribution based on need was absolutely incompatible with a market economy, and the guaranteed minimum wage only destroyed the work motivation of laborers and induced employers to reduce their wages to the minimum, or less. In short, the Speenhamland system was a well-motivated but misdirected attempt to improve economic conditions for the laborer; instead, it prevented the development of a labor market. In this view, the Poor Law Reform of 1834 represented the triumph of the competitive labor market. Once the "right to live" or guaranteed minimum wage was abolished, and relief was provided only to those who absolutely could not work anyway, labor would be forced into the wrenching but ultimately beneficial market, wherein each worker was a mobile element, similar to a commodity.[79]

Careful analysis of the Speenhamland system has shown that it had almost none of the effects commonly attributed to it in the classic view.[80] The system was adopted not nationally but only by some counties, apparently those where agricultural wages were already extremely depressed by an oversupply of labor and insufficient "pull" from urban industrial centers. Many counties abandoned the system within thirty years, but even among those that kept it longest, there is no evidence that their general pattern of rise and decline in relief expenditures differed from that of counties without the minimum wage. The rise in relief expenditures was due to a long period of bad harvests (1795–1818), and the decline in expenditures after 1818 went along with a series of good harvests. But the conventional wisdom of the time attributed the state of the economy to the advent and abandonment of the Speenhamland relief system—a typical case of attributing changes in the state of nature or the economy to chronologically proximate changes in public policy.

Thus, Speenhamland, a totally need-based system, was itself a response to bad economic conditions and an admission by its advocates that the old work-based system, with categorical restrictions on alms and relief, was not working to keep people from starving or to increase productivity among the ablebodied. When it appeared that Speenhamland didn't "work" either, it was abandoned as well—not so much because there was good evidence that it wasn't working as because the makers of economic policy were ideologically blinded by the belief that relief undermines effort and productivity.[81] The essence of the Reform of 1834 was a reassertion of the work-based distributive system with categorical exemptions, even though this system hadn't worked prior to 1795. The legislation of 1834 has a spirit of firm resolve, as if to say, "This time we are *really* going to enforce the principle of work-based distribution." The fact that policymakers would revert to the categorical system in spite of their own fairly recent historical experience indicates the strength of their belief in the importance of work incentives. And for all the conviction expressed in official (statutory) policy that need-based relief was to be eliminated, the policy as implemented provided outdoor relief to a variety of constantly expanding categories, and in many instances to vagrants and ablebodied workers as well.

Thus, the picture of halfhearted implementation that emerges after 1834 shows that policymakers did not have terribly strong faith in their own remedies. What had been intended as an absolutely rigid denial of the need principle in distribution ended as a combination of need and work, where the boundaries between the two systems were drawn in accordance with the categories whose development we have traced. The categorical welfare system as it stood in 1900 was the resolution of a series of shifts back and forth between work and need. Before 1795, the system was largely work-based, with a few exceptions for needy categories. The Speenhamland system represented a shift to an absolute criterion of need. Its implicit diagnosis of the failure of the earlier Poor Law was not that the need-based component was too liberal but that it was not liberal enough. The Reform of 1834 was intended to be a return to an absolute criterion of work, with very stringently enforced exceptions. What resulted in the next several decades, however, was a combination system in which the categories were used to delineate the boundaries between work and need. Thus, the categories provided a resolution to the old dilemma of work versus need by allowing the two systems to coexist.

Whatever else it accomplished, the categorical system was expressly designed to place certain limits on the mobility of labor. The categories of English welfare policy evolved out of a system of vagrancy controls whose chief purpose was not so much to provide for the needs of the poor as to prevent ablebodied workers from pursuing their self-interest to the possible detriment of employers. Laborers could move around in search of higher wages or better jobs only if they could count on receiving alms in times and places between attachment to specific employers; otherwise, leaving a place of employment and a community where they were part of a social network would have been a very risky proposition. In the context of a general system of alms, however unofficial and unorganized, was movement in search of work and higher wages feasible.

The categories solved the work/need dilemma by limiting alms or relief to precisely the people who could not move around anyway: the acutely ill, the physically and mentally disabled, the very old and the very young. Those people who had the potential to move were the ones against whom the prohibition against outdoor relief was directed; they could receive relief only by being immobilized in a workhouse. In the categorical system of Poor Law policy, the basic method of drawing a boundary between work and need was thus *literal confinement*: one was either confined by one's own physical limitations or confined in a workhouse. The workhouse may have been a validation device (the "workhouse test"), but it was also a method of containment.

The conventional interpretation of Speenhamland and the Reform of 1834 is thus wrong for another reason: far from being a restoration of the labor market after the "disaster" of Speenhamland, the Reform of 1834 was expressly designed to prevent labor mobility, not encourage it. If anything, the Poor Law Reform was meant to attach the worker more firmly to his employer, to force him to accept low wages, and to prevent him from becoming a self-interested, welfare-maximizing individual. In spite of economic doctrine that the pursuit of self-interest was the engine that would drive the national economy to prosperity, self-interest was to be allowed only to merchants and employers, not to common laborers.

Finally, the history of English welfare policy demonstrates that the unitary category of "disability" in contemporary social policy (particularly social insurance) began as a series of separate conditions more unified in the notion of vagrancy than in any concept of common cause. The concept of need embodied in these categories was the mirror image of the concept of work. Social aid for the needy was designed to provide exactly what work provided for the ablebodied themselves (physical subsistence) and for society (productivity). The needy were by definition, therefore, those who could not, under ordinary circumstances, provide for their own sustenance or contribute to the national economy. The workhouse was a remedy for both of these problems.[82]

The essence of the categorical solution is classification. From the first mandate to separate the ablebodied from the impotent poor, relief schemes evolved ever more elaborate systems of classifying the needy. In many such schemes, the categories were arranged in a hierarchy of legitimacy; the point, after all, was to allocate social aid, and allocation requires that priorities be set.[83] The problem of vagrancy was tackled by dividing the poor into different classes and providing each class with appropriate treatment.

This mode of thinking generated some fantastic schemes for employing the disabled, in which particular tasks were matched to particular disabilities. Juan Luis Vives, in the sixteenth century, described a model workhouse where the blind would be set to work making "little boxes and chests, fruit baskets, and cages," or making music, or working the treadmills and treading the wine presses, all according to their particular talents.[84] Jeremy Bentham concocted an amazing plan in 1797, under which the blind would knit, and children would be harnessed to a seesaw apparatus designed to pump water as a by-product of their play. The unpleasantness of living with the disabled would be minimized by another type of matching: lunatics would be housed next to the deaf, and the physically deformed next to the blind.[85]

English Poor Law policy dealt with disability as a variety of very separate conditions. What they had in common was their reduction of people's ability to work, but social reformers were careful to differentiate these effects. It was only the need for a common administrative mechanism and an accurate validation device that pushed these categories together under one heading.

German Social Insurance

The German Invalidity and Pension Law of 1889 was the third program in a trio of social insurance laws passed under Chancellor Otto von Bismarck. It followed a compulsory national health insurance scheme in 1883 and an industrial accidents law in 1884. The German program represents a critical point in the development of the disability category, not only because it was the first but because it became a model, explicitly or implicitly, for all subsequent social insurance programs. There is ample evidence that policymakers from several countries consciously examined the German system during the phase of study and legislative drafting in their own countries.[86]

In order to understand the political significance of the disability pension program, it is necessary to understand the political context in which it was created. Germany had become a unified empire only a short time before (in 1870), having been a loose collection of independent principalities until its defeat of France under the leadership of Prussia. In the period preceding and during the era of social insurance legislation, the government was making a concerted effort to industrialize, partly driven by its realization that Germany was behind much of the continent in its economic development. The national government was at the center of the industrialization campaign: the state owned and operated the railroads, canals, mines, and utilities; it provided a very large proportion of the capital for private industrial development in both heavy industry and manufacturing; and it supported both its agricultural and its industrial sectors with protective tariffs.[87] The social insurance programs must be seen as part of a larger strategy to unify the country politically and strengthen it economically.

Social insurance was created entirely on the initiative of the central government and primarily at the behest of Bismarck. Gustav Schmoller, a historian and member of the Conservative Party at the time, has said that if Bismarck had not mobilized support for the social insurance legislation, the country would have waited generations for the program.[88] This assessment of Bismarck's role is widely accepted, even by historians of different political persuasions.[89]

Bismarck gave three explicit rationales for his social insurance program. One was that a program of insurance, and particularly pensions, would make the worker realize that his future was tied to the future of the state, and therefore he would be less likely to join the Social Democratic Party or be otherwise politically rebellious. In a famous speech before the Parliament in 1881, Emperor Wilhelm said:

> Past institutions intended to insure working people against the danger of falling into a condition of helplessness owing to the incapacity resulting from accident or age have proved inadequate, and their insufficiency has to no small extent contributed to cause the working classes to seek help by participating in Social Democratic movements.[90]

Social insurance benefits were explicitly conceived as a material benefit whose costs to the state were infinitely repaid in the political loyalty they secured. For this reason, Bismarck was insistent that the state should play some role in financing the programs; if the benefits were financed entirely by contributions from employers and employees, then the political value of insurance would be entirely lost to the state.

The program was also built on an underlying philosophy of government that emphasized the duty of the state to rule in accordance with Christian ethics and to promote the welfare of its members.[91] Bismarck used this philosophy of the paternalistic role of the state to exclude the possibility of a compulsory insurance program run through private companies. Because only the state has the power to coerce, he said, it would not be fair to impose compulsory insurance on people without offering something in return:

> If compulsion is enforced, it is necessary that the law provide at the same time an institution for insurance, which shall be cheaper and securer than any other. We cannot expose the savings of the poor to the danger of bankruptcy, nor can we allow a deduction from the contributions to be paid as dividend or as interest on shares.[92]

Of course, the benevolent sentiments in this statement, however sincere, coincidentally also justified the policy that would best serve the state's political interests. If insurance benefits created political support for the institution that provided them, then the state should try to capture a monopoly on this resource.

A third rationale for the program was that the state should reduce the burdens of poor relief for local governments by assuming the costs of pensions for invalids and the elderly. In the second reading of the bill before the legislature, Bismarck said that the parishes and counties (*Kreise*) would be considerably helped if the poor law charges were distributed more evenly among larger units.[93] Because of a lack of data, it is impossible to know whether a reduction in local relief expenditures actually occurred. Nevertheless, the centralization of fiscal responsibility for welfare was certainly consistent with Bismarck's political goals of strengthening the central government vis-à-vis local governments and of making individual workers directly dependent on the state.

The Law of 1889

The term "invalid" in German usage was borrowed from the French, where it was used in the beginning of the eighteenth century to describe men unfit to be soldiers.[94] It first appears in official German usage in an 1887 social insurance bill. In that proposal, invalidity was defined as the total incapacity to work, without regard to age. A disabled person was in turn defined as someone who "*because of his physical or mental condition* is neither in a position to perform regularly his previous work . . . nor to *earn the minimum invalidity pension* through other work *corresponding to his strengths and capabilities and existing job opportunities.*"[95] This proposal contains all the elements of the current definition and exemplifies all the principles of the concept of disability in German social insurance law.

First, from the very beginning, disability has been defined with reference to *earning capacity*. It has always been a dual concept, linking the inability to earn some specified minimum level with a medical condition. In German law, the earnings levels were established by the legislature and initially pegged to four "wage classes" set up to determine the weekly contributions owed by workers to social insurance.

Second, the notion of *boundaries* was an explicit part of the concept of disability. The law set two particular boundaries for the program—one to establish the class of people for whom participation in the scheme would be mandatory, and who therefore would have to contribute to it from their wages; the other to establish when members of the scheme would be entitled to collect a disability pension. Both were conceived as earnings levels, or an imaginary boundary through the wage distribution, so that the term *Grenze* (limit, boundary) in German usage made intuitive sense. In the Law of 1889, the boundary for obligation to insure (*Versicherungspflichtgrenze*) was set at one-third the average daily wage in the locality of employment. Insurance was compulsory for workers earning below that amount. The boundary for entitlement (*Invaliditätsgrenze*) was originally set at one-sixth of the applicant's prior earnings (technically his wage class, rather than his actual earnings); he would be deemed disabled only if he could not earn at least this amount.[96] The entitlement boundary might be seen as a floor below which no worker could fall.

Political discussion of the pension program during the legislative phase centered on the locations of these boundaries. The Social Democrats were caught in the classic dilemma of working class parties confronted by proposals for either state-sponsored or employer-sponsored labor protection programs. They did not want the state or employers to take over insurance functions, something they had hoped to capture for trade unions, but they could hardly oppose social insurance for the working class. As a result, the political conflict focused on the exact level of the two boundaries. Discussion of the meaning of disability took the somewhat bizarre form of a debate over fractions: should the boundary be one-quarter, one-third, or one-half? Of course, the Social Democrats pushed for a higher entitlement boundary or protective floor. One Social Democratic deputy commented ten years later, when the program was up for discussion again: "The entitlement level was set in such a way that a worker would not receive a pension until he was so far down that he was a long-time alumnus of the poor law."[97]

The third element of the original definition of disability was its provision that the incapacitated worker could be *required to perform other suitable work*. This requirement was at the heart of most political controversy over the program from its inception. While the law assumed that an injured person could be transferred to other jobs, it did not, like American disability insurance, make any pretense of forcing him to the last resort. He did not have to accept "any job in the entire national economy," as the American standard was originally phrased. He could be expected to take on a new job only within a certain "sphere of activity" (*Kreis der Tätigkeit*). That sphere was to be defined by his skills and qualifications as well as by his previous work experience. The notion of a "sphere of activity" also connotes boundaries and suggests that the function of the disability category was intimately connected with the drawing of social boundaries within the occupational structure. The chief political question in the administration of the program became: to what extent can a person be forced to perform other types of jobs (after he is incapable of performing his own) and what factors will be taken into consideration to define the sphere of occupational change?

The original proposal of 1887 included a provision that the state of the current labor market should be a relevant consideration in determining what other jobs the incapacitated worker could be asked to perform. This element was the one feature of the proposal that was dropped from the final bill (and has never been reintroduced), on the grounds that the tightness of the job market had nothing to do with the concept of physical and mental capacity to work. Besides, argued the regime, "the purpose of the proposal is not to provide insurance against unemployment, but rather, against disability."[98] As we will see, this same debate was reenacted in the United States Congress some sixty years later.

Evolution of the Disability Category

The invalidity pension program covered manual laborers (including day laborers, domestic servants, clerks, assistants, and apprentices in handicrafts and trade) as well as clerical and administrative workers earning less than RM 2,000 per year (about $250). It was administered by a group of mutual associations called *Landesversicherungsämte* (LVA). Bismarck had originally hoped to have the program administered directly by the Imperial Insurance Office, which had been set up with the accident insurance program, but the Catholic and Conservative majority in the legislature strongly opposed such centralized bureaucratic control.[99] As a result, the Imperial Insurance Office was given a supervisory function over the LVAs, rather than a direct administrative role, and it also served as an administrative court for hearing disputes between employees and the LVAs. The LVAs were in theory mutual associations managed jointly by employers and employees, but were in fact so dominated by the employers that workers saw their relationship to the LVAs as adversarial rather than participatory.[100] The Imperial Insurance Office was the court of last resort for decisions on pension eligibility. It in turn came under the supervision of the Ministry of the Interior until 1917, when it was transferred to the Ministry of Labor.

Bismarck had also wanted the state to play the major role in financing the program, but he lost on that issue as well. All the major parties in the legislature (Conservative, Catholic, Liberal, Social Democrat) agreed that both employers and employees should contribute to the pension program, though they disagreed on the exact proportions. Nevertheless, their agreement on the issue extended far enough to prevent the state from becoming the major financer, and in the end, the state's financial contribution was limited to a nominal per capita subsidy.[101] Policy for the invalidity pension program thus evolved through the interplay of two major institutions: the legislature which enacted major reforms in 1899, 1911, and 1957; and the administrative agencies (the LVAs and the Imperial Insurance Office),[102] which strongly influenced policy through the development of common law in the hearing of claimants' cases.

In 1899, the regime decided that the original definition of disability was no longer working, and it submitted a new proposal to the legislature. In particular, it rejected the old two-part definition, in which different earnings levels were used to determine the obligation to insure and entitlement to a pension.[103] In the new law, the earnings level for compulsory insurance remained at one-third, but the level for pension eligibility was raised from one-sixth to one-third, so that the two criteria were now the same.

Even more important than this liberalization of the earnings level for eligibility, however, was a new emphasis on the question of occupational transfers. A new phrase was introduced into the law: from then on, a person would be considered disabled when he or she, because of a physical or mental condition, "could no longer earn at least one-third as much as a mentally and physically healthy person with similar education and work experience in the same region, in any suitable job corresponding to his strengths and capabilities *and taking into reasonable consideration his education and former occupation.*"[104] Such "reasonable consideration" obviously left a wide latitude for interpretation, and it was thus a double-edged sword that could be used either to restrict or to expand eligibility.

The motive behind the legislative revision of 1899 was clearly a desire to expand the number of pensions. The regime argued that a disabled worker should not be forced to accept a job that was "completely foreign to him, mentally or physically unsuited to him, or . . . far distant from his former place of employment." In a rare instance of the triumph of common sense over bureaucratic sophistication, the regime criticized the previous definition of disability, saying it had led to such excessive severity that pensions were denied to "people who deserved them according to customary usage of the term 'disability' and according to common sense views."[105] The Imperial Insurance Office issued a clarification of policy six months later, in which it said that the LVAs could not deny an invalidity pension merely on a showing that the applicant was not occupationally disabled; they must also investigate whether there existed some other wage labor corresponding to his "strengths and capabilities as well as his education and other life circumstances."[106]

Not surprisingly, the number of invalidity pensions awarded jumped dramatically between 1899 and 1900, from roughly 96,000 to over 125,000. Since this meant an increase in the amount of subsidy provided by the federal government, the Ministry of Interior (which included the Imperial Insurance Office) almost immediately began to issue warnings that the system was in danger of bankruptcy. It conducted a series of investigations of the LVAs to find out why the number of pensions was growing, and suddenly, in the regions that had been investigated, the number of pensions awarded fell back just as dramatically.[107] A ministerial report of 1905 essentially blamed the physicians. It said that they were confusing the concept of disability in the health insurance program with disability in pension insurance, and that they were mistakenly applying the (more liberal) criteria of sickness insurance to applicants for disability pensions.[108]

In 1911, the statutes for the three social insurance programs were consolidated into a single "Imperial Insurance Code" known as the RVO (*Reichsversicherungsordnung*). The Social Democrats tried repeatedly during the discussion of the bill to raise the eligibility criterion for disability pensions from one-third to one-half; that is, they wanted a worker to be able to receive a pension as soon as he was incapable of earning at least half of the lowest wage class amount. They even offered to accept an increase in employee contributions to the scheme in exchange for the rise in the entitlement floor, but their proposal was defeated for lack of support from any of the other parties or the regime, which was particularly worried about the extra subsidies the Social Democratic proposal would entail.[109]

The formal definition of disability remained essentially the same, with one minor exception. The new code said that in considering a person's capacity to hold other suitable jobs, the LVAs must consider "the entire labor market." The meaning of this requirement was yet to be worked out in practice.

Also in 1911, the Reichstag established a separate pension insurance scheme for white collar workers; those earning less than RM 2,000 had been included in the program from the beginning, and by

1903, 58 percent of all male and 92 percent of all female white collar workers were compulsorily insured under the existing program. In 1911, a special distinction was made between the two types of insurance, and in 1922, white collar workers were transferred to a new and separate insurance fund administered directly by the Imperial Insurance Office. This change represented the beginning of a class distinction in German social insurance policy that was to persist formally until 1957, and informally until today. The separate administration of pension policy for the two groups—white collar and blue collar workers—was important because it enabled the application of different eligibility criteria (or disability definitions), and these definitions in turn amounted to a different labor policy for the two groups.

The separate scheme was established primarily at the behest of the white collar workers themselves. Between 1900 and 1911, there were about fifty different associations of white collar workers, all of which were in conflict over the goals and strategies to be pursued on behalf of their members. The one goal that united them was the desire for a separate pension program.[110] They wanted it not only because of the low benefits of the general insurance scheme but also, in Tennstedt's words, because "there was a danger for a white-collar worker that he would be forced into a manual labor job before he could obtain a disability pension."[111]

The Ministry of the Interior went along with the idea and developed the legislative proposal, which it justified with two main points. First, it said that to develop separate wage classes for white collar workers within the general scheme would "create financial difficulties for the carriers and disadvantages for the remaining insured people." Second, it said it placed great weight on the wishes of the white collar workers themselves. Critics of the separate program maintained that the regime was using it for political purposes, in the same way that it used social insurance in general: namely, to reward a social class that had been politically loyal to the government and to undercut any motivation of this class to join the "red camp."[112]

Once the separate scheme for white collar workers was established, there were two major differences in the definition of disability used to determine eligibility. White collar workers needed to demonstrate a loss of only one-half of the earning capacity of a comparable healthy worker, while blue collar workers still needed to demonstrate a loss of two-thirds. And when disability pension applications were examined for other possible employment, the range of options considered acceptable was drawn much more narrowly for white collar workers; for blue-collar workers, the "entire job market" was considered.

The question of transferability was paramount in the definition of disability in German social insurance. Whereas the English notion of disability grew out of a concept of deficient but faultless states of being that should carry exemption from certain civic punishments, the German concept was both more individualized and more intrusive, being tied in complex ways to *individual occupational experience*. When a person applied for a disability pension, his application was examined first for clinical evidence of a mental or physical condition that prevented him from doing his old job, then to determine whether the person could perform other "suitable" work, given his education and background.

Throughout the period between 1911 and 1957, there were no important statutory changes, but the concept of disability was shaped through a series of administrative law decisions that carefully delineated boundaries of "allowable occupational transfers" (*zumutbare Verweisungen*) for different social groups. Different criteria were applied to skilled, unskilled, and white collar labor, as the Imperial Insurance Office worked somewhat inductively through individual cases.

In order to give some systematic underpinning to the common law decisions about requiring occupational transfers, the Director of the Division of White Collar Workers of the Imperial Insurance Office, Hermann Dersch, developed the notion of the "transferability cross." On the horizontal dimension were different occupational groups, and the policy question was which of these constituted appropriate reference groups for any given white collar worker. The cross for any particular occupation would contain the acceptable or permissible occupations to which a person could be required to transfer. The vertical dimension of the cross represented different levels of qualification or skills within the same occupation. For example, could a "senior bookkeeper" be required to accept a less strenuous job as a lower-level bookkeeper?[113]

In Dersch's formulation, the question of occupational transfer was determined by the "inherent" nature of the occupations. In deciding on a pension application, the LVA or administrative law judge would examine a group of similar occupations and the nature of the tasks and skills required in each. The "suitability" of some alternative employment for a disabled worker would be determined by a consideration of his skills, education, and background and of the skills required in the possible new occupations. But very quickly, the criterion of *social status* came into explicit consideration. An important LVA decision of 1932 said that "one can expect a skilled worker in general to accept only a job in which he will continue in an essentially similar social position."[114] In 1935, the Imperial Insurance Office held that accountants and cashiers could be required to accept the less strenuous position of "bookkeeper," as long as the change did not involve "a significant social decline."[115] From this point on, the phrase "significant social decline" became an explicit criterion in the disability insurance program.

For the unskilled laborer, however, eligibility for a disability pension was still determined by whether or not he or she could be transferred to any occupation within the entire labor market. In 1957, in a major reform of social insurance legislation, the legislature moved to equalize the insurance benefits of manual and white collar workers.[116] But the actual statutory changes, which ostensibly called for the same definition of disability in both insurance programs, were contradictory and unclear. In the implementation of the reform, the old distinctions prevailed and the law remained a way of protecting the existing social hierarchy.[117] The Minister of Labor (now responsible for the social insurance programs) issued a commentary on the new law in which he argued that because common law had already expressly reduced the permissible "sphere of activity" for transfer of white collar workers, the new law must follow suit.[118]

Moreover, in 1959, two key decisions of the Federal Social Court with respect to blue collar workers applied new criteria to the phrase "significant social decline," so that in effect it did not protect manual laborers from drastic occupational change in the same way it protected white collar workers. In one case, the court said that a skilled mason could be expected to work as an unskilled assistant inspector of motorcycle engine housing, because such a job was still a "responsible activity that would only be entrusted to reliable and smart workers."[119] The concept of "responsible activity," which is so vague as to be meaningless, enabled the LVAs to force manual laborers to accept virtually any kind of work. The second decision held that a worker could be expected to accept employment in a totally new and different occupation as long as it was not too strenuous and the worker "would not enjoy a significantly lower reputation in the eyes of the world."[120] These two decisions, by giving the LVAs the ability to assess permissible transfers in terms of the "responsibility" of jobs and general "public opinion" about the prestige of various occupations, stripped the criterion of "significant social decline" of any firm meaning, and thus of any protective value for manual workers.

The Significance of the German Concept of Disability

German pension policy from the very beginning anchored disability to the inability to earn a certain amount, rather than to a total incapacity to earn or to certain recognized diseases and handicaps. The central question then became: when a person can no longer practice his former occupation, what kind of alternative work should he be expected (or forced) to do? How much of a change in jobs, skills, training, and social status should he be forced to undergo before becoming eligible to receive a disability pension? Thus, the disability category is used to define the nature and degree of labor mobility within the occupational and social structure. It is used to preserve the occupational hierarchy and social status relationships by granting disability when an occupational change would result in "too great" a social drop.

The concept of disability is fundamental to defining the spheres of social status within which an individual is protected. The courts, in handling disability pension cases, came to "respect legitimate individual achievement of a life position" in the same way that they protected private property.[121] The disability pension is used to protect what a person has *already* earned in the work-based system. In this sense, one can see the disability pension program as a system of valves designed to prevent people from "slipping back" into a lower social position. The system is artfully constructed to preserve the existing social hierarchy: in the white collar occupational structure, there are only one-way valves, permitting upward movement and spaced very close together; in the blue collar structure, some of the valves are two-way, and even the one-way valves are placed relatively far apart. Unskilled manual workers are allowed to fall the furthest, skilled workers an intermediate distance, and white collar workers only a very short distance.

Disability in German policy, as in English policy, serves to demarcate the boundaries between the work and need systems, but the boundaries are defined very differently. In Poor Law policy, the purpose of the categories was to keep people in the work-based system as long as possible so as not to lose their productivity. Disability was thus defined very narrowly, and restricted (originally) to a small set of recognizable conditions that permanently incapacitated a person or totally incapacitated him or her temporarily. The Poor Law concept allowed people out of the work-based system and into the need-based system only when they were absolutely devoid of productive ability. In German social insurance, the effect of the category was to preserve very fine distinctions in the internal occupational hierarchy. The German definition of disability thus let people out of the work-based system when keeping them in would disrupt the social hierarchy.

How can one account for the differences between the two systems? Two factors would appear to be important. First, the two concepts grew from entirely different ideological backgrounds. Social insurance in Germany was born of a tradition that sees a positive value to the state in providing social welfare benefits to its people. Welfare was conceived as a quid pro quo, a material benefit that would make citizens both physically and psychologically dependent on the giver. In this view, welfare benefits were an instrument to create political loyalty, and their value as a political resource far outweighed their financial cost. In the English mercantilist tradition, welfare benefits were viewed as a drain on the state. Not only did they involve direct financial costs and a hardship for the ratepayers, but they also symbolized (and created) the loss of productive workers from the labor force. Given these two constrasting beliefs, it is no surprise that German policy would draw the boundaries of disability much more broadly.

The second factor has to do with the nature of the disability category as a regulatory instrument. The German system was forged at a time when the newly formed central government was pursuing a policy of economic planning for rapid industrialization. In such a situation, a government would want to be able to coerce workers into accepting the necessary variety of jobs. The disability definition enabled the regime to have a great deal of control over labor mobility; through the explicit consideration of alternative occupations, disability applicants (especially manual laborers) could be compelled to accept changes of occupation in accordance with available positions in the labor market. The disability category enabled a carefully controlled direction of occupational mobility while still preserving the tightly defined social structure.

England's more gradual industrialization was conducted under the doctrinal aegis of laissez-faire. As we have seen, Poor Law policy defined its categories so stringently that pursuit of self-interest was scarcely permitted to the average laborer. This was a system that crystallized under conditions of a shortage of agricultural labor and then evolved through a period of considerable rural unemployment. Perhaps the categories were designed to force unskilled agricultural laborers out of the countryside and into the cities; for that purpose, the administration of a strict definition would serve.

The German disability insurance program highlights a particular aspect of the disability concept as a boundary-maintaining device. Not only does the definition of disability serve to delineate the boundary between work and need, but it also gives official recognition to *internal divisions* within the occupational structure. In the German case, the definition of disability is explicitly occupational and therefore tied to a particular map of the hierarchical organization of labor. The implementation of disability pension policy thus contributes to enforcing the particular hierarchy. Although other disability programs (such as the American Social Security, Veterans, and Workers Compensation programs) may be less explicitly tied to occupational definitions, all of them necessarily contain this element of enforcing an occupational hierarchy. As we will see, an occupational definition was explicitly rejected by the framers of Social Security Disability Insurance, yet in practice the program requires consideration of what other jobs an injured worker can be expected to perform.

The American Social Security Disability Insurance Program

The United States has often been called a laggard in welfare policy, because it was the last of the industrial states to introduce social insurance. Even once social insurance and welfare programs were introduced, the federal government played a smaller role than that of other major national governments in their respective welfare systems, and the proportion of the national budget devoted to welfare expenditures has been lower than in many other countries.[122] The pattern in disability insurance is no exception. Social insurance for the aged was not introduced until 1935, and not until the 1950s was disability added to the Social Security program as an insured contingency. Disability pensions were introduced in a very limited fashion and expanded gradually, and the federal government's role was reduced by assigning responsibility for disability determination to state agencies. The definition of disability and the mode of determination in individual cases were at the heart of the controversy over the establishment of the program.

The evolution of the concept of disability in American social insurance is strongly marked by the fact that disability insurance was always discussed in the context of *expansion* of an existing program. By the time it appeared on the American policy agenda, there were already several programs for income maintenance or compensation of disabled people that could serve as models and would shape policy ideas. Besides an extensive system of disability pensions for veterans, there were the Railroad Retirement program, Civil Service disability pensions, and state Workers Compensation programs, as well as disability provisions in collective bargaining contracts and in commercial life insurance policies. In addition, the elements of the Social Security program were already in place, so that there was never any question that disability insurance would fit within its basic framework as a contributory program with earnings-related benefits. The major question was whether Social Security would be expanded to include disability as a contingency of coverage.

Thus, the reason for an examination of the origins of American Social Security Disability Insurance is not that it was the first time government recognized disability as an administrative category of entitlement; the program is of interest rather because the controversy over its introduction centered on the *definition* of disability and the process of disability *certification*. The issue of drawing a boundary was discussed more explicitly in this program than in any other, and the connection between the workability of a definition and political acceptability of the program is clearest.[123]

The impetus for expansion came primarily from the Social Security bureaucracy itself. Almost from the moment of passage of the original Social Security Act in 1935, President Franklin D. Roosevelt contemplated expanding the program; in the same year, he appointed an Interdepartmental Committee to Coordinate Health and Welfare Activities to study the possibility of including medical care and disability benefits. If there was consensus among the program executives on anything, the strongest agreement was on the worthiness of social insurance in general and the desirability of constantly improving and expanding the existing system.[124] Whether the urge to expand was derived from liberal, humane, and altruistic values (as Eveline Burns maintains) or from the inherent tendency of any bureaucratic organization to seek to expand its power (as Robert

Myers maintains),[125] there is no question that program executives were the major force behind the studies and proposals for new additions to the program.

The Social Security Administration (called the Federal Security Administration in the early years) was supported in its goals by organized labor, a number of liberal Congressmen, and to some extent by the citizen advisory councils that formed part of the Social Security organizational network. These councils consisted of representatives of labor, business, and "the public," although they were always heavily slanted in favor of the liberal positions of the Social Security Administration itself. The first councils, appointed in 1937, 1947, and 1953, were ad hoc groups created at moments when an important Congressman or administrator feared that a contemplated expansion might be "railroaded through." Beginning in 1956, the Social Security amendments called for advisory councils as a matter of statute. Under both systems, the councils came to be advocates of the Social Security Administration position; they were used to test the political waters with their own reports and recommendations, and to legitimate the policy initiatives of the SSA.[126]

In her history of Social Security, Martha Derthick argues that the major conflict was the question of whether to expand the existing system. Ultimately, the issue of expansion was a fundamental question about the proper role of government—especially the federal government—in social aid, and about the proper scope of redistribution. But because the issue was fought out in the context of pressure group politics, and because the initiative came from an existing bureaucracy, the issue was debated as one of incremental change rather than one of principle.[127]

While it is essential to an understanding of the concept of disability in American social insurance that the legislative history be viewed in this context of bureaucratically induced expansion, there is another aspect that requires explanation. The history of the disability insurance program is a particularly fascinating study in policymaking because the people concerned with drafting the policy actually foresaw all the problems currently plaguing the system and being discovered anew. There is nothing that we now know with hindsight that the legislators, the advisory committees, and even the system's administrators, did not also know. The puzzle is to figure out why these people went ahead and passed a disability insurance program which, they had every reason to believe, would develop precisely the problems that policymakers now are trying to correct.

Policymakers knew, first, that disability insurance (or "invalidity insurance," as it was sometimes called, following the European terminology) was the most problematic of all types of social insurance. Edwin Witte, Executive Director of the Committee on Economic Security that recommended the initial Social Security program as well as directions for expansion, explained later why the committee did not recommend disability insurance as part of the original program:

> The problems of the disabled were never given any real consideration by the Committee on Economic Security. . . . The Technical Board discussed this subject and reached the conclusion that invalidity insurance is the most difficult of all forms of social insurance and should, therefore, be considered as one of the items to come last in a complete program for economic security.[128]

The Advisory Council appointed in 1937 was asked to consider the feasibility of disability insurance, and it, too, concluded that although disability benefits would be "socially desirable," the foreseeable additional costs and administrative difficulties warranted some delay.[129] The Social Security Board then adopted the Advisory Council's position in its 1938 report:

> The Board recognizes that the administrative problems involved are difficult, although it does not believe them insuperable. It also recognizes that provision for permanent total disability would increase the cost of the system both now and in the future. For these reasons it is not making any positive recommendations on this matter at this time.[130]

Thus, for the first several years after the passage of the Social Security Act, there was consensus even among the expansionist program executives and advisory council members that disability insurance was somehow an administrative can of worms that ought to be avoided, especially while the basic social insurance program was being established. Despite all the discussion of disability insurance, the studies commissioned by the Federal Security Administration, and the strong liberal consensus that disability benefits "ought" to be part of social insurance, the Social Security Board did not formally recommend disability insurance until 1943.

The policymakers recognized, second, that the crux of the problem lay in *definition*. In its 1938 report, the Social Security Board said: "The extent to which costs would increase depends on the definition of disability which could be made effective. If a fairly strict definition were adopted and maintained, the Board believes that additional costs would be kept within reasonable limits."[131] Already an informal committee of the advisory board had attempted to define disability and had reluctantly concluded that mental disability should be excluded because it was too hard to determine.[132]

The 1947 Advisory Council, whose report is generally acknowledged to have set the basic framework for the future disability program, also saw the definitional issue as crucial: "The definition of 'disability' used in a disability program will in large part determine the feasibility of administration and the costs of the program. The proposed definition is designed to establish a test of disability which will operate as a safeguard against unjustified claims."[133] The report went on to suggest a definition of disability, but at the same time recommended that its details be left to administrative regulations.

The third piece of foresight shown by the early policymakers was their recognition that any program of disability insurance was likely to expand. The inherent tendency for benefit programs to expand, even when they begin with strict eligibility definitions, was particularly a concern of the opponents of disability insurance. This concern was voiced in a minority report, published as a dissent accompanying the 1948 Advisory Council's report. Robert Myers, the Social Security Administration's chief actuary, constantly warned against what he saw as inevitable bureaucratic expansionism.[134]

In 1938, one did not need any social science theories of organizational behavior to predict liberalization and expansion of disability insurance. Policymakers could observe the experience of commercial insurers as well as the government's own War Risk Insurance program for veterans of World War I.

The record of Congressional testimony and reports shows that Congressmen did indeed examine these other programs.[135] During the 1955 hearings, in which Congress considered offering cash benefits to disabled people, representatives of the insurance industry were called upon to testify about their experience with disability insurance. The main theme of their testimony was that the *courts* had liberalized the definition of disability, despite the industry's use of a narrow standard in its written contracts. The industry had honestly attempted to define disability clearly as an inability to engage in any occupation or perform any work for compensation.

> Courts and juries, though, rewrote the clause, interpreting it so that if an insured [person] was unable to follow his occupation, he

> became entitled to have his life insurance premium waived and monthly total disability benefits paid.
>
> Total, permanent disability became partial disability; it became professional disability; it became unemployment insurance; and at times it became retirement insurance.[136]

Of course, Congressmen and Social Security officials had reason to take such testimony with a grain of salt: the industry had a huge stake in keeping the government out of the disability insurance market, and especially in preventing a compulsory and universal coverage program from emerging. Nevertheless, judicial construction of insurance contracts through the adjudication of controversies between policyholders and insurance companies was a matter of public record, and on this point, the insurance industry was reporting what had in fact occurred.

Disability clauses became fairly standard in life insurance policies in the decade of 1910. The majority of companies defined disability very narrowly as a condition in which a person is "wholly and permanently disabled by bodily injury or disease, so that he is and will be permanently, continuously and wholly prevented from performing any work for compensation or profit."[137] One company introduced a "professional man's clause" in 1922, under which disability was defined as "inability to perform the duties of [one's] occupation," and such clauses became more common during the 1920s. However, the state insurance regulatory agencies, through the vehicle of the National Association of Insurance Commissioners, essentially eliminated these clauses at its 1929 convention by adopting "standards" for life insurance policies. The standards were in turn recommended by two committees, one composed of insurance department actuaries and the other of insurance company representatives.[138] The new standards, which became effective July 1, 1930, prohibited the use of the professional man's clause, which defined disability with reference to an individual's own occupation.

Insurance companies may have preferred the strict interpretation of disability because under it they would have to pay out less frequently, but from a purely theoretical point of view, they probably had no inherent reason to prefer one type of clause over another. They could simply set their premiums to reflect the actuarial costs of awarding pensions on the basis of the general or occupational definition. The companies did face a dilemma of collective action, however: if some of them used the more liberal professional man's clause, these more favorable policies would probably give them a market advantage. Thus, it was in the interest of the companies to use the device of state regulation to foster collective, cooperative action.[139]

Although insurance companies were behind the move to eliminate the professional man's clause, and although they later complained vehemently about "judicial subversion" of the stricter definition, the companies were all too willing to take advantage of the market potential of the more liberal occupational clause. In the period between announcement of the new standards by the insurance commissioners' convention and the effective date of those standards, the companies wrote a flood of new policies with the soon-to-be-eliminated occupational definition. Salesmen used the impending regulation as a sales tactic to persuade people to buy the liberal policies while they were still available.[140]

It was after 1930, when the occupational definition of disability had been eliminated, that courts began to interpret the general disability clauses more broadly. The standard clauses required the insured to be "wholly" or "totally" incapable of working, but the courts generally took the position that a person need not be in a totally helpless and hopeless mental or physicial condition in order to collect. The courts generally reasoned that if the strict clauses were interpreted literally, people would be denied protection in exactly those situations for which they had purchased insurance.[141] One court offered a vivid hypothetical example: "If a person should suffer the loss of his arms and legs, his eyesight and his hearing, he might have his trunk conveyed to a busy street corner and make a little money by selling small objects such as post cards, candy, or cigars."[142]

The insurance industry, in its testimony on Social Security disability insurance, described its serious financial difficulties during the 1930s and attributed them to the judicial liberalizaton of the disability definition. The industry claimed that because of judicial construction, it was forced to pay out more on policies than predicted by its actuarial calculations, which were based on a strict but fair interpretation of the disability clause. In fact, the serious losses of this period were the result of the industry's own rush to write policies with professional man's clause before July 1, 1930, coupled with poor underwriting practices and a failure to raise premiums adequately.[143] Thus, although there was more to the story than their testimony revealed, the experience of private insurers during the 1930s, and the tendency of courts to interpret disability provisions as "occupational disability," stood as clear harbingers of developments in any public disability insurance program.

If the policymakers were tempted to believe that a *public* insurance program would somehow be immune to judicial construction and that the experience of the private sector was therefore irrelevant, they had only to turn to the federal government's War Risk and Government Life Insurance programs for contrary evidence. War Risk Insurance was established in 1917 to provide life and disability coverage to members of the armed services, because the cost of commercial insurance was prohibitive, given the foreseen risks of World War I. The Government Life Insurance program was established two years later, in 1919, to allow policyholders under the War Risk program to convert their term policies to a permanent plan.[144] The judicial history of the definition of disability under War Risk Insurance told much the same story as the experience of commercial life insurance.

The program rested on the narrow and strict definition of disability stated in the regulations of the Bureau of War Risk Insurance. Total permanent disability was defined as "any impairment of mind or body which renders it impossible for the disabled person to follow continuously any substantially gainful occupation. . . ." Disability was to be deemed "permanent" whenever it was "founded upon conditions which render it reasonably certain that it will continue throughout the life [of the disabled person]."[145]

Yet almost from the beginning, the courts broadened the definition in favor of the claimants. Instead of interpreting literally the phrase "*any* substantially gainful occupation," they held that a person must be "adapted" or "fit" to follow some other occupation, not merely physically capable. And they insisted that the determination of disability must take into account the ability of the applicant to hold a job in a competitive labor market. The phrase "to follow continuously" was also interpreted generously, so that a person would still be deemed permanently disabled even if he could work for short intervals or at very light occupations.[146]

The fears of the conservatives about the uncontrolled expansion of a disability insurance program were clearly well founded. Even if they thought that Social Security officials would try to constrain the program within the tight bounds of a very narrow definition of disability, they had reason to worry that the courts would expand the scope of the program while they stood helplessly by.

The original drafters had foresight about one other crucial phenomenon—the tendency for labor market conditions to influence both the rate of applications and the adjudication of disability claims. Many members of the Advisory Council of 1937 expressed the fear that people would file for benefits whenever they became unemployed, particularly during a depression.[147] Albert Linton, president of the Provident Mutual Life Insurance Company and a member of both the 1937 and 1947 Advisory Councils, warned the 1937 council that "if you want to adopt a Machiavellian plan to wreck the whole Social Security, just put in disability and let it run, especially during a period of depression."[148]

Linton was a staunch opponent of the disability insurance program and a coauthor of the dissenting report of the Advisory Council of 1948. He argued, on the basis of the experience of commercial insurers during the Great Depression, that people tended to look on disability benefits as a right, whether or not they were disabled, and that they intensified their demands for benefits during a recession. The dissenting report expanded on the tendency for disability claims to rise with rising unemployment, and even suggested that a disability program would give *employers* an incentive to "lay off inefficient workers who later would be represented as unable to work because of alleged disability."[149] Since there were many reasons for the increase in disability benefits during the 1930s, the entire expansion cannot be blamed on an increase in applicants. But there was a general consensus among insurance industry representatives that policyholders' perceptions of their own disabilities, their propensity to apply for benefits, and their willingness to pursue claims in court all increased during periods of high unemployment.[150] Nevertheless, the majority report, while acknowledging that "the number and duration of disabilities may reflect somewhat the state of the labor market," dismissed the experience of life insurance companies as "important but not conclusive."[151]

Even if the proponents of disability insurance were distrustful of the testimony of commercial insurance representatives on the question of unemployment as a factor in increasing disability applications, they had evidence from War Risk Insurance on this point, too. A 1949 study of that program concluded that there was a "high inverse correlation between disability claim rates and the level of economic activity and prosperity."[152] And on the eve of passage of the first disability component of Social Security, in 1954, the Bureau of Old Age and Survivors Insurance indicated its awareness that a disability program was likely to be responsive to labor market conditions.[153]

In other words, the planners of disability insurance had at their disposal the basic outlines of every current (1980s) policy analysis of the disability insurance program. They were in the unique situation of being able to use hindsight in designing policy, because they had access to the accumulated experience of other programs with disability insurance provisions. They knew that disability insurance was difficult to administer; that its scope and costs were dependent on the definition of disability; that any program was likely to expand; that the courts would be a strong force for liberalizing the definition of disablity; and that any such program was likely to be sensitive to economic conditions, even if the formal definition of disability were very strict.

Why, then, did they adopt a disability program for which all of the dire predictions came true? One explanation is that the liberals essentially tricked the conservatives with a policy of gradual expansion. As Derthick argues, "incremental change in whatever institutional setting has less potential for generating conflict than change that involves innovation in principle. That is why program executives, even when undertaking an innovation in principle, tried to cut and clothe it in a fashion that made it seem merely incremental."[154] In this view, disability insurance was built by a process of gradual accretion. The first trick was to propose a "disability freeze" instead of actual cash benefits. The freeze was the equivalent of a waiver of premium in private insurance; if a person were deemed disabled, he would not have to make Social Security contributions during the period of disability in order to remain eligible for an old-age pension at age 65. The very major change in principle—a legal recognition of disability as an administrative category in social insurance—was buried in a seemingly minor administrative technicality: the waiver of Social Security contributions for a short period. The 1954 amendments to the Social Security program, in creating this disability freeze, took the first step down a slippery slope.

The second trick was to assign the task of disability determination to state agencies rather than to the Federal Security Administration (or some other federal agency). This device allayed the fears of conservatives who thought that the federal government should be involved as little as possible in the administration of programs. It also soothed the fears of the American Medical Association, which had passed a resolution in 1949 stating that "a federal disability program would represent another step toward wholesale nationalization of medical care and the socialization of the practice of medicine."[155] (In 1955, as Congress was considering adding a cash benefits provision, physicians from virtually every state medical society, as well as from specialty organizations, came before the Senate Finance Committee to argue, among other things, that disability insurance would lead to socialized medicine.)

With local administration, however, the skeptics were persuaded that "doubtful or fraudulent claims . . . would be held to a minimum."[156] Just to ensure that the states really did administer the program with all the strictness conservatives thought necessary, two provisions for federal supervision were added. The government would set guidelines for disability determination so that there would be uniformity among the states. And the Federal Security Administrator would have the authority to reverse positive findings of disability by state agencies, but not negative findings.[157]

Once the idea of the disability freeze had been accepted and the mechanism for determination was in place, the growth of the program was simply a matter of adding apparently incremental changes. Wilbur Cohen, an advocate and architect of Social Security, described his strategy as "the principle of salami slicing, which is to take a piece of salami and slice it very thin and then pile slice upon slice so that eventually you have a very good sandwich."[158]

The 1956 Social Security amendments introduced cash benefits for disabled people between the ages of 50 and 65. The discussion over the age limit "obscured the threshold nature of the change involved in providing actual cash benefits where formerly there had been only a waiver of contributions."[159] The 1958 amendments extended cash benefits to wives, children, and dependent husbands of disability beneficiaries. The 1960 amendments eliminated the age restriction and provided for benefits to people under age 50. And the 1965 amendments changed the definition of "permanent disability" from a condition with a "long, continued, and indefinite duration" to one "expected to continue for at least 12 months."

If the strategy of innovation through incremental change was successful, the question arises as to why the proponents of disability insurance were willing to ignore the evidence of expansionist tendencies and their understanding of the difficulty of preserving a narrow definition of disability. What was the source of their faith that a disability program could be carefully controlled and monitored? What made them believe they could succeed where private insurance and War Risk Insurance had (allegedly) failed?

The answer is to be found in the report of the 1948 Advisory Council, which grappled directly with the problems detailed in the dissenting minority report. The underlying concern was to prevent the abuse of any disability insurance. The authors repeatedly discuss the need for "strict" tests to eliminate the possibility of awards based on purely subjective perceptions of need. The report is full of phrases conveying exclusion, such as "strict test," "safeguard," "strict eligibility requirements," and "carefully circumscribed and restricted program." But the council established a tone of confidence in the possibility of solving the problems and offered a series of detailed criteria to make the program workable. The crux of their plan was the use of clinical judgment to determine disability:

> The Council recommends that compensable disabilities be restricted to those which can be *objectively determined by medical examination or tests.* In this way the problems involved in the adjudication of claims based on purely subjective symptoms can be avoided. Unless demonstrable by objective tests, such ailments as lumbago, rheumatism, and various nervous disorders would not be compensable. The danger of malingering which might be involved in connection with such claims would thereby be avoided.[160]

Earlier definitions of disability recommended by the Social Security Board and its Advisory Councils had not included the criterion of "objective medical determination";[161] that was an innovation of the 1948 council. Its members clearly had faith that medical science was capable of objective determination of disability and that medical examination could distinguish the genuinely disabled from the malingerers. In its formal recommendations, the report gave a definition of disability based on clinical judgment: "A 'permanent and total disability' for the purpose of this program should mean any disability which is medically demonstrable by objective tests, which prevents the worker from performing any substantially gainful activity, and which is likely to be of long and continued duration."[162] And it specified that medical examination would be the basis of eligibility determination.

> Claims should be disallowed if the claimant refuses to submit to medical examination, and benefits should be terminated if the beneficiary refuses to submit to reexamination. Provision should be made for periodic reexaminations so that benefit payments can be terminated promptly when the beneficiary is no longer disabled."[163]

The possibility of objective determination by physicians was one of the major themes of testimony on various versions of the disability insurance program considered by Congress between 1949 and 1956.

A few physicians supported the idea. In 1949, a doctor testifying on behalf of the AMA recommended a definition in which disability "is medically demonstrable by objective tests," by which "are meant the things that can be *observed or proved in the findings of an examination . . . from a physical standpoint.*"[164] The director of the Union Health Center of the International Ladies Garment Workers Union said the disability program of the garment industry was evidence that "an equitable and efficient system for determining total and permanent disability can be developed on a sound medical basis."[165] And a representative of the Physicians Forum told the Senate Finance Committee that the difficulties were not really so great if the program would make a conceptual distinction between determining impairment and performing a vocational evaluation.[166]

But the overwhelming majority of physicians testified against the disability insurance program and attempted to persuade Congressmen that physicians could not possibly provide the kind of objective determination desired by program advocates.[167] The medical profession had several objections: some were technical, based on knowledge of the practice of medicine; others, which might be called political or economic, were based on claims about the impact of the program on the organization of medicine.

The technical objections were of three sorts. First, physicians asserted that disability determination is inherently subjective, and that honest physicians could legitimately disagree about whether a person is disabled. Many argued that medical science is incapable of determining whether people can or cannot work. Over and over again they told Congress that "medicine is not an exact science," and that disability is a social and psychological problem not amenable to exact definition by physicians. As a representative of the American Academy of General Practice put it:

> Unfortunately, medical science has not reached the point of being able to unerringly state whether or not a man is totally and permanently disabled. . . . Is the delivery boy who loses both legs totally and permanently disabled? Or is the certifying doctor supposed to point out that he can still run a drill press and probably make more money?[168]

Second, doctors said that the very process of labeling a person as disabled would weaken his incentive to recover and rehabilitate himself, and that income awards on the basis of disability would only encourage malingering. One doctor, speaking for the Medical So-

ciety of Delaware, claimed: "The greatest danger to the Nation in this plan is the danger of the people's being educated to regard injuries as opportunites for financial gain."[169] Others were less melodramatic, but virtually all the testifying physicians expressed the belief that malingering is a widespread and serious problem, and that disability payments can be *therapeutically* harmful by interfering with the motivation to recover. Several physicians propounded a sort of "reservoir theory" of disability. It holds that there are many people currently in the labor force despite physical and mental handicaps, and that the availability of disability benefits would draw these people out of the labor force by sapping their will to work. A disability insurance program would "give hundreds of thousands of malingerers the kind of opportunity they've been seeking for years."[170]

Third, most physicians testified that the process of certifying disability would put them in an uncomfortable, if not conflictual, role. Disability certification for the purposes of cash benefits set the physician up as having to mediate between the interests of their patient and the government. They described certifying physicians as "caught in a squeeze," "policeman for the government," and having to "serve two masters." Patients, they said, could simply shop around for a doctor willing to accommodate their request to be certified. And friends and family of the patient often put unbearable pressure on the physician, reducing his or her ability to make good clinical judgments. Introducing such tensions into the doctor-patient relationship would undermine the doctor's therapeutic effectiveness.

Physicians argued from their experiences in certifying people for other disability programs—those of commercial insurance companies, Workers Compensation, Civil Service, Veterans Administration, and the armed services—that clinical definitions of disability were not very workable. Most of them used the standard professional device of describing particular cases to show either that determination was impossible or that a disability pension *caused* a person to remain out of work.

Many of the physicians attempted to illustrate the impossibility of medical determination by discussing particular diseases. Congressional testimony in 1955, when Congress was contemplating the introduction of cash benefits, is replete with examples of "elusive disabilities"—conditions which physicians believe are very common, frequently disabling, and impossible to determine: severe chronic headaches, heart disease, heart attacks, rheumatic diseases and arthritis, drug and alcohol addiction, backaches, neurotic conditions, epilepsy, and anxiety. In speech after speech, doctors attempted to explain the complexity of these conditions and their relationship to the ability to work. One brave soul, at the risk of making his profession look somewhat foolish, cited a poll of heart specialists about whether Eisenhower was "physically able" to serve as President after his heart attack: 114 specialists had said "yes," but 93 said "no." Such disagreement, even among specialists, was typical in all fields of disability determination, the doctor asserted.[171]

Physicians kept telling Congress that the proposed definition of disability simply would not work, but Congress was reluctant to accept such a conclusion; at many points during the hearings, a Congressman would read the definition from the legislative draft and then ask the physician-witness whether it would work. In one of these interchanges, Senator Alben Barkley asked whether the doctor could make a determination based on the definition. When the doctor said "no," he was asked whether the medical profession could provide the committee with a workable definition. The doctor said he thought the task impossible. Yet Senator Barkley later said, "I don't know of anybody as well qualified as the medical profession to pass on a man's disability. Is it not a medical question after all?"[172] And in spite of the testimony about the difficulty of certifying for veterans' programs and insurance companies, Senator Barkley asked yet another physician why the question of disability should be any more difficult in Social Security than in the Veterans Act or in insurance companies.[173]

One doctor, trying to get the Congressmen to understand the role of individual will in disability, said, "Disability is almost—to some extent—a philosophy." Senator Russel B. Long then read him the formal definition of disability from the bill and asserted that the wording left no room for a person to be certified purely on the basis of subjective complaints: "Doesn't it seem to you that that is pretty closely drawing the net as far as preventing any malingerer or person who does not want to work very much from drawing disability?" The doctor replied, "It may appear that way to you, Senator, but not to me," and went on to explain that many people with backaches, anxiety, neuroses, and other problems are legitimately disabled even though their condition is not medically demonstrable. The Senator handed the doctor his copy of the legislation, had the doctor read the definition again out loud, and then the two of them argued about whether the definition included alcoholism as a disability.[174]

No matter what the physicians said, nothing could shake Congressional belief in the ability of the medical profession to make reasonably accurate judgments of disability. In a revealing and prophetic comment, Senator Barkley said to the physician-witness:

> I agree with you and all of those who have testified that there is a danger that this thing might break down of its own weight some day. . . . But I am not willing to concede that after all the years of experience and growth and investigation and practice in the medical profession that they cannot with some reasonable degree of certainty arrive at a medically determinable point where a man is totally and permanently disabled."[175]

Not disabused of the notion of medical objectivity by physicians' testimony, the social insurance advocates ultimately incorporated the definition of disability based on medical determination in both the freeze provision of 1954 and the cash benefits provision of 1956. This faith in the objective vision of medicine was repeated in numerous reports and statements about disability insurance over the next several years. A House Ways and Means Committee report on the 1954 amendments proposed to limit the program by asserting that "there must be a *medically determinable impairment of serious proportions*."[176] The Bureau of Old Age and Survivors Insurance in 1958 even expressed its faith that clinical judgment could protect the disability insurance program from the influences of the economic environment:

> A person may become unemployed or remain unemployed for a number of reasons other than disability—individual employer hiring practices, technological changes in the industry in which the applicant has been employed, local or cyclical business and economic conditions and many others. [But] the applicant *must establish by medical evidence* that his impairment results in such a lack of ability to perform significant functions . . . that he cannot, with his training, education and work experience, engage in any substantial gainful activity.[177]

Thus, it was faith in the techniques of medical examination and the powers of clinical judgment that allowed even the most reluctant policymakers to swallow their fears and support first a disability freeze and then a cash benefit program based on the determination of "medical disability." Yet even as they drafted the legislation, they revealed unresolved paradoxes in their formulation of the concept of disability and doubts about the trustworthiness of physicians.

One paradox was that although program planners wanted disability to be a medical concept, they also wanted it to reflect the individual's ability to earn. In 1946–47, the Bureau of Old Age and Survivors Insurance, in formulating some basic underpinnings of the program, had defined disability as an incapacity to work, but the operational measure of incapacity to work would be "residual earning capacity," which in turn would be based on medical, social, and vocational factors.[178] Only six years into the program, the issue of untangling medical problems and employment problems surfaced. A House Ways and Means Committee Report of 1960 pointed to the problem:

> It is essential that there be a clear distinction between this program [disability insurance] and one concerned with unemployment. . . . The Department should make a thorough study of this situation to see if criteria can be developed which retain the basic emphasis of the program on major medical impairment but at the same time allow for a more realistic assessment where there are multiple bars to employment, e.g. age, employer bias in hiring, and other factors that limit job opportunity.[179]

The difficulty of reconciling disability as a purely medical concept with disability as an economic (or vocational, social, and personal) concept stands out as the critical problem in contemporary evaluations of the program.[180]

Another paradox was that the planners wanted disability to be determinable in some simple and objective way, yet they explicitly rejected the use of rating schedules or other systematic devices to eliminate the need for individual assessment. The Bureau of Old Age and Survivors Insurance, in making basic policy decisions in 1946, had rejected a schedule approach in favor of individual assessment "because of the failure of the schedular approach to give consideration to the individual's social and vocational factors as well as the medical."[181] It is noteworthy that although the Bureau had made a commitment to the inclusion of social and vocational criteria (as yet unspecified), the 1948 Advisory Council Report somehow neglected to mention these criteria. Instead, the report came out strongly in favor of a disability definition based strictly on medical criteria. If there was a trick in the passage of disability insurance legislation, this was surely it. The Social Security bureaucracy explicitly contemplated a concept of disability encompassing social, vocational, *and* medical criteria, but the program was sold as one with a strictly medical definition.

The illusion that clinical methods can somehow objectively determine disability persists, even when disability is acknowledged to be a vocational concept. In a statement somewhat reminiscent of the emperor's new clothes, Commissioner Robert Ball told a House committee in 1959 that the phrase "by reason of any medically determinable physical or mental impairment" is "the part of the definition that administratively . . . gives us the most trouble and yet is really absolutely essential to the definition."[182] By 1960 it was clear that the definition of disability was highly problematic, and the Ways and Means Committee report cited earlier (generally called the "Harrison Subcommittee Report") urged the Social Security Administration to promulgate regulations to clarify it. The committee, expressing the same fear of judicial expansion that planners had foreseen when they considered adopting the program, warned: "The distinct possibility exists that if the situation remains unchanged, the courts rather than the Department [of Health, Education and Welfare] or Congress will set the standards."[183]

Indeed, the courts had begun to expand the definition of disability. Courts varied in their interpretation of the phrase "unable to engage in substantial gainful activity," particularly in their willingness to allow consideration of the job market and of the applicant's occupation and experience. Some were verging on an occupational definition of disability; others were placing the burden of proof on the government to show what other kinds of jobs the applicant could do.[184]

By 1967, Congress had become extremely concerned about the expansion of the disability program. In a new set of amendments, it tried to reassert control by specifying a strict definition to make disability independent of job availability:

> An individual . . . shall be determined to be under a disability only if his physical or mental impairment or impairments are of such severity that he is not only unable to do his previous work but cannot, considering his age, education, and work experience, engage in any kind of substantial gainful work which exists in the national economy, regardless of whether such work exists in the immediate area in which he lives, or whether a specific job vacancy exists for him, or whether he would be hired if he applied for work.[185]

And still, Congress relied on clinical judgment to save the program from broad expansion. The Senate and House committee reports said that they were trying to "reemphasize the predominant importance of medical factors in the disability determination."[186] To that end, they clarified the role of clinical judgment: "Statements of the applicant or conclusions of others with respect to the nature and extent of impairment or disability do not establish the existence of disability . . . unless they are supported by clinical or laboratory findings or other medically acceptable evidence confirming such statements or conclusions."[187] In other words, the truth is to be found in clinical medicine. Evidence presented by applicants and "others" is to be disregarded unless it can be confirmed by clinical methods and meet the canons of clinical knowledge.

The 1967 amendments changed the wording of the law to include more clinical language, as though an elaboration of medical jargon could somehow accomplish what previous definitions had not: "For purposes of this subsection, a 'physical or mental impairment' is an impairment that results from anatomical, physiological or psychological abnormalities which are demonstrable by medically acceptable clinical and laboratory diagnostic techniques."[188] And the courts, although playing the lead role in expanding the definition of disability to include vocational factors and market conditions, also bought into the myth of objective clinical determination. In a Supreme Court decision of 1976, Justice Powell said:

> In short, a medical assessment of the worker's physical or mental condition is required. This is a more sharply focused and easily documented decision than the typical determination of welfare entitlement. In the latter case, a wide variety of information may be deemed relevant, and issues of witness credibility and veracity often are critical to the decisionmaking process. . . . By contrast, the decision whether to discontinue disability benefits will turn, in most cases, upon routine, standard, and unbiased medical reports by physician specialists.[189]

The Significance of the Social Security Concept of Disability

By the time the American Social Security disability insurance program was established, there were a number of precedents for disability-based benefit programs in both the United States and Europe. The idea of disability as an administrative category was hardly novel. What was novel was the recognition that the *definition of disability* was the central problem. The legitimacy of excusing the disabled from work requirements was hardly at issue, but considerable debate occurred about whether the disabled should be provided with income or, instead, with rehabilitation services—almost as though the two options were mutually exclusive.[190] The primary question in the American debates, however, was how to define disability so as to avoid the problems of individual abuse and judicial expansion already evident in other disability programs.

The planners foresaw all the problems now plaguing the system. Analyses of disability insurance from the 1930s and 1940s contain all of the theoretical issues of contemporary analyses. The planners explicitly searched for a solution to these problems and believed they had found it in the notion of medical determination. Reports and testimony of the period illustrate how vigorously planners insisted on this solution, how strongly they believed in it, and how clearly they connected clinical judgment with the creation of a tight boundary.

It is remarkable how that faith in clinical judgment persisted despite overwhelming testimony from physicians. One can only marvel—or despair—at the technicalization of a political issue even when the technical experts themselves insist on the inability of their science to perform the tasks expected of it. The virtual unanimity of the profession on this issue—on the sheer technical question of whether physicians can determine disability—is rare in technical policy issues. And if Congress was unwilling to listen to experts in a situation where the experts presented a uniform opinion, one can only wonder about the ability of technical experts to influence policymaking in any rational way when there is more professional disagreement.

How can this rejection of professional expertise be explained? The statements of Congressmen during hearings on the various bills reveal a paradoxical attitude toward the medical profession: on the one hand, they had an abiding trust in the judgment of physicians; on the other hand, they rejected the judgment of physicians that the profession was incapable of determining disability. One explanation might be that the lay perception of science as objective dies hard. Policymakers' belief in the capabilities of clinical medicine had a nearly religious quality; it was a faith which could not be shaken by empirical evidence.

Another explanation might be that given political pressure for a disability insurance program covering the general population, policymakers needed *some* definition and seized on the best one they could find, however imperfect. Since numerous special groups were already receiving the privileges of disability insurance, Congress and program executives could not deny these privileges to the general population. If disability could be determined for veterans, government employees, and commercial insurance policyholders, how could politicians possibly maintain that it could not be determined for everyone else? Even though they knew that the definition of disability was a problem for these other programs, they thought they could at least improve on the definition for Social Security. They were satisfiers, not perfectionists.

Finally, it is likely that the medical profession, for all its uniformity on the technical issues, lost credibility with policymakers because of its position on the political and economic issues. Medical testimony on the technical question of disability determination was intermingled with a variety of arguments about how a disability insurance program would lead to socialized medicine. The medical profession rendered its opinion on the technical issues in the context of a broader political campaign to resist national health insurance and, in particular, the then current threat of disability insurance. The American Medical Association orchestrated this campaign, using its usual weapons of resolutions, mailings of informational packets, and intensive lobbying. The physicians who testified before Congress were almost entirely representatives of the American Medical Association and state medical societies; few came as independent experts.

The party line of organized medicine was that a federal program of disability insurance would be the entering wedge of socialized medicine. If the program were to require medical certification, so the logic went, then the government would have to provide free medical examinations to applicants. The government would therefore use government-employed physicians, such as those working for the Veterans Administration and the Public Health Service, to conduct the examinations. More and more physicians would come to be employed by the government; government employment would mean socialized medicine.[191] Because the professional testimony on the technical issue of definition was presented by physicians admittedly hostile to the program for reasons of professional self-interest, and because the profession itself chose to speak on the technical issues and the political issues in the same breath, the technical testimony lost much of its persuasiveness. Comments of many of the Congressmen during hearings indicate that they discounted the profession's opinion on the technical question because the political motives were so clear.

This last explanation leaves some grounds for optimism about the use of technical expertise in policymaking. Perhaps professional judgment can be incorporated into policy decisions if it is not tainted by crass and obvious political self-interest. But as we will see in the next chapter, the faith in medicine manifested by the planners of Social Security has its roots in a much deeper cultural system; and the virtue of the medical profession manifested in their humble assessment of their own capabilities was easily corrupted when they were presented with a concrete program.

3

Disability as a Clinical Concept

In the previous chapter, we saw how disability came to be formulated as an administrative category out of a collection of separate conditions understood to be legitimate reasons for not working. The legal evolution of the category shows how the concept of disability was intimately connected with the control of labor. The category could be used, as in England, to determine which people would be entitled to relief without working; it could be used, as in Germany, to make even finer distinctions about enforced occupational transfers. In the United States, the very techniques of defining the category were essential to its political acceptability.

The other major historical question is how the concept of disability came to be associated with clinical medicine and clinical reasoning. The notion of disability meant "inability to work" (which is the literal term used in German). Why is it that we think of disability as a medical phenomenon to be ascertained by clinical methods (at least in the first instance), rather than an educational phenomenon to be ascertained by teachers, or a legal phenomenon to be ascertained by judges? In England, lay magistrates decided whether paupers were to be considered "sick" or "lunatic" before the responsibility was shifted to medical officers. In the United States, the first national system of compensation for veterans with service-connected disabilities used *judges* to examine the injuries and ascertain the extent of disability; Congress placed responsibility in the U.S. Circuit Court System. How is it that disability as recognized by the state—that is, as a legal entitlement to some form of social aid—should come to be dominated by clinical concepts?

The argument of this chapter is that the clinical conception of inability to work was the result of two important developments. First, during the nineteenth century, just as the system of categorical exemptions was being tested as a solution to the work/need dilemma, there was a major change in the medical concept of disease that absolved the individual from responsibility for, or control over, his condition. Second, at the same time, disability was seen as a condition with both genuine and artificial forms. In its genuine form, it was indeed beyond the control of the individual, but it was also a condition that could be feigned or brought on by self-mutilation. Scientific medicine offered the promise of new diagnostic methods that could distinguish between genuine disability (or inability to work) and feigned disability. Clinical medicine, then, offered a model of illness that gave legitimacy to claims for social aid, and it offered a method of validation that would render administration of the category feasible.

Disability and Fault

The most important change in theories of disease in the nineteenth century was the idea that each disease was caused by a specific agent. In the period from roughly 1840 to 1890, scientists and doctors attempted to explain contagious disease with a variety of new theories predicated on the transmission of an identifiable, specific disease-producing agent. The difference between the theories lay in the nature of the agent: self-reproducing particles of organic matter, organic secretions derived from albumen, poisonous substances, diseased matter derived from normal protoplasm, or living microorganisms (as in "germ theory" proper).[1]

As early as 1840, the German scientist Jacob Henle proposed that contagious diseases were caused by microorganisms, but this theory was not widely accepted for another forty years, after Louis Pasteur, Robert Koch, and others had more convincingly shown the connection between specific bacteria and specific diseases.[2] Fundamental to the methods of the bacteriologists was a demonstration that the agent could and did exist *outside* the human body, and that it could produce disease in animals as well as humans. Koch's method for establishing a cause-and-effect relationship between a microorganism and a disease, known as "Koch's postulates," was based on this separation of the organism from the individual. His method required that the organism always be present in the diseased parts; that it be cultivated outside of the body; and that it produce disease when inoculated into a "susceptible animal."[3]

The physical separation of a disease-producing agent and the deliberate production of specific diseases in animals challenged the conception of individual responsibility previously associated with disease. Germ theory marked a major break with earlier nonorganic theories that attributed disease either to spiritual forces (it was a punishment for sinful behavior) or to mechanical forces (it was the result of an imbalance of "humours" or fluids in the body). If disease were a form of punishment by the gods, then it was also a visible revelation of some past transgression for which the sick person could certainly be held responsible. And if disease were the result of an imbalance of humours, the cause was often sought in the behavior of the individual that might have created the imbalance. But the germ theory rested on the assumption that each disease had its specific causative agent and that medical treatment should seek to attack the agent rather than the whole person.[4] Germ theory was also rooted in the Darwinian concept of evolutionary struggle, and thus it conceived of disease as a struggle between two organisms, one human and the other not.[5] The outcome of the struggle had nothing to do with virtue; rather, it was a matter of superior "weaponry," and the treatment of disease was conceived as a minor military campaign to eradicate the nonhuman invader. (Many observers have noted the persistence of the military metaphor in medical language, even today).

Germ theory also implied a very different role for government than did a model of disease that located cause in personal habits and moral choice. In both England and the United States, for example, it was a change in the understanding of the cause of cholera that led to the creation of municipal health boards and the expansion of their powers where they already existed.[6] During the epidemics of 1832 and 1849, cholera was thought to be caused by a life of vice or a weak personal character. Even those who granted the contagious nature of the disease were able to retain a role for virtue in their causal model by invoking the notion of host receptivity: cholera might be transmitted by some sort of atmospheric miasma, but people actually became ill because something in their character or living habits made them more receptive to it. By 1849, "the connection between cholera and vice was almost a verbal reflex,"[7] and the response of most communities to the epidemics was to step up exhortations to the poor about cleanliness.

Then, in 1855, Dr. John Snow published his famous study demonstrating the connection between cholera outbreaks and contaminated water sources. Even though the cholera bacterium was not isolated until 1883, pressure for strict government health measures began to mount. Snow spearheaded a campaign, joined by physicians in England and America, to create governmental sanitary institutions with broad authority. By the time of the epidemics in the late 1860s, local governments were much more likely to confront them with organized efforts at street cleaning, storehouses of disinfectants, brigades for disinfecting stricken homes, compulsory reporting of cases, and provisions for sanitary burial of victims. Although acceptance of the amoral germ theory of causation was by no means universal, it did provide the impetus for the creation and expansion of public health institutions. The connection was not lost on public health reformers: in Australia, yet untouched by cholera, doctors and public health officials noted that their country's immunity was a mixed blessing, for they did not have the support of an aroused public opinion for sanitary reform.[8]

The shift in understanding of disease causation certainly did not occur all at once, and changes in the intellectual concepts of disease did not lead ineluctably to the conclusion of personal innocence. Many public health officers still insisted on the role of personal hygiene and living habits in disease transmission and continued to see disease as an individual problem to be remedied through education, rather than as a social problem to be remedied by government health activities. Even after Koch had identified the cholera bacterium, there was resistance to germ theory; Pettenkoffer and his associates in Germany still embraced the "environmental theory" of transmission and swallowed live cultures of the bacteria to show that other factors besides a germ must be present to produce a case of cholera.[9]

The new theory of specific etiology, with its denial of individual responsibility for disease, profoundly challenged the existing social structure, and in particular, the boundary between work and need. Every identification of a specific agent in effect pushed another category of sick people over the border, to the side of the "deserving poor," and excused them from responsibility for their condition. So it is no wonder that there was often social resistance to medical discoveries that later provided the basis for highly effective treatment.

The way identification of a pathological agent undermines the ideological justification for social hierarchy is nowhere more evident than in the case of hookworm in the United States. In 1902, Dr. Charles Wardell Stiles first publicly attributed the "chronic anemia" or "continuous malaria" prevalent in the American South to a parasite.[10] The disease manifested itself in two notable symptoms—dirt-eating and lethargy. Far more than cholera, hookworm stayed within the confines of a single social class: it affected the rural poor in the South but, for some reason, not blacks. The disease made people listless, tired, disinclined to work, and apparently also mentally less alert, if not slow-witted. But what Stiles saw as symptoms, the popular conception saw as the malady itself. "Poor white trash," it was held, were dirty and lazy. That was enough of an explanation for the socioeconomic position of the white rural poor, but should anyone feel compelled to explain their apparent sickness, then the "anemia" or "malaria" was alleged to be the consequence of bad moral habits.

By the time of Stiles's discovery, the germ theory of disease had been firmly established, and specific microorganisms had been isolated in cholera, tuberculosis, pneumonia, plague, anthrax, typhoid fever, diphtheria, gonorrhea, influenza, leprosy, malaria, and many other diseases.[11] Yet Stiles's assertion that dirt-eating and lethargy were actually caused by a parasite (whose eggs he found in fecal samples) was ridiculed in the press as a discovery of the "germ of laziness." Cartoons, jokes, poems, ditties, and songs facetiously celebrated the discovery of a medical excuse for sloth. It seemed the germ theory and its advocates had gone too far for the public. The reaction was censure not only of Stiles, for his denial of the moral basis of backwardness, but of the entire germ theory, for its undermining of the determinative role of character in human affairs.

The strength of public incredulity in the face of Stiles's demonstration of a parasitic cause is all the more striking in light of the greater visibility of the hookworm than of the cholera bacillus. But what is more interesting about the hookworm story is that the public, by and large, reacted to Stiles's report as if *threatened* rather than relieved. Stiles may have found a 50-cent cure for hookworm, but his discovery meant that the successful and well-to-do southern elite not only had to stop blaming the "poor white trash" for their laziness but could no longer take quite so much credit for their own socioeconomic positions. Microorganisms and parasites thus posed radical challenges to merit-based justification of the political order.

Given the understanding of disease that rapidly took hold during the last part of the nineteenth century, it is easy to see why the category "sick" in English Poor Law policy came to refer primarily to "acute infectious diseases," and why the sick should be exempted from the prohibition against outdoor relief. Infectious disease was a model that had little room for individual will or deception in its theory of causation or, therefore, for education and moral virtue in its treatment. It is also easy to understand why the sick should have been provided with better conditions in the workhouse than laborers on the outside, in contrast to the prevailing philosophy of least eligibility. If sickness was a struggle between the virtuous human and the enemy microbe, society should certainly take the side of the human and aid his struggle. Medical care for the poor in this context had something of the flavor of foreign aid.

The new concept of the role of will in sickness that was embodied in the infectious disease model gave impetus to a major change in the political meaning of the sick category in the late 19th century. Historically, people on relief had been denied certain civic rights—especially the right to vote for elected officials. This provision had been common in the early voting laws of many counties or boroughs and was incorporated into the Reform Act of 1832, which significantly extended the franchise. The Poor Law reform of 1834, in addition to revising the principles of relief, established a stronger system of medical services for the poor. The sick wards of workhouses were gradually opened to and used by people who were not indigent by Poor Law standards but could not afford medical care. Poor Law medical officers increasingly provided care for the nonpoor in their districts—such services as emergency and accident care, childbirth attendance, and vaccinations. The question arose whether these *sick* people receiving public care should lose their citizenship rights, or, in the lingo of the times, be forced into "pauper status." The policy of the central authority was that anyone who received relief, medical or otherwise, would be considered a pauper, but many reformers believed that medical relief should be made separate from the rest of the Poor Law precisely so that the sick poor would not have to become paupers.[12]

Exemption of the sick poor from formal pauper status did not happen until 1885, although a small change in that direction occurred in 1841. After England had suffered a smallpox epidemic and Edward Jenner had come up with an effective vaccine, the desire of public officials to get people vaccinated led to the Vaccination Act of 1840. It designated the Poor Law medical officers as "public vaccinators," who would provide free vaccinations to all at public expense. A year later, the act was amended to exempt from pauper status all those who accepted vaccines from the public vaccinator.[13] The automatic reduction to pauper status for those who accepted any other kind of medical relief remained until 1883. Then, on the heels of a cholera epidemic, Parliament made a special exception for people suffering from infectious diseases:

> The admission of a person suffering from infectious disease into any hospital or hospital ships provided by the managers, or the maintenance of any such person therein shall not be considered to be parochial relief, alms, or charitable allowance to any person and no such person or his parent shall by reason thereof be deprived of any right or privilege, or be subject to any disability or disqualification.[14]

This law was a temporary emergency measure designed to encourage people to enter the hospital during a severe cholera epidemic. But it reflected a larger public discussion about universal access to treatment for infectious diseases. The move to make treatment available for all social classes, because all were susceptible, virtually required the creation of exemptions from pauper status. These exemptions were soon extended not only to people with infectious diseases but to those with any kind of sickness. In early 1885, the Medical Relief Disqualification Act provided that indigents receiving any kind of medical or surgical care could still vote in Parliamentary elections, though not in elections of Poor Law guardians. The distinction between medical relief and other kinds of relief for the purposes of the franchise marked a formal legal recognition of the no-fault status of disease.[15]

The germ theory clearly explains why people with acute infectious diseases would be a proper group for the categorical welfare system, but what about people with chronic, noninfectious mental and physical problems, the group that makes up the bulk of the current category called "disabled"? Here, too, the germ theory had its influence. Though somewhat slow to catch on, the theory profoundly influenced thinking about disease and was often extended beyond the bounds of empirical demonstration of its validity. By the 1890s, many physicians were relying primarily on the findings of bacteriological examination, rather than symptoms and medical history, to diagnose tuberculosis, cholera, and diphtheria. The medical profession began to apply the model of infectious disease everywhere, finding bacteriological causes for nonbacteriological diseases, and medical research concentrated on the search for "magic bullets" or specific antidotes to each disease-causing agent.[16]

The *metaphor* of infectious disease shaped public thinking about the nature of all illness. Even if a specific microbe had not yet been isolated for a disease, people assumed that such a microbe existed and had only to be discovered. And the tremendous success of the medical profession in reducing the morbidity from infectious diseases created a belief in the ability of physicians to detect diseases invisible to the average person. The sudden extension of voting rights in England not only to people with infectious diseases (in 1883) but to people receiving any kind of medical care (in 1885) suggests that the understanding of infectious disease led to a rapid extension of the presumption of lack of individual responsibility in other medical conditions.

Infectious disease was one major model that influenced the concept of disability. The recognition of industrial accidents as another peculiar kind of disabling phenomenon also profoundly influenced the growth of the disability category. Industrial accidents were usually the very first contingency to be insured in the creation of national social insurance programs,[17] and the reason for this early recognition is also to be found in a new notion of causation that absolved the worker of responsibility.

The introduction of workers' compensation around the turn of the century was preceded by vigorous discussions about the causes of industrial accidents.[18] The prevailing method for handling compensation had been adversarial tests of employer liability, which required that the injured worker be able to pinpoint the cause of his injury and demonstrate definitively that the employer had been negligent. English common law, followed by American common law, provided such a variety of defenses to the employer that proof of negligence was extremely difficult. The general assumption of the law was that the worker should bear the costs of his own accident unless he could show that it was caused by the employer's negligence. He had to surmount a number of legal hurdles to prove negligence and shift the costs to the employer.[19] But with the growth of large scale industry using a variety of hazardous machinery, injuries increased dramatically, and the courts became more sympathetic to the worker. Courts realized that large factories and corporate ownership made it increasingly difficult for workers to demonstrate that their employers were personally at fault. Yet accidents were incontrovertibly increasing, and the theory that they were due to worker carelessness was less and less tenable. One by one, the traditional defenses for the employer were eliminated, and juries began granting major awards to workers. Once employers were faced with large but unpredictable liability costs, the entire system seemed to be "in crisis," and it was at this point that proposals for reform usually sprang into being.

In Germany, Britain, and the United States, the debate generally followed the same broad outlines: should the problem of increased worker injuries be dealt with through an extension of employer liability within the adversarial framework, or should the entire system of liability be jettisoned in favor of an insurance system that would compensate without regard to fault? The proponents of insurance argued that no amount of tinkering with the legal or administrative framework of liability law would help, since the whole legal structure was predicated on an outdated concept of causation: liability law presumed that the causes of accidents could be traced to identifiable individuals and their specific actions. Instead, the advocates of insurance argued, industrial accidents were simply a natural concomitant of industrial development: "The extended use of tools, mechanical implements and appliances in all employments creates an element of inherent hazard unknown to the simpler working conditions of the past, unavoidable by human precaution. . . . [T]his risk, inherent in the way the world does its work, is not likely to decrease."[20] Or, in the more detached economic language of the 1940s, industrial accidents were the "'human overhead'. . . which is an inevitable part of the cost—to someone—of doing industrialized business."[21]

The ideological argument for insurance was that it would spread the costs of industrialization (or, more precisely, the costs of industrial accidents) equitably among all employers, and ultimately all consumers, instead of letting the costs fall on a few unfortunate victims of circumstance.[22] If the causes of industrial accidents were anonymous, then the costs, too, should be borne anonymously.

The reasons for acceptance of industrial accident insurance were probably more economic than ideological. Insurance, with its periodic payment of fixed premiums, made the cost of industrial injuries more predictable for employers than the quixotic system of liability suits. It substituted small regular payments by all employers for infrequent but enormous damage payments by a few. For employers, then, insurance removed a great deal of the risk of doing business that had been created by the liability system. For workers, it substituted a greater likelihood (if not certainty) of small payments to all injured workers for the small chance of successful litigation and a large award to a very few injured workers. At least in the

United States, the case for economic motivation has been made convincingly.[23]

The motivation for industrial accident insurance may have been economic, but the prior debate forced a public discussion about the *causes* of the most visible source of inability to work. Whatever shifting of the allocation of economic costs occurred in the transition to industrial accident insurance, there was also a cultural shift in the attribution of moral responsibility. In the rhetoric of the new programs, accidents could no longer be attributed to worker carelessness, any more than they could be attributed to employer negligence.

The movement towards insurance compensation thus had an effect similar to that of germ theory in medicine: it reduced the importance of individual behavior as a causal factor. Germ theory worked to decrease individual responsibility by attributing disease to specific, nonhuman, external agents; the industrial accident controversy decreased individual responsibility by attributing job injuries to the anonymous, collective forces of industrialization. But both had the effect of enlarging the sphere of conditions under which a person would not be held responsible for his inability to work.

Changes in the understanding of the causes of disease and injury were one very significant reason why disability became an administrative concept in welfare policy, and why its association with clinical medicine was so strong. The association was buttressed by another major transformation in medicine: new diagnostic techniques that offered a validation device superior to all previous eligibility tests.

Disability and Validation

The problem of distinguishing those who *cannot* work from those who *will not* work has plagued society for centuries. Alexis de Tocqueville predicted that the English Poor Law Reform of 1834 would founder on precisely this dilemma, and no one has stated more vividly the difficulty of setting a boundary between work and need:

> Nothing is so difficult to distinguish as the nuances which separate unmerited misfortune from an adversity produced by vice. How many miseries are simultaneously the result of both causes! What profound knowledge must be presumed about the charac-

> ter of each man and of the circumstances in which he has lived, what knowledge, what sharp discernment, what cold and inexorable reason! Where will you find the magistrate who will have the time, the talent, the means of devoting himself to such an examination? Who would dare to let a poor man die of hunger because it's his own fault that he is dying? Who will hear his cries and reason about his vices? Even personal interest is restrained when confronted by the sight of other men's misery. Would the interest of the public treasury really prove to be more successful?[24]

The first official necessity for making such a distinction came about with the antivagrancy law of 1388, which required local officials to distinguish between "those impotent to serve" and "those able to serve or labor."[25] Vagrants were asked to give their reasons for traveling, and it is because there are official records of these reasons that historians are able to glean some picture of vagrants in rural England. As described in Chapter 2, only people with valid reasons were allowed to beg, and even they were controlled through a system of licensing or badging.

The *testimony of acquaintances* was the first primitive form of validation device to determine eligibility for begging licenses. In many cases, magistrates checked the stories very thoroughly in an attempt to detect lying. Witnesses and former employers were contacted, even those living at some distance.[26] Juan Luis Vives, in his influential sixteenth-century treatise on poverty, offered a similar method for checking up on the poor. They were to be registered, and then investigated by parish officials. "It will be easy to learn from the neighbors what sort of men they are, how they live and what their habits are," he wrote, but noted that "evidence about one poor person should not be taken from another, for he would not be free from jealousy."[27]

The art of detecting the motivation of beggars from the testimony of witnesses eventually grew into elaborate forms of *social inquiry* directed at the applicants for relief. A description of poor-relief practice in Hamburg in the late eighteenth century shows to what extent the inquiry had evolved:

> Our overseers had printed interrogatories, which they were to propose to each poor family. The answers were written upon the white column of the page, and verified by a personal visitation, and the evidence of their neighbors, and many queries were

> formed to discover the average earning of each member of the family; but this was not a point made easily. *Few answers were sincere*. . . . The state of health was determined by a visit from a physician and a surgeon.[28]

In France, the Baron de Gerando published his *Manuel du visiteur du pauvre* in 1820, setting forth the importance of the home visit in the detection of cheating. His basic idea was that agencies of welfare could not take the self-description of applicants at face value; instead, applicants should be subjected to close scrutiny in their own homes. Gerando wanted to substitute something like detached, scientific inquiry for emotional response: "In order to distinguish between genuine poverty and artificial indigence, it is preferable to probe into the life of the poor rather than being moved by the sight of ragged clothing and open sores."[29]

If social welfare agencies of the early nineteenth century conceived of the poor as a kind of wild animal to be investigated through direct observation in its natural habitat, the agencies of the late nineteenth and early twentieth centuries took social investigation one step further and introduced deliberately contrived *experiments*, designed to create situations in which the deceiver would "give himself away." Three techniques illustrate this new mode.[30] The first is the "circular approach to the family": the investigator gathers information from acquaintances and associates of the family before actually confronting its members. Thus, he or she has independent sources of information to serve as a check on the truth of the applicant's story. The second is "separate and contradictory questioning": the investigator poses a series of questions and tries to catch the applicant in inconsistencies; moreover, members of the family are questioned separately so that they cannot coordinate their stories on the spot, and the investigator can use the information provided by one member to confront another. The third is "practical verification of the family's way of life": the investigator engages in a little friendly snooping around the house to examine furniture, clothes, food, bedding, and other clues to the applicant's true assets. As the historian Jacques Donzelot so quaintly says, "It was not considered inappropriate, either, to raise the lids of a few cooking pots."[31]

Another type of validating device is the *revelatory sign*: officials construct a situation in which the applicant is required to perform, and the person's behavior reveals, according to some predetermined rule, whether he or she is truly incapable of working or merely feigning inability. The "workhouse test" of the 1834 Poor Law Reform was a form of revelatory sign. Under the principle of least eligibility, conditions inside the workhouse were to be made absolutely minimal and even abhorrent, and applicants would be given the choice of receiving relief inside the workhouse or not at all. The framers of the law had faith that when confronted with such a decision, applicants would reveal the true state of their needs:

> Into such a house none will enter voluntarily; work, confinement, and discipline will deter the indolent and vicious; and nothing but extreme necessity will induce any to accept the comfort which must be obtained by the surrender of their free agency, and the sacrifice of their accustomed habits and gratifications. *Thus the parish officer, being furnished an unerring test of the necessity of applicants, is relieved from his painful and difficult responsibility; while all have the gratification of knowing that while the necessitous are abundantly relieved, the funds of charity are not wasted upon idleness and fraud.*[32]

When the Poor Law Board instituted its campaign to be more stringent after 1871, it not only exhorted local officials to adhere more strictly to the workhouse test but complained that the workhouse itself was an insufficient test. In parishes where outdoor relief was allowed, a "labor test" was used instead. Applicants for relief were made to "break stone and pick oakum," and their willingness to perform this back-breaking labor was to serve as evidence of their true motivation. For this purpose, the parishes were told to create stoneyards. And because the guardians even distrusted the labor test, they instructed local overseers that the homes of these men "should be visited by the relieving officer at least once a fortnight."[33]

The workhouse and labor tests, coupled with home investigations, still did not succeed in curbing relief to the satisfaction of the commissioners, so yet another revelatory device was tried. This was a "test" workhouse strictly for the ablebodied poor, in which work requirements and living conditions would be even harsher than in the general workhouse. The accepted explanation for the failure of the general workhouse to stem relief was that too often, because the aged and sick were not segregated from the ablebodied, the necessarily relaxed discipline actually made the workhouse attractive to many paupers. To remedy this problem, test workhouses exclusively for the ablebodied were established in London (the so-called Poplar Union Workhouse) and other large cities; there they could be subjected to "such a system of labor, discipline, and restraint as shall be sufficient to outweigh . . . the advantages" that the inmates enjoyed.[34]

Revelatory signs as a validation device persist in twentieth-century social policy in the form of status requirements for social insurance. These specify that an applicant for social insurance benefits must have a prior work record of a certain length of time, as evidenced by payment into the social security scheme. In part, these requirements support the notion that social security benefits are earned by the recipients and are a form of saving rather than a social handout. But they are also a test of intent: the record of prior work is taken as a sign of current willingness to work. Similarly, the requirement typical of unemployment insurance programs, that beneficiaries must register periodically with employment offices, is a revelatory device. The willingness to seek employment is taken as evidence of the willingness to work, and therefore evidence that the applicant's unemployment is beyond his control. William Beveridge explicitly promoted the idea of labor exchanges as a substitute for the workhouse test when he advocated unemployment insurance in Britain at the turn of the century.[35]

One last type of validating device is the *adversarial test*. Claimants are asked to prove the legitimacy of their need for aid by providing evidence and, in a sense, engaging in a contest. As already noted, adversarial tests were the classic form of decision in compensation for industrial accidents under systems of employer liability, and were used when the question was one of causation, rather than ability to work. One of the standard arguments against workers' compensation, or even a liberalization of liability laws, was that workers were careless and not terribly concerned about injuries, particularly if they knew that an injury could lead to compensation.[36] Because liability suits were lengthy and expensive, the process itself was alleged to serve as a deterrent to frivolous suits on the part of injured workers.

The growth of welfare programs based on the disability category represents a substitution of *clinical judgment* for earlier forms of validation. Medical criteria have by no means replaced other criteria as eligibility tests for social welfare benefits, but the tremendous growth in the relative importance of disability-based income transfer programs reflects a concomitant growth in the importance of clinical judgment as an administrative tool in the welfare state.

Why was clinical judgment so attractive, and why does it continue to be? Why did it come to replace earlier forms of detection of human motivation, most notably the social investigation so prominent in the social-work/philanthropy institutions, the revelatory tests of the workhouse and labor exchanges, and the adversarial tests of industrial accident law? Clinical judgment was seen to have certain advantages over other validation devices. It was a new technology for accomplishing the same purpose, but without some of the defects of earlier methods.

While the administration of social welfare was undergoing a transformation in the methods of detecting genuine poverty, clinical medicine was undergoing a development that was curiously parallel and ultimately more successful. In both fields, there was a quest for methods of examination that would be independent of the will of the person being investigated. In medicine, this quest took the form of technological development of instruments to give the physician information about the body and its processes without his having to rely on the patient's description of himself.[37] Much of the debate about diagnostic technique during this period centered on the question of the relative merits of physical examination, on the one hand, and traditional patient interviews and observation of external signs on the other.

The first breakthrough in "objective" diagnosis was the stethoscope. Its inventor, the French physician René Laënnec, published a treatise on diagnosis of chest diseases through auscultation (or acoustic signals) in 1819, which started a long controversy over the utility of his methods. Laënnec specifically promoted his new technique as freeing the physician from dependence on the patient, whose information was likely to be distorted by "prejudice or ignorance."[38] His followers extolled the stethoscope for similar reasons: it enabled the physician to avoid the problems of a patient's willful simulation or concealment of disease, and exaggeration or minimization of symptoms.[39] The advent of the stethoscope amounted to a revolution in medical diagnosis and care:

> The effects of the stethoscope on physicians were analogous to the effects of printing on Western culture. . . . auscultation helped to create the objective physician, who could move away from involvement with the patient's experiences and sensations, to a more detached relation, less with the patient but more with the sounds from within the body. *Undistracted by the motives and beliefs of the patient, the auscultator could make a diagnosis*

> *from sounds that he alone heard emanating from body organs, sounds that he believed to be objective, bias-free representations of the disease process.*[40]

Here, in medicine, was exactly the sort of technique welfare administrators were so desperately trying to achieve for their own purposes.

During the rest of the nineteenth century, physicians developed other new instruments and techniques for visualizing the interior of the body and measuring physiological processes. The ophthalmoscope and the laryngoscope enabled them to look directly into the body. The microscope permitted examination of body tissue, revealing structures and microorganisms previously invisible. And the X-ray allowed physicians to look "right through the skin" into any part of the body. Together, these instruments gave medicine a new kind of vision, both literally and metaphorically. Even the stethoscope, whose name Laënnec composed of the Greek words for "chest" and "I see," was regularly described as an instrument for "seeing" into the chest.[41] The medical historian Lester King also emphasizes that percussion and auscultation were so important because they "affected the physician's capacity to observe." The stethoscope required special skill, which meant that only the physician could interpret the sounds. Henceforth, certain data about disease would be available to the physician but not to the patient.[42]

Each new instrument engendered its own controversy, and each one met with some initial resistance that was eventually overcome. And in each case, the proponents of the new technology emphasized its ability to free the physician from the information and judgments of the patient and to diagnose the presence of disease even before the patient manifested any symptoms or complaints. They were also quick to advertise the usefulness of the new technologies for disability certification. An article on legal medicine in 1862 touted the ophthalmoscope's ability to reveal feigned nearsightedness among would-be evaders of military service.[43] The inventor of the spirometer, a device for measuring lung capacity, suggested that doctors could use it to judge fitness for military and other public duties.[44] Thus, medical judgment appeared as a new kind of vision, enabling human beings to look inside other human beings to determine what was "really there." It seemed to be a more powerful kind of investigative device that magnified and made visible things formerly invisible.

This view of clinical judgment pervaded popular thinking as well as the profession itself. The X-ray in particular caught the popular imagination and stimulated a number of fads. Young couples had their clasped hands photographed; people sent X-ray views of themselves as mementos; one woman even used X-rays to locate a ring she had lost in some bread dough. But coupled with this somewhat frivolous exploitation of the new magical powers of medicine was a vague popular fear that X-rays would invade the privacy of both body and home.[45] This image of the special vision of doctors is evident even in contemporary popular culture. In a recent popular song, "Turning Japanese," a skeptical lover sings, "I've got your picture . . . I want the doctor to take a picture so I can look at you from inside as well."[46]

There were other reasons why clinical judgment was so attractive as an administrative device, though the image of its special vision was undoubtedly the most important. Medical judgment was seen as nonintrusive. By the time "lifting a few pot lids" came to be seen as too much of an infringement on privacy, medicine was holding out the promise of providing the same kind of in-depth, inside view, without physically violating the homes of the poor. To ask an applicant for social aid to submit to a medical examination did not seem nearly so great an imposition as a home investigation. Hence, the American Social Security Advisory Council could recommend in 1948 that "claims should be disallowed if the claimant refuses to submit to a medical examination.[47]

An investigation conducted under the rubric of a medical examination also created a context of voluntarism and therapy for what was essentially an eligibility test. The doctor-patient relationship is normally a voluntary one, in which the patient seeks the advice of the physician and submits to medical tests and physical examination entirely by free choice (even though much of what physicians do to patients might be seen as torture or assault in other legal contexts). Moreover, patients generally agree to examination and tests with the expectation that a diagnosis will lead to therapy, some form of care to alleviate the symptoms that brought them to the physician in the first place. By using medical examinations as the primary eligibility determination device for a set of welfare programs, the state could take advantage of these cultural associations. Although the applicant for social aid would actually be undergoing a mandatory examination for the purpose of determining his motivation and ability to work, the test had all the trappings of a voluntary, patient-initiated, therapeutic encounter.

Finally, clinical judgment appeared as a politically neutral mechanism. The growth of scientific medicine brought with it an image of decisions based on pure, objective, unbiased expertise. To base eligibility on clinical criteria gave the illusion of taking politics out of a redistributive program. The conversion from a conflict model to an administrative model was most evident in the field of industrial accidents, where decision-making methods were changed from an adversarial dispute over liability to a simple administrative decision: a matter of locating a particular claimant within a "schedule" of injuries, to which fixed monetary amounts were attached. Finding a claimant's position in a schedule was in turn simply a matter of observation, albeit the special observation of the clinical eye.

The clinical concept also de-politicized the redistributive issues of social insurance for people whose disability was not connected with an identifiable job-related injury. The central problem of such a program was how to identify people with legitimate reasons for their inability to work. The definition of eligibility was highly controversial (and still is), but in the beginning, a reliance on medical criteria as the preliminary screen at least thwarted much of the conflict that might have prevented disability insurance from emerging.

The appeal of apolitical medical judgment found its expression in a peculiar literary genre of medical utopias, societies where clinical and scientific decisions would substitute for controversial political decisions. Ernest Tarboureich, a French physician who played a leading role in establishing workers' compensation in France, was so enthralled with the administrative solution to the industrial accidents conflict that he proposed an entire state that would be regulated primarily by medical decisions. Children would be required to undergo medical examination upon reaching maturity, and physicians would control permission for marriage, reproduction, and sexual union.[48]

The Clinical Concept of Impairment

The assessment of eligibility for American disability benefit programs is dominated by a concept called "impairment." Virtually every medical article or text on the subject of disability evaluation begins with liturgical cant distinguishing between "impairment" and "disability." The medical profession takes the position that impairment is a purely medical phenomenon, while disability is a medical-administrative-legal phenomenon. In this view, physicians can attest to impairment, but they cannot certify or even identify disability; that is the province of administrative agencies.[49]

The literature on disability evaluation provides innumerable classifications and definitions of the phenomenon, but all are predicated on a three-part distinction. First, there are some physiological changes in the human body that are observable and objectively measurable but may have nothing to do with the ability of a person to work or perform other social roles.[50] Second, some of these physiological changes also cause changes in the person's ability to perform particular tasks or simply to function as an organism—for example, there may be a decrease in the range of motion of a joint, in visual acuity, or in respiratory capacity as compared with the functions of a "normal" or "standard" person—but again, not all of them are significantly related to working ability. Such changes are called "impairments" or sometimes "function losses." Finally, there are some physiological changes that do indeed restrict the ability of a person to work because they dovetail with the physical requirements of a job. These are called "disabilities." This three-part classification of physiological, functional, and work-related phenomena probably does justice to most attempts to define disability.[51] The clinical concept of impairment, as used by the medical profession, is an attempt to work at the second level.

All disability benefit programs rely to a greater or lesser extent on the medical evaluation of impairment. In addition, they take into consideration a variety of social, economic, and environmental factors such as age, education, job training and experience, availability of different types of jobs, or the need to support dependents. Different national programs for accident compensation or disability pensions emphasize these nonmedical factors in varying degrees, but the common denominator of all programs is the requirement that inability to work—in any socioeconomic context—be caused by a demonstrable medical condition. Thus, evaluation of impairment is the critical element in public decision-making about access to disability benefits; medical impairment is the necessary condition for eligibility.

How did this concept of impairment come into being and how did it come to dominate disability evaluation in public programs? It is worth noting that there are other concepts of disability in use by public agencies. Only the benefit-granting agencies rely primarily on impairment for their definition of disability. In epidemiological studies of disability conducted by government agencies, interviews are generally used (rather than medical examination), and the classification of people as disabled is made on the basis of whether they *say* they have limitations on their normal activities.[52] A second type of disability definition is used by public rehabilitation agencies. Here the focus is on the rehabilitation potential of applicants, rather than their current earning capacity, the origins of their inability to work, or the causes of their condition.[53] The emphasis on potential earning capacity and "marketability" of applicants came about largely because vocational rehabilitation agencies were funded out of general revenues and constantly needed to justify their actions in public budget-setting contexts; in order to show profitability, these agencies would engage in cream-skimming, or selecting out the clients who were easiest to rehabilitate.[54] The use of criteria other than clinical judgments is important, not because they are any better or worse than clinical criteria but because their use demonstrates that a medical conception of disability is not the only possible conception, and that in fact public agencies do use other definitions when the purpose of their programs is not primarily distributive.

The transformation of the idea of "inability to work" into the clinical concept of impairment is a fascinating intellectual story. There are basically two approaches used in evaluating impairment, corresponding to the two administrative approaches of granting benefits for either partial or total disability. The first approach, used in Workers Compensation and Veterans Administration pensions, rests on the the creation of schedules or lists. These schedules translate particular biological phenomena (such as amputations, or laboratory findings) into levels of impairment expressed as percentages. Early schedules used by commercial insurers and workmen's compensation programs were typically based on an image of anatomical wholeness; impairment was conceived as a "missing part." The second approach is used primarily in the Social Security Disability Insurance and Supplemental Security Income programs, both of which provide benefits only in cases of a "total incapacity to engage in substantial gainful activity." This approach also creates a list, but this time a list of impairments deemed totally incapacitating; in addition, the SSA provides "guidelines" for the identification of conditions which are not on the list (don't "meet the listings" in SSA parlance) but are "equivalent" (see Chapter 4).[55]

The earliest schedules for the assessment of disability presumably came from commercial insurers and European mutual aid societies under old systems of employer liability. Public programs adapted them, and there was a great deal of cross-national borrowing in the design of both social insurance programs and specific schedules. The state of California, for example, patterned its first workmen's compensation schedule after a Russian schedule of 1907.[56]

The intellectual foundations of the concept of impairment are to be found in these industrial accident schedules. There are lists of physical or medical conditions, with a percentage of loss attached to each condition. Thus, the early schedules share two assumptions essential to the impairment concept. First, they postulate a correspondence between a concrete bodily condition and a more abstract loss. Some purport to describe loss of "earning capacity," others focus on loss of "working capacity," actual "economic loss," or "loss of function." But they all presume a link between bodily condition and some more abstract notion of performance. Second, the schedules all assume that a person (or more properly, a person's ability to function) is a collection of arithmetically manipulable separate entities. Human performance is divided into percentiles, so that disability is conceived in terms of missing parts. Impairments become entities to be subtracted from the presumed wholeness of the individual.

A third element of the impairment concept, the idea that the purely *medical* judgment of impairment is separable from the more subjective and value-laden judgment of disability, crystallized in a set of disability guides created by the American Medical Association to assist physicians in their certifying role. Between 1958 and 1971, the AMA's Committee on Medical Rating of Physical Impairments produced a series of thirteen "Guides to the Evaluation of Permanent Impairment," each one devoted to impairments of a particular body system.[57]

According to Henry Kessler, an influential member of the committee and author of a widely used disability evaluation system, the main purpose of the guides was to standardize medical decision-making on disability by grounding evaluation in measurable factors. He thus hoped to bring more respect to the medical profession in an area where lawyers and judges, in particular, were cynical about the reliability of doctors' opinions.[58]

> One can observe the [medical] damage as an objective physical fact and often can classify and measure it. . . . Clearly so long as the objective is strictly limited to accurate description of the damage, *the medical "factor" remains distinct from all else and can be reduced to a scientific procedure of unquestionable validity.*[59]

But beyond this quest for an objective science of disability evaluation, a latent function of the guides was to make disability evaluation accessible to the average practicing physician. The guides' assessment of impairment is based entirely on information normally collected during the course of diagnosis and treatment. According to William Roemmich, the Chief Medical Consultant to the Social Security Administration from 1956 to 1974, program officials wanted to develop an administrative concept of disability that would derive from normal clinical practice: "It was hoped [early in the program] also that the operation would not make heavy demands upon the medical profession of the Nation [*sic*] and that decisions could be made from the evidence which was adduced and recorded in the process of medical care."[60]

At the time of the advent of Social Security Disability Insurance, the American Medical Association's major concern was whether disability evaluations would be provided by practicing doctors or by disability experts on the government payroll. Doctors, of course, were adamantly opposed to the latter. The basis of the AMA's concern was a desire to protect the existing (distant) relationship between government and the profession by resisting any program that would increase the number of physicians working directly for the government. One major objection to a federal disability insurance program was the lack of "assurance that the family physician of the potential beneficiary will be permitted to have any voice in the determination of disability"; instead, the proposed plan would give the Social Security administrators broad discretion in selecting physicians, and they might "utilize physicians who are employees of the government, such as salaried physicians of the Veterans' Administration or of the United States Public Health Service."[61] Thus, the development of a clinical concept of impairment served an important strategic purpose: it grounded the determination of disability in the office-based practice of the typical physician (the bulk of the

AMA constituency) instead of in a bureaucratic agency of staff physicians who might develop criteria totally outside the realm of clinical experience.

The interest of the AMA in creating a concept of disability based on clinical practice did not derive from any direct economic motivation to make sure that practicing physicians got a "piece of the pie"; no one foresaw that disability evaluation was going to be a terribly large or lucrative aspect of medical practice. Indeed, disability certification was not a task the profession wanted to assume. Most physicians believed that medical science was not capable of assessing disability, and that adoption of the certifying role would only create enormous tensions between doctors and their patients. Thus, when the American Academy of General Practice sent in its representatives to testify against the proposal for disability-based cash benefits (see Chapter 2), the essence of its argument was the folly of a disability program at all, not the wisdom of assigning disability certification to general practitioners.[62] Once the legislation for a disability program had passed, however, the American Medical Association's interest was to prevent the creation of a corps of government physicians who might eventually come to rival independent practitioners, and who in any case would be the entering wedge of socialized medicine. The best way to accomplish this goal was to create a method of disability evaluation relying on the existing system of medical care.

In the end, the AMA Guides did not become the primary basis for disability evaluation under Social Security; for that purpose, the SSA's own guidelines are determinative. The AMA Guides are used more commonly by physicians evaluating clients for Workers Compensation, veterans' pensions, or liability suits, all of which make use of the concept of partial disability implicit in the guides. (Social Security Disability Insurance requires permanent and total disability.) But the guides influenced other public schedules; for example, the Social Security Administration's techniques for measuring restricted motion are based on the AMA's Guide to the musculoskeletal system.[63] Moreover, they are important for their articulation of one of the central premises of disability evaluation: the separation of impairment as a medically determinable phenomenon. And they are illustrative of how the medical profession, legal profession, and disability bureaucracies *think* about disability.

The professional concept of impairment represents an effort to define and quantify the elements of inability to work, while recognizing that working ability is a relative phenomenon. The profession steadfastly maintains that "inability to work" itself is not quantifiable, at least by doctors. What is quantifiable (and allegedly quantified) in the AMA Guides is functional capacity. But since the agencies that grant benefits on the basis of disability certification rely primarily on medical certification, for all practical purposes the concept of impairment stands as a proxy for disability or inability to work. Despite its insistence on the conceptual distinction between impairment and disability, the Committee on Medical Rating of Physical Impairment admitted that "permanent impairment is, in fact, the sole or real criterion of permanent disability far more often than is readily acknowledged."[64]

The AMA Guides are based on a pervading faith that a phenomenon of functional impairment, totally independent of context, can be precisely measured. This doctrine is so important in the disability field that it is worth quoting the committee at length:

> The Committee on Medical Rating of Physical Impairment believes that permanent impairment *cannot vary because of the circumstances of its occurrence or the geographic location of the patient at the time*. Furthermore, unlike disability, permanent impairment *can be measured with a reasonable degree of accuracy and uniformity on the basis of impaired function as evidenced by loss of structural integrity, pathological findings, or pain substantiated by clinical evidence.*[65]

The guides enable physicians to translate clinical criteria into *percentage* disability. The rationale given for the use of percentages is that numerical values avoid some of the "difficulty in communication and variability in interpretation of such terms as 'slight,' 'marked,' and 'moderate.'"[66] More likely, the committee was compelled to use percentages if the guides were to be of use to the practicing physician, because the state Workers Compensation agencies and the Veterans Administration were demanding information in the form of percentage disability ratings. This basic requirement that impairment (or whatever concept the committee chose) be expressed as a percentage of a whole had a profound impact on the concept. The guides perform some ordinary arithmetic manipulations and apply ordinary mathematical ideas to the concept of impairment, but these ordinary ideas become absolutely bizarre in the context of the underlying issue—the ability of a human being to work.

The guides begin with a concept of "the whole man" and assume that medical conditions operate to reduce the whole by some percentage. Each type of disease within a given anatomical system is then divided into *classes of severity*. The severity classes are really just groupings by percentage, but for some curious reason, the guides do not make use of the full continuous scale. For example, the four severity classes for organic heart disease are subtitled 0–15% (class 1), 20–40% (class 2), 50–70% (class 3), and 80–95% (class 4). What happened to the percentages between these categories is a mystery.[67] Even more curious is that when the committee made the transformation from the 100 percent scale to the categories, the same categories were not used for every type of disease. For vascular diseases affecting the extremities, the categories are 0% (class 1), 5–25% (class 2), 25–50% (class 3), 50–75% (class 4) and 75–90% (class 5). The specifics of the categories are not important here, but the inconsistent translation between integers and classes is revealing. Clinical criteria may be able to group people reasonably well into broad categories, but the committee was straining to meet the administrative demands for a more precise integer scale.

The guides then proceed to list important clinical signs for each of the major diseases of a system and to express each sign on a quantitative scale. Where an integer scale is already in use (as in temperature, pulse rate, blood pressure), the signs can be expressed as such. For other clinical signs, the guides resort to the same imprecise language previously decried by the authors—"intermittent," "average," "of moderate degree," "marked," "persistent."

If a physician wants to assign a patient to a severity class, he must first perform an examination to elicit the clinical signs, history, and symptoms used in the guide. For any given disease, the physician will always look at the same set of clinical variables—for example, the ability to walk and climb stairs, the ability to engage in prolonged exertion, blood pressure, or urine tests. Then the Guide gives rules for classifying a patient on the basis of these findings, by specifying either a threshold value for a particular variable or a minimum number of clinical characteristics that must be present. In vascular disease, for example, one of the necessary characteristics for impairment is "intermittent claudication (lameness) on walking." The criterion is made increasingly stringent for the different severity classes by adding a distance: walking 100 yards (class 2), 25–100 yards (class 3), less than 25 yards (class 4). For hypertensive vascular diseases, impairment requires a diastolic blood pressure of at least 100 mm. plus various "quorums" of other clinical findings—none for class 1, any one of several for class 2, any two of several for classes 3 and 4.

The mathematical precision necessary to derive percentages is thus gained by using measurable physical properties (temperature, blood pressure, distance) and then defining those properties as entities that can be added together. What results, however, is not a continuous scale but a categorical scale with four, sometimes five, groups. The guides provide illustrative examples of real clinical cases, but their classification is not always self-evident. A hypothetical man who has a history of rheumatic fever and the presence of a heart murmur but is otherwise "asymptomatic and leads a normal life without limitation of activity" is classified as 5% impaired.[68]

Those are the basic rules. Use threshold values of clinical signs and minimum quorum values of signs in combination to locate an individual within broad severity classes. Pick a percentage to the nearest 5% within that class. (At this point the classification is a judgment call, but because of the way the classes are defined, the physician cannot err by more than 20 percentage points.) A few supplementary rules liven up the game a bit. A person automatically gets additional points for an amputation due to peripheral vascular disease, for example. These bonus points, listed in a separate table, range from one additional percentage point (for amputation of the little finger at the distal joint) to 70 percent (for a forequarter amputation).[69]

Finally, taking all possibilities into account, the guides provide a rule for combining multiple impairments. The principle is that "each impairment acts not on the whole [person] but on the portion which remains after the preceding impairment has acted."[70] Impairments are assumed to be independent and cumulative, though not strictly additive. "The source and the chronology of the impairment values are immaterial." Thus, if a person who is already 50 percent impaired sustains a second injury which normally produces a 20 percent impairment, the two combined will yield a total of 60 percent, not 70 percent, impairment—according to the formula for combining two impairments, a and b:

$$a + \frac{b(100 - a)}{100}$$

This same method is also used to combine different types of function loss in the same limb, such as motion, strength and coordination of a hand.

In sum, the guides begin with constructs from clinical practice that have real validity as measurements—temperature, blood pressure, blood chemistry analyses, electrocardiogram readings, and so forth—but combine these measurements in ways that make no sense (like adding apples and oranges) in order to yield identifiable categories. The physician performs arithmetic operations on clinical measurements to yield some numbers, but these numbers do not measure anything real.

The evaluation of impairment is thus full of errors of reification and false precision. It assumes a direct correspondence between physiological processes and functional abilities. It conceives of functional ability as a single but composite entity that can be measured on an integer scale. Finally, it assumes an equivalence between different anatomical or physiological systems, so that, for example, a loss of either 20 percent of normal respiratory capacity or 20 percent of normal musculoskeletal function yields a 20 percent impairment.

It would be grossly unfair to suggest that medical professionals are oblivious to these errors or totally comfortable with the systems of evaluation they have invented. The professional literature is replete with disclaimers about the complexity of the phenomenon of disability and the importance of the interplay of social, economic, psychological, environmental, and medical factors. Even so staunch a defender of the idea of objective measurement of impairment as Henry Kessler says that his practical experience has taught him "there is no great correlation between physical injury and ability to earn a living."[71] He concludes his text on disability evaluation with an assertion that schedules are "pure fiction":

> To summarize, it is important to understand that the entire pension scheme and disability rating scheme are pure fiction if we feel that the rating table expresses in a scientific way the economic, or psychological or physical effects of these injuries. At best they can only be arbitrary agreements, expressing not physical effects but reflecting the cultural forces or pressures of the nation at large. These arbitrary schedules have a definite and indispensable place, but they must be recognized for what they are, and equity lies in their consistency since it applies to all the people.[72]

But notwithstanding the disclaimers, the quest for an objective method of medical evaluation of disability has a long history and continues into the present.[73] The new science of "ergonomics,"—which attempts to measure human work capacity and the requirements of jobs, using objective techniques—is also being put to the service of disability programs.

The concept of impairment is certainly an imperfect rendition of the phenomenon of the inability to work. And while the classification method presented above appears somewhat foolish in many respects, we would do well to remember that the problem of translating complex human experiences into administratively manageable categories is not unique to the evaluation of disability. Virtually every private and public agency must make judgments about selecting clients (or patients, residents, suspects, prisoners) and about providing appropriate treatment. In doing so, these agencies must translate a complex conception of need for services into a set of operational rules.[74] The problem of surrogate measures is pervasive.

The intellectual problem for the scholar of social policy, therefore, is not simply to ferret out the existence of surrogate measures but to understand how such measures distort social reality and why particular distortions come about. Granting that there are always multiple understandings of a particular social phenomenon such as disability, and that there can never be a perfect correspondence between a measure and the underlying phenomenon it is trying to capture, one can try to examine how particular constructs and measures *systematically* exclude certain understandings and include others, how they serve the political interests of some groups at the expense of others, and how they work to produce particular types of policy results.

The clinical concept of impairment certainly served the interests of the organized medical profession, albeit not without certain costs. If the profession was able to use its concept of impairment to capture disability evaluation for its members and to resist the development of public employment of physicians, it was also stuck with all the problems of mixing a certification role with its traditional therapeutic role. And if society at large benefited from the development of a workable redistributive method, it, too, was stuck with a concept full of problems.

4

Mechanisms for Restricting Access to the Disability Category

The purpose of the disability category is to keep everyone in the work-based distributive system except for the very neediest people, those who have legitimate reason for receiving social aid. Like any mechanical device, it had to be deliberately designed to accomplish its purpose. This chapter examines the restrictive elements of that design. The example of American Social Security Disability Insurance is used throughout this chapter and the next, largely because it makes sense to study the mechanism of boundary control at close range. This program is ideal for a case study because it has always placed so much emphasis on the role of clinical judgment in determining disability. At the same time, the experience of this program is not irrelevant to the analysis of others in which clinical criteria play a less prominent role, since even for those programs where reduced earning capacity is the chief criterion, a medical condition is always the *sine qua non* for disability certification.

The most important element of the disability category as a restrictive mechanism is, of course, the reliance on a formal definition of disability based on clinical criteria—the "medically determinable by objective tests" requirement in the Social Security program. If the motivation behind the development of the clinical concept of impairment by the AMA was to keep disability evaluation within the purview of private medical practice, the motivation from the point of view of the Social Security executives was to find a definition of disability that would be immune to influence by applicants.

As we have seen, legislators and then program executives looked to clinical medicine to provide such a definition.

The SSA made a second important decision by creating a presumption of disability for those physical conditions generally recognized as causing total inability to function. The idea behind this presumption is that certain conditions are so incapacitating that an individual examination is not necessary to determine whether a person is impaired. Instead, the SSA would draw up a "Listing of Medical Impairments" based on these conditions, and any person who produced medical evidence of a condition on the list would automatically qualify for benefits.

Thus, a formal definition of medical impairments had to be created by the program. Disability insurance was run by the Division of Disability Operations, under the Bureau of Old Age and Survivors Insurance (BOASI). Within the division, two groups worked on the listings: the Medical Consultant Staff, physicians employed by the division who were responsible for reviewing cases as they came up from the states and for drafting medical criteria to resolve the ambiguities in actual cases; and the Medical Advisory Committee, appointed by BOASI in 1955 to provide guidance on the development of medical standards. The committee was composed of fifteen physicians, representing both general practice and specialties as well as preventive medicine and vocational rehabilitation; this group acted as a sounding board for the Medical Consultant Staff.[1] The Medical Consultant Staff, with the advice of the Medical Advisory Committee, drafted the standards for disability determination, variously referred to as "standards," "guides," or "medical listings," and then circulated these drafts to subcommittees with specialty expertise.

Early in the program, the expectation was that most awards for disability would be made on the basis of the listings. There was, however, provision for people who did not "meet the listings" (have exactly the conditions described) but who "equaled the listings" (had conditions with equally incapacitating results). The Medical Advisory Committee suggested that certain nonmedical factors would also need to be considered in some cases: age, education, training, experience and other individual factors.[2]

The basic principle followed by the Medical Consultant Staff was to separate clinical data into parts that could and could not be manipulated by the patient, and to ensure that the definition of impairment was not based entirely on the manipulable elements. Since the nineteenth century, the medical profession had made a distinction between "signs" and "symptoms." Symptoms were sensations or observations of disease perceptible only to the patient; signs were sensations and observations perceptible to the physician.[3] The Medical Advisory Committee therefore was guided by the principle that every impairment in the listings be recognized primarily by clinical signs rather than by symptoms.

William Roemmich, Chief Medical Director of the Bureau of Disability Insurance for fifteen years, later explained that this distinction was one reason why he had confidence that the listings could in fact "do a fairly accurate job in separating the able from the disabled by reason of impairment":

> Of the *three* types of medical data, symptoms, signs, and laboratory findings, only symptoms can be moulded by the applicant to his advantage. For that reason, symptoms alone cannot by themselves describe an impairment that meets the medical standards. Sets of medical data always include signs or laboratory findings. The latter cannot be fashioned by the applicant, the examining physician, nor the decision-maker.[4]

In 1961, the Social Security Administration published regulations that further elaborated the concept of "medically determinable impairment." They, too, sought to distinguish between subjective reports of claimants and objective findings of physicians:

> There should be evidence that medically ascertainable anatomical, physiological, biochemical or psychological aberrations exist. Allegations of inability to work as a result of impairment such as dyspnea [shortness of breath], pain, lack of musculoskeletal function, decreased vision or hearing, decreased memory, etc., should be shown to result from structural physiological or psychological changes which can be identified by the use of clinical and laboratory diagnostic techniques. *An alleged impairment is medically determinable only if it can be verified by the use of clinical and laboratory techniques.*[5]

At the same time that the program rested on a faith in the ability of stringent clinical standards to maintain a tight boundary around the disability program, its executives betrayed a profound distrust of physicians. They realized that the interests of applicants and those of the program were in some sense in conflict, with physicians cast in the role of mediator. Applicants wanted to receive money from the program; administrators wanted to conserve money, both to make sure the program served the most needy applicants and to protect the public treasury. Physicians had the power to determine whether a person would receive money simply by indicating whether the person was "clinically impaired."

For all the expression of confidence in the ability of clinical criteria to distinguish between genuine medical incapacity and malingering (or other nonmedical reasons for unemployment), the Social Security Administration was unwilling to *publish* its medical listings for many years, precisely because it feared that both patients and their physicians could use the listings to advantage. In a revealing comment, the Commissioner of Social Security, Robert Ball, gave as one reason for not publishing the listings that "it would not be desirable for examining physicians throughout the country to have available to them exactly what it is that makes it possible for a person to qualify."[6] The SSA feared that if the specific criteria were available, applicants might fabricate the requisite symptoms, and physicians might report whatever was necessary to make the patient eligible for benefits. SSA policy on disability determination was published only in an internal manual (the Disability Insurance State Manual) not available to the public or even to physicians and attorneys representing claimants.

Under pressure from both Congress and practicing attorneys, the SSA finally did publish its regulations on disability determination in 1961,[7] but omitted any specific numerical values of clinical tests or performance (such as the percentage of limitation in joint motion), even though such quantitative criteria were given in the manual.[8] Quantitative criteria were not published until 1980, when the SSA issued updated listings for the first time since 1968.

Thus, to ensure stringency in eligibility, the program used two methods whose assumptions were absolutely contradictory. The first was to define disability in terms of objective clinical findings so that neither patients nor physicians could manipulate them. The second was to keep the criteria secret, just in case patients and their physicians *could* manipulate them.

A third restrictive mechanism was the institution of "consultative examinations." In theory, the program uses these second opinions simply to supplement the medical evidence given by the claimant's own physician, so that the eligibility decision will be better informed. Social Security regulations state that consultative exams will be required under three different conditions: when the medical evidence from the treating physician is insufficient; when the evidence required is too technical or specialized to be provided by the treating physician; or when there are conflicts or differences in opinion in the medical evidence submitted by the claimant.[9] Consultative exams are usually purchased from physicians by the state agencies. Since the federal and state agencies have very limited in-house medical capabilities (that was part of the original bargain—no new corps of government physicians), the exams are performed by physicians in private practice who serve the disability program on a contract basis.[10]

There is little consensus in state agencies about what constitutes "adequate documentation" of a claim and, therefore, about when consultative exams are necessary.[11] Instead, they seem to be used as an administrative control device, another means of making the program restrictive. Program officials *believe* that they help keep costs down, and it is clear that the agencies use them to that end. In 1979, the General Accounting Office, in one of its many supervisory reports on the program, noted that consultative exams are "cost beneficial," since "the denial rate goes up as the consultative examination rate goes up." To make the point even more convincing, the report contrasted the cost of a consultative exam ($107) with the cost of an average disability pension ($29,000), implying that the program could save a lot of money with each exam.[12] In 1981 hearings, the Associate Commissioner for Operational Policy and Procedures testified that "the incidence of denials increases the more you get consultative examinations," but the evidence for his assertion was hardly convincing.[13]

Consultative examinations have gone in and out of fashion as the program has evolved. During the decade of the 1960s, they were purchased in roughly one-third of all cases. In the period from 1971 to 1975, the SSA tried to minimize their use to save time and money in processing claims, and to save scarce medical consultants for the really difficult cases. In those years, consultative exams used in initial claims declined to about one-quarter or one-fifth of all cases,[14] but since then, their use has increased steadily—from a rate of 19.7 percent of all cases in 1975 to 34.6 percent in 1980.[15]

In the quest for more consultative exams, most states have made arrangements with "volume sources" or "volume providers"—physicians or institutions who agree to dedicate a portion of their practice to providing disability evaluation services for the Social Security program. State administrators give several reasons for the trend toward specialized volume providers. One is that the state determination agencies were overburdened with claims after the introduction of black lung benefits in 1969 and Supplemental Security Income in 1972. Compounding the problem of increased workload was an inability to attract physicians to the consultative role because of its low fees, lack of reimbursement for missed appointments, and agency requirements that the physician be able to provide extensive written reports in a fairly short time.[16]

The demands for rapid availability of appointments and rapid processing of reports were in turn a product of federal "processing time targets" imposed by the SSA on state agencies at the urging of the General Accounting Office (GAO)—all part of the general campaign to solve the disability problem through administrative reform. The GAO's campaign began in earnest in 1976, when it published a study showing inconsistency in disability determination among the states. It circulated descriptions of some two hundred cases to ten state agencies and asked them to adjudicate the claims. The study found that there was complete agreement among the agencies in only 22 percent of the cases. This result was widely publicized and then used to justify further evaluation of the state determination processes.[17]

This and several later GAO reports urged the Social Security Administration to establish claims-processing standards, including "processing time goals," and to provide better supervision of state agencies.[18] The SSA did establish national accuracy and processing time standards in March 1977, and then required the state agencies to produce "action plans" describing how they would meet these goals. But the GAO was still unsatisfied, because, it said, the goals were arbitrarily set, the states were given little guidance in achieving the goals, and states were encouraged to meet statistical targets rather than the substantive aims of the program.[19]

The advent of volume providers brought its own problems, however. There were reports of abuses, such as billing for services not performed, misrepresentation of services, perfunctory examinations of applicants, and inadequate written reports. In one widely publicized case, seven claimants won a suit in which they maintained that the services of a volume provider used to deny their claims were fraudulent. The SSA temporarily suspended the use of that provider while it investigated the charges. Although the SSA found no evidence of fraudulent practices and reinstated the medical group, it did issue new standards for consultative exams and guidelines for state agency monitoring of volume providers.[20]

This rather long story about consultative exams illustrates the failure of medical determination as a restrictive mechanism and the consequent need for repeated buttressing: first a set of strict medical criteria was established; then it was kept secret. Even so, disability awards increased "too much," so consultative exams were brought into play. When there were not enough physicians to provide enough consultative exams, arrangements were made for "volume providers." Then volume providers were thought to be abusing the system, so new criteria for consultative examinations were established. Tennessee, the state where the "scandal" described above took place, even set up its own standards to supplement the national standards. Its requirements have a certain Alice-in-Wonderland quality:

1. There must be a minimum of 15 minutes spent examining each patient.
2. The physician's office should look like a physician's office.
3. Equipment used in the course of the examination must be accurately calibrated and clean and make a positive influence on the patient.
4. The report must accurately reflect what occurred during the examination.[21]

Clinical definition and clinical methods of determination were the primary mechanisms built into the program to restrict access to income through the social insurance disability program. Other mechanisms are also of interest, not because they contributed to the formation of the clinical concept but rather because they demonstrate both the *intent* for a very restrictive program and the understanding of policymakers that clinical criteria by themselves could not be restrictive enough.

The first of these other mechanisms was the insurance status requirement. The very first recommendation of the Advisory Council of 1948, when it initially advised the development of a disability program, was that a person "should be required to meet strict tests of recent and substantial attachment to the labor market" in order to be eligible for benefits.[22] The council recommended a minimum of forty quarters of coverage; one quarter of coverage for every two calendar quarters after age twenty-one; and two quarters of coverage within the four quarters preceding the onset of disability. The jargon of "quarters of coverage" obscures the fact these criteria are essentially work requirements. Translated, they mean that a person had to have worked for at least ten years, for at least half of his or her adult life, and for at last half a year in the year preceding the disability. When the 1954 disability freeze was passed, the requirements were only slightly changed: a person needed twenty out of forty quarters, six of which must be in the thirteen quarters ending with the onset of disability—that is, recent. (The six-out-of-thirteen requirement was repealed in the 1958 amendments.)

Another restrictive requirement is that an applicant for disability benefits must be willing to accept rehabilitation and/or treatment of his disabling condition. Mandatory rehabilitation was also one of the recommendations of the 1948 Advisory Council.[23] Similarly, a Ways and Means Committee report on the 1954 amendments said that one reason for locating disability determination at the state level was to encourage "rehabilitation contacts by disabled persons."[24] Willingness to accept rehabilitation or treatment is the modern analogue of the workhouse test; it is intended to reveal the applicant's true motivations.

Rehabilitation was a concept that appealed to everyone, and united conservatives and liberals on the disability insurance issue.[25] Like most such concepts, it was ambiguous enough to mean different things to different people. To the liberals, it meant that the work of vocational rehabilitation agencies would be expanded and more people would have a chance at a productive life. But to the conservatives, it meant a safeguard against abuse of the system. During the 1956 debates on the introduction of cash benefits for disability, one of the sponsors of the legislation, Senator Walter George, explained that beneficiaries would be required to accept rehabilitation services from state agencies. "Could the requirement be made any stronger?" he asked rhetorically.[26]

All of these requirements were clearly intended as obstacles to entry into the program. Senator George tried to win opponents over by portraying the eligibility criteria as seven separate requirements: 1) the test of work history and contributions to Social Security; 2) the "unable to engage in substantial gainful activity" test; 3) the "medically determinable impairment" test; 4) the 6 month waiting period; 5) the "age 50 or over" requirement; 6) the "proof of existence" test, wherein the applicant must furnish proof of his or her impairment; and 7) the willingness to accept rehabilitation test. Senator Albert Gore added that these requirements would ensure that the type of person who received benefits would be "not an itinerant worker, not a spasmodic job holder, but a man or woman who had demonstrated by his or her longevity of service, a reliable and sustained employment in industrial life."[27]

Social Security regulations also stipulate that a beneficiary must follow treatment prescribed by his physician; if he fails to comply, he will not be found disabled, or will have his benefits cut off.[28] Even the medical listings include certain requirments for treatment as part of the very definition of "total and permanent disability." The listings contain many phrases that define a medical condition in terms of failed treatment: "despite prescribed therapy"; "in spite of prescribed treatment"; "despite treatment for at least 3 months"; "under continuing surgical management"; "after definitive surgery"; "not controlled by surgical or medical treatment"; "not healed following at least 3 months of prescribed medical or surgical therapy"; "inoperable or beyond control by other modes of therapy" (applies to cancer). A person has the right to refuse treatment only under certain conditions—among them, when the treatment conflicts with one's religious beliefs, when it involves a significant amputation, and when it is very risky. Both the disability insurance and supplemental income programs recognize alcoholism and drug addiction as disabling conditions, but SSI requires "*whole-hearted participation* in a treatment program."[29] (Imagine enforcing that requirement!)

In addition to agreeing to submit to medical treatment and rehabilitation, the recipient of disability benefits must agree to a *reexamination* under some circumstances. Certain conditions defined in the listings (kidney transplant, for example) specify that a person is to be reexamined at some set time interval. But the SSA has the right to call in any beneficiary for reinvestigation.[30] Reexamination, like the other safeguards, was already contemplated by the 1948 Advisory Council, and the requirement dates from that time. The recipient also has a legal obligation to inform the Social Security Administration if his condition improves, if he returns to work or increases the amount of his work, or if he increases the amount of his earnings.[31]

Finally, the program as it was initially designed made use of all the standard methods of insurance programs to discourage abuse: waiting periods, income offsets, and low benefit levels. A waiting period of six months between the beginning of the disability and the time a person could claim benefits was contemplated in the 1950 proposals and ultimately written into both the freeze legislation (1954) and the cash benefits amendments (1956). Offset provisions stipulated that benefits would be adjusted to take account of any income from Workers Compensation, but this requirement was repealed in the 1958 amendments. In theory, the benefits of disability insurance are always less than a person could make by working; they are calculated at a "replacement rate" or percentage of prior earnings, and that ratio is supposed to be less than one. In practice, however, the replacement rate may be greater than one for a particular worker because of the nontaxability of disability benefits, special allowances for dependents, and cost of living increases pegged to general economic indicators (rather than to what workers in the claimant's particular occupation actually received).

Problems with Clinical Criteria as a Restrictive Mechanism

Like that of the AMA Guides, the Social Security Administration's process of defining and determining disability rests on a distinction between disability and impairment. The Medical Advisory Committee (as well as the entire SSA) takes the position that only physicians can judge impairment, but that a finding of impairment does not necessarily mean that the person is disabled. Only a state disability determination unit or an administrative hearing officer can render a valid judgment on disability. The Medical Advisory Committee also believes that judgments of impairment can be done accurately and fairly, with a high degree of consistency,[32] and that a system of eligibility determination based on impairment assessment can separate people who are capable of working from those who are not. The extent to which actual determinations fail to meet standards of accuracy and consistency constitutes a problem of *implementation*, not problems in the concept of impairment itself. Hence, the SSA responds to criticisms of its determination process, such as those of the General Accounting Office, by providing more training, more guidelines, and more supervision.

But there are important reasons why a concept of disability based on clinical criteria is bound to fail—why it cannot be perfectly objective and why, therefore, as a determination mechanism, it is highly flexible and inevitably subject to manipulation. Moreover, these problems with clinical criteria are not unique to Social Security; they plague all of the many redistributive programs that use certified disability, based on a notion of clinical impairment, as their eligibility criterion.

First, clinical tests can provide a measure of some phenomenon, but no single test can tell whether a person is "impaired" (whatever that means) or "disabled" or still able to work. Someone has to *decide* what level of any measurement is indicative of inability to function and how the information from different tests ought to be combined. Should disability be presumed when someone meets any two of a set of criteria, or any three?

Although the listings were allegedly based on strictly physiological criteria, they were formed by a process of consensus that was no more objective than the informal molding of a group opinion. A memorandum of the BOASI in 1955 described the proposed standards as a listing that would include "a description of medical conditions concerning which *doctors will in general agree* that an individual so impaired and not engaged in substantial gainful activity" ought to be considered disabled under the law.[33] Roemmich's description of the formation of the standards also portrays an exercise in formalizing the informal opinions of a group. In his 1976 testimony, he said:

> The medical standards were created by analyzing the collective experience of hundreds of physicians. These physicians had behind them a vast medical literature not only describing the many impairments but the physical and mental restrictions produced by such impairments. . . . The medical staff in the central agency assembled these collective physician judgments into *sets* of symptoms, signs, and laboratory findings. . . . These sets of symptoms, signs, and laboratory findings represented what *in the collective judgment of several hundred physicians* in all geographic areas *believed* to represent the critical medical data separating applicants who retained ability to meet job demands from those who had lost such ability [*sic*].[34]

Nowadays, social psychologists have systematic techniques for collecting and merging the opinions of experts into one single opinion or prediction.[35] But no matter how primitive or how sophisticated such techniques are, the resulting judgments are still only the product of personal opinion. Like the AMA Guides, which artfully produced estimates of impairment by applying arithmetic operations to clinical data, the listings for Social Security Disability Insurance are at bottom the collected medical opinion on the relationship between clinical signs and ability to function. Ultimately, the question of which groups of people should be included in a disability benefit program is a political judgment, and the decision to set criteria in a certain fashion is a choice among competing alternatives, not something dictated by the clinical measurements themselves. And the manipulation of criteria by physicians, lawyers, and officials to include or exclude whole classes of individuals is far more potent than any strategic behavior on the part of individual applicants.

A second reason why clinical criteria cannot protect eligibility decisions from manipulation is that the diagnostic decisions on which judgments of impairment rest are themselves subject to an enormous degree of uncertainty. The evaluation of impairment rests on physicians' observations and interpretations of basic clinical findings: the medical history (elicited by interviewing the patient); auscultation (listening to chest sounds through a stethoscope); blood pressure, pulse, and temperature measurements; electrocardiograms; X-rays; and laboratory tests (especially urinalyses, blood cell counts, and blood chemistry analyses). These building blocks of clinical practice are as much art as science, and numerous studies have demonstrated significant variations among physicians and laboratory technicians in interpreting them.

The problem of human error in medicine has troubled physicians since at least the early twentieth century.[36] No sooner had the advent of diagnostic "machines" (the stethoscope, microscope, and X-ray) promised a new accuracy than physicians began to recognize, or re-emphasize, the important contribution of human observation even to machine-aided diagnosis. Studies of diagnostic error, conducted in virtually every field, almost always found high rates of disagreement among physicians and laboratory technicians.

Moreover, studies of laboratories themselves showed alarming discrepancies in test results, even for serious communicable diseases where identification of a specific pathogen is the diagnostic criterion. These investigations were not the work of renegade physicians or people hostile to the use of diagnostic technology. The Boston Public Health Department conducted a major study of laboratories in 1919, and found wide disparities in the analysis of identical samples.[37] U.S. Public Health Service studies in the late 1930s concluded that "many laboratories have not met the minimum standard of efficiency of serologic test performance."[38] Similar surveys continued into the 1960s, usually with similar findings. In short, both the medical profession and Congress had ample evidence that the "laboratory tests" proposed as objective criteria in disability determination were subject to significant degrees of human error.

Problems in the reading of X-rays were also documented, beginning in the 1920s. A major study in 1947 found that doctors "differed with the film interpretation of their colleagues about a third of the time, and upon a second review of films even with themselves about a fifth of the time." Several studies of other diagnostic techniques were available before the passage of the disability freeze in 1954; they reached similarly negative conclusions about accuracy and consistency in judging the need for a tonsillectomy (1930), accuracy in history taking (1951), and the diagnosis of emphysema (1952).[39]

As the Social Security bureaucracy dug in its heels and committed itself to the use of impairment as its eligibility criterion, the medical literature continued to document the unreliability of clinical judgment. A 1958 study of the ability of general physicians (not cardiologists) to read electrocardiograms found that ten physicians could agree unanimously on only about one-third of one hundred tracings.[40] These results are telling, since the premise of disability evaluation in both the AMA Guides and the Social Security Listing of Medical Impairments is that assessment can be done by the average practicing physician in the course of everyday treatment of patients. Studies of diagnostic consistency among physicians continued to produce results in the same vein, showing disagreement in anywhere from a tenth to a third of all cases. A comprehensive review of studies up to 1975 concluded that physicians "almost always disagreed at least once in ten cases, and often disagreed more than once in five cases, whether they were eliciting physical signs, interpreting roentgenograms, electrocardiograms or electroencephalograms, making a diagnosis (from incomplete information), recommending a treatment or evaluating the quality of care."[41]

The levels of disagreement uncovered by these studies are not so surprising, especially to anyone who has ever performed a simple laboratory test or listened through a stethoscope. What is surprising is that despite the volume of these studies, their authorship by respected scientists and government agencies, their publication in major medical journals, their sometimes wide publicity, and their availability to both Congress and government officials, Congress still passed and expanded a piece of legislation predicated on the illusion of objective medical determinations. No less surprising is that the Social Security Administration's chief medical consultant could reassure Congress in 1976 about the validity of disability determinations based on the listing of impairments by asserting that clinical signs cannot be molded by the patient or the physician.[42]

In fact, a third problem with clinical criteria is that patients do have an enormous degree of influence over the results of many clinical tests. A number of important methods of disability determination, including cardiac "stress tests" and pulmonary function tests, require the subjects to perform in some way; the result is dependent on their efforts. It is also well known that the physiologic constitution of an individual changes over short periods of time, and the same test performed at intervals may yield different results. Digestion, emotion, work, and weather cause changes in body chemistry and therefore also in the outcome of laboratory tests.[43]

The field of pulmonary disease can be used to illustrate all three of these problems. Pulmonary disease is one of the major sources of disability. It is also an area where several clinical tests and X-ray studies are widely used, so that the dependence on patients' and physicians' subjective judgments should be minimized. Yet even the leading physicians most involved in developing criteria for impairment emphasize the "softness" of their evidence. One researcher in pulmonary disability stated that "most of our data is [*sic*] gotten from the history; only 5 percent comes from the physical exam."[44] Even if this is just a casual estimate, it is disturbing in the light of one British study of history-taking in the evaluation of lung disorders: it found that even when physicians were asking patients simple yes-or-no questions, there was significant variation in the responses different doctors obtained from the same patient.[45]

Pulmonary specialists emphasize that individual reactions to physiological changes are highly variable and depend on what each individual thinks is "normal" for himself. One person might experience shortness of breath, make the symptom disappear by changing his behavior, and conclude that he is normal; another person with the same symptom might visit a physician, exaggerate the symptoms, and seek disability compensation. It has been well documented that patients evaluated for disability compensation complain of more severe dyspnea (shortness of breath) for a given degree of physiologic impairment as measured by lung function tests than do patients being evaluated for other reasons.[46] Despite the recognition by physicians that shortness of breath and painful breathing are highly subjective symptoms, the Veterans Administration uses these as the criteria for assigning grades of disability.[47]

Physical findings—including the quality of breath sounds (wheezing, crackles), cyanosis (turning blue), and finger clubbing (distortion of fingertips due to oxygen insufficiency)—might yield more objective evidence of impairment. Yet even if they were not also subject to the problems of observer error described above, they are inconsistently related to the presence of severe disease.[48] For these reasons, disability compensation programs often specify criteria based on the "more objective" evidence of X-rays and measurements of pulmonary capacity. The black-lung disease compensation program bases eligibility on the reading of X-rays. But in diseases with chronic airflow obstruction, "the appearance of the chest roentgenogram often bears little relationship to severity and may be entirely normal in the presence of severe obstruction"[49] Moreover, interobserver variation in reading lung X-rays is very high.[50] The Social Security Disability Insurance program, where concern for objective medical evidence is highest, uses pulmonary function tests (so-called "spirometric measurements") as its criterion for determining total impairment due to respiratory disease.[51] But even these tests depend to a large degree on patient cooperation, because they ask the subject to inhale and exhale "with maximum effort" and then measure various results.[52]

Even if one accepts that lung function tests give a reasonably objective measure of physiological capacity, there is the problem of deciding at what level of results a person should be considered impaired or disabled. This is a matter of pure judgment and can only be decided by some process of consensus. Different systems of evaluation, including those of the Social Security Disability Insurance program, the AMA Guides, and the Department of Labor (which administers the Federal Mine Safety and Health Act of 1977), all specify different norms or levels of test results as criteria for disability[53]—which means that people with the same clinical test results will be found eligible for disability benefits in one program but not another. One might argue that the problem of setting levels is not important in a program, such as Social Security, that compensates only for total disability. But given the overwhelming judicial opinion that a person does not have to be totally "helpless and hopeless," on his deathbed, or reduced to having his "trunk conveyed to a street corner" to be considered disabled, the issue of a cutoff point for "total" disability remains very sticky.

Thus, one can trace in one particular type of disability—respiratory disease—a hierarchy of criteria from highly subjective to more objective. But ultimately, even the most objective criteria are subject to manipulation, and in the end the decision about what constitutes a legitimate medical impairment is still a matter of judgment. Given this analysis of factors that influence clinical judgment, it is not surprising to find substantial inconsistencies in disability determination in a program whose definition rests on clinical judgment.

There have been three major studies of the accuracy and consistency of determination within the Social Security disability program. The first, and still the most comprehensive, used clinical teams to make independent disability evaluations of actual applicants and compared these results with the SSA determinations. The findings, according to the author, cast serious doubt on the validity and equity of SSA decisions: of a total sample of about 1,500 cases, the clinical teams and agency teams came to *opposite* conclusions on more than one-third of the cases; of the people who were found "fit for work under normal conditions" by the clinical teams, 26.9 percent were allowed benefits by the SSA teams; and of the people found "not fit for work" by the clinical teams, 27 percent were denied benefits by the SSA teams.[54] The second study, conducted by the General Accounting Office in 1976, has already been described: in a sample of 221 cases submitted to ten state agencies, there was complete agreement on disposition in only 22 percent of the cases.[55] The third study was conducted in 1978–79, by the SSA Office of Research and Statistics, as part of an effort to evaluate the impact of the new vocational guidelines of 1979 (see Chapter 5). The study selected a random sample of 504 actual claims and submitted them to disability adjudication teams in eight states. It found that there is about one chance in eight that two examiners within the same state will reach a different decision, and about one chance in six for examiners from two different states.[56]

These are fairly high levels of discrepancy for a program that allocates public benefits as a matter of right. But it is unlikely that the accuracy and consistency of disability determination decisions can be improved very much, given the limits of the diagnostic technology on which they are based. Nevertheless, the predominant response to these findings is essentially a call for improved management techniques—clearer guidelines, better training, and tighter supervision.[57]

The Special Problem of Pain

That the clinical concept should fail as a restrictive mechanism is not surprising, because in an important way it sidesteps the key issue of disability: what is it that prevents people from working? In most instances, the cause is not some identifiable physical phenomenon but a complex set of interacting factors involving individual and family history, the state of the economy, and cultural and psychological as well as biological factors. The whole notion of impairment rests on a mechanical metaphor suggesting some "outside force" that acts on a person to "prevent" him or her from working. Yet even in the narrow medical sphere, if we look only at physiological processes as the last in a chain of causal events, the ultimate obstacle to work is the subjective experience of the individual. As Roemmich wrote in 1961:

> Most diseases which we encounter in our program prevent work because they produce in man an uncomfortable sensation when he works. These sensations are dyspnea, pain, fatigue, or a combination of all three. . . . There are no biological techniques at present which can measure dyspnea, pain or fatigue. There are biological sequelae of physical exercise in health and disease but so far these have defied predictable patterns.[58]

Pain, fatigue, shortness of breath—and, one might add, anxiety—are all real and very powerful subjective phenomena, but they defy measurement. Disability evaluation manuals and texts have also wrestled with a variety of other subjective experiences that crop up in disability claims: tenderness, numbness, weakness, stiffness, coldness, loss of sight, hearing, smell, changes in taste, and nervousness.[59]

The concept of impairment represents an attempt to translate these subjective experiences into objective phenomena, or at least to correlate subjective experience with observable physiological phenomena. That is why the clinical discussions of impairment place so much emphasis on the distinction between signs and symptoms, and why judgments of disability are supposed to rest on signs to the greatest extent possible. But the paradox is that symptoms, or subjective experiences, are much more important than signs in determining whether people can or will work.

In trying to measure some objective phenomenon of impairment, clinicians and administrators must rely on one of two strategies. They can assume that impairment creates a *permanent transformation* of the human body, so that a reduction in work ability will show up in a test given at any moment in time. This is the assumption of lung function tests, or tests of joint motion, vision, and hearing. But this model of disability holds true for a very small number of conditions and is obviously based on an image of disability as anatomical imperfection.

Alternatively, examiners can assume that impairment is a sporadic malfunction that appears only under stress, and that it affects people through subjective experience rather than through a direct reduction in the body's mechanical abilities. In this case, the appropriate test is to "stress the person" (in the disability evaluation lingo)—to submit them to some kind of rigorous exercise that approximates conditions of work in a meaningful way—in order to produce *visible manifestations* of pain, fatigue, shortness of breath, or other subjective symptoms.

Pain is only one of the many subjective factors involved in the inability to work, but it warrants a lengthy discussion here for three reasons. First, it is one of the most common subjective complaints in disability claims. Second, it is probably the most difficult to measure of the subjective symptoms. And third, there has been a great deal of formal policy discussion in legislative testimony, agency regulations, and judicial opinion about the significance of pain in disability determination.

The clinical literature frequently discusses the problem of distinguishing genuine from faked pain and thus repeats, in its own language, the larger social problem of distinguishing genuine from feigned inability to work. There is fairly wide agreement that clinicians can successfully recognize patient deception, and numerous texts give specific indicators of "real" pain—facial expressions, color of skin, clamminess, and dilated pupils, to name a few. One medical text for lawyers states that "pain is the most easily pretended symptom and among the most commonly feigned," but that if it is marked, it will "produce symptoms which cannot be simulated."[60] Another gives a description of the behavior manifested in true pain: "The facial expression of true pain—the pinched features, the pallor, the clammy skin, the dilated pupils, the knotted brow—cannot be imitated by the malingerer: these, with the intermittent involuntary cry or groan and the characteristic writhing or bodily contortions, present an unmistakable picture of suffering."[61]

In some areas, the assessment of impairment takes on the character of looking for a revelatory sign. The clinical test is designed to convert a subjective symptom of pain into an objective manifestation of pain. The patient is asked to perform a maneuver known to cause pain under conditions of "true" injury or impairment; presumably, if the patient then displays the "correct" behavior for pain, he is to be believed. The use of tests to elicit pain is probably most common in assessment of lower back injuries, which are one of the most common bases of disability claims. Such tests are euphemistically called "signs," and each one is named after its inventor—thus, Bragard's sign, Cram's sign, Goldthwait's sign, and so on. Some of these are merely tests of reflex reactions, but by far the majority are tests in which the presence or absence of pain determines the existence of true disease or injury.[62]

Disability assessment, when the claim is based on pain, thus relies on two methods to determine the validity of subjective reports: simple observation of the claimant, and deliberate production of pain, followed by observation. Some clinicians have gone even further in the attempt to produce objective tests, suggesting that pain can be measured:

> There are various degrees of pain, and the degrees have been established to be: Slight, which is up to one-third of total pain; moderate, from one-third to two-thirds of total pain; and pronounced or severe, more than two-thirds of total pain. The examining physician, with the cooperation of the patient, will be able to define the degree of pain in one of the three categories, and also to establish the character of the pain, its frequency and location.[63]

These authors apparently do not define "total pain," but the intellectual process by which they arrive at their notion of measurement is exactly that of the AMA Guides. They assume an abstract entity of 100 percent pain (like the whole man assumed in the guides), and then divide that entity into equal thirds. They have neither defined the endpoints (what is total pain, and what is total absence of pain?) nor wrestled with the question of whether pain is simply additive (is the first 10 percent painful in the same degree as the fifth 10 percent?) Such questions sound like medieval sophistry, but they are generated by the arbitrary application of arithmetic concepts to subjective experience.

As one might expect, modern technology has been pressed into service to help provide objective measures of subjective experiences. Thermography, a method of producing images of temperature variations on the skin (used for example to detect breast cancer) has more recently been applied to the detection of pain, on the theory that "true" injuries are always accompanied by temperature increases around the affected body part.[64] Measurement of myoelectric impulses (the electric energy of muscle tissue) while a person performs a strenuous task is used for distinguishing true fatigue.[65]

When eligibility for disability benefits is based on pain, three questions become important. First, does the claimant "really have" pain? Second, how much pain should society expect a person to tolerate? And third, should society expect all people to tolerate the same amount of pain? (One could apply the same questions to each of the other subjective bodily sensations thought to prevent people from working.) Framing the issue in this way highlights the nature of the enterprise of disability determination. Each determination involves an attempt to assess as objective something that is really subjective, a complexly determined personal experience. And each also involves a *social consensus* about what personal experiences, or individual interpretations of personal experience, ought to count as legitimate for public purposes.

The courts, in mediating disputes over disability claims, have wrestled with these questions. Despite the Congressional intent to make eligibility contingent on purely objective, medically determinable factors, and despite the Social Security Administration's regulations translating that intent into formal criteria, the courts have insisted that the subjective experience of pain must be taken into account, although there is disagreement on what level of pain should qualify a person for disability benefits.

A District Court in Arkansas specifically rejected the idea that Congress meant to deny benefits to people disabled by pain:

> There is nothing in the statute or the legislative history which indicates a Congressional intent to exclude disability caused by pain, as contrasted to other types of disability, such as disability resulting from loss of limbs or sight or from mechanical dysfunction of the limbs, joints, or other organs of the body.[66]

While it is undoubtedly true that Congress did not mean to exclude compensation for disabilities caused by pain, it most definitely did mean to exclude those disabilities whose *only manifestation* is subjective pain. Another case in the same year illustrates how much the assessment of disability turns on trust: is the claimant to be believed about pain and discomfort, or isn't he? The court, in sustaining a rejection of the claim, stated:

> There is no evidence of any attempt on the plaintiff's part to work. *Only his belief that he cannot.* He refused two jobs that were offered which under the medical evidence he was physically able to do. He *testified* he has not been without pain since 1952, and *says* he cannot work long in one position, either standing or sitting. . . . *I do not believe* he would have been more uncomfortable on these light and sedentary type jobs than when at home periodically doing house, yard, and carpentry work, between periods of resting, as he testified he did.[67]

In general, however, the courts have shared the view of the medical profession that the subjective experience of pain is in fact objectively determinable, that it necessarily "leaves its stigmata,"[68] and that true pain will manifest itself with or in proportion to objective clinical and laboratory findings.[69]

The issue of how much pain a person should be expected to tolerate has been debated almost exclusively in the courts. In a famous decision on a War Risk Insurance claim, Judge Learned Hand said that "a man may have to endure discomfort or pain and not be totally disabled; much of the best work of life goes on under such disabilities; if the insurance had been against suffering, it would have read so."[70] These words are often cited to support a strict view that mere pain is not enough to justify giving a person social aid. At the other end of the spectrum, a 1961 Appeals Court decision held that while a little pain might indeed be beneficial, "the purpose of much social security legislation is to ameliorate some of these rigors that life imposes."[71] There has been a general trend toward the more liberal view, but courts, as might be expected, have taken every position in between. Thus, the issue of how much pain an individual can be expected to endure is simply a more precisely stated version of the fundamental distributive question: under what conditions should individuals be given aid on the basis of need? The reduction of the concept of inability to work to impairment or even to pain hardly makes a determination philosophically more simple or practically more feasible.

Despite the intentions of the framers of disability benefit programs to make them highly restrictive through the vehicle of clinical criteria, the boundaries between ability to work and disability remain extremely flexible. Disability determinations depend on diagnostic judgments which are themselves not overly reliable and are subject to manipulation by patients and physicians. The criteria for disability must still be formulated by a process of group consensus. And the essential problem of the relationship between subjective experience and inability to work remains unsolved. This indeterminacy and resultant flexibility of the disability category as an administrative device means that it is particularly subject to external pressures.

5

The Pressures for Expansion

The clinical concept of disability was intended to place a very tight boundary around need-based distribution. It was certainly not to be the only boundary, but the legislative history and administrative development of the Social Security disability program show a clear intention to ensure that this category would be very narrowly defined. The grounding of the definition in the clinical concept of impairment and the use of medical evidence as the method for determination are the primary mechanisms through which disability-based programs seek to maintain tight boundaries.

Yet the disability concept is in fact highly flexible. Despite all efforts, even the medical concept remains very loosely defined, and the mechanism for determination of disability offers many opportunities for purposeful manipulation. The assignment of citizens into the work-based and need-based distributive systems remains a highly political issue which is not readily resolved by the creation of formal administrative schedules or the delegation of decisions to the medical profession (or any other technical experts). Thus, there is a constant struggle over the boundaries, which manifests itself in shifting pressures for expansion and contraction of the disability category.

The pressures come from three major sources: individuals seeking aid, who put pressure on the boundary by applying to programs and acting to receive a favorable decision; the gatekeepers of the programs, who actually make eligibility decisions, and who put pressure on the boundary by applying to individual cases their own professional norms and biases about distributive justice; and high-level policymakers—the legislators, administrators, and judges who create the general rules by which disability programs operate and who thereby design and redesign the boundary-maintaining mechanism.

The Pressures from Individuals

Individual applicants exert pressure on the boundary mechanism in three ways. First, every decision to award disability benefits must begin with the initiative of the individual; thus, a decision to apply for benefits is the crucial factor that sets up pressure for an entrance into the need-based system. Second, the individual has a fair degree of control over how he or she presents the case, and that self-presentation influences how disability determiners will respond and which specific rules and procedures will be applied. Third, the individual is also the major promoter of the case, and his or her persistence and cleverness in pursuing it will have a significant impact on the outcome.

The initial step in every disability determination is the individual's application, which must be preceded by a conscious self-perception of disability. Social policy, particularly the policy of the Social Security program, is predicated on a naive view that disability is purely a medical phenomenon, and that it will be legally recognized for purposes of entitlement only if it rests on some biological impairment. But the popular conception of disability is much broader; many people who are not disabled according to the definition of the program still *define themselves* as disabled. This disparity between the popular and programmatic concepts of disability, and the resulting excess of self-defined disabled people over "legally qualified" disabled people, is one source of enormous pressure.

The disparity between the popular and legal conceptions has been well documented. Population estimates that depend on self-definition or self-classification always yield much higher numbers of disabled people than the number actually receiving benefits from disability based entitlement programs. For example, the most widely used survey of disability in the United States found that 14.6 percent of non-institutionalized adults consider themselves disabled (that is, as having some work limitation resulting from chronic health conditions).[1] But only a small proportion of these were actually receiving any kind of social welfare based on disability—between one-quarter and one-third were receiving Social Security disability benefits. Even among those people who responded that they were *totally* unable to work, and were therefore more likely to meet the SSDI definition of total impairment, only about half were receiving Social Security disability benefits.[2] In a 1966 survey, of those who ascribed their disability to a work accident or other work-related cause, only 22 percent had ever received Workers Compensation benefits.[3]

The disparity between self-defined disability and legally qualifying conditions is almost certainly not an artifact of the particularly strict program definitions in the United States. A West German survey that compared fourteen different definitions, ranging from informal self-definition to medical definitions and legal program definitions, found similar results: of all the people who might be considered disabled under some one definition of disability, only 22 percent met legal program criteria.[4]

Although there is clear evidence that the popular conception of disability is much broader than the narrow clinical conception adopted in social policy, the exact nature of the public conception is less clear. In fact, there are probably many different popular conceptions. But in order to understand exactly what kinds of pressures are put on disability programs, it is important to know how popular conceptions differ systematically from program conceptions.

There have been two basic approaches to this question, broadly deriving from sociology and economics. The sociological tradition, taking the perspective of disability as a social role, asks what characteristics of individuals will lead them to adopt the "disabled role." Until recently, the disabled role was seen as a long-term version of the "sick role," so that the same factors used to explain why people define themselves as sick and seek medical care were used to explain why people define themselves as disabled.[5] In general, level of education, income, ethnic background, and social class have been shown to influence what people think of as "medical problems" and to influence their propensity to seek medical care or advice.[6] But ironically, the findings of most sociological studies indicate that the popular conception of illness (at least, illness requiring medical care) is *narrower* than the professional medical conception; that is, people seek medical care (or say they would seek medical care) in fewer circumstances than the medical profession would deem appropriate. Thus, these models do not help explain why and how the popular conception of disability is *broader* than the official definitions.

Economic theory takes the perspective of the welfare-maximizing rational man and suggests that people will define themselves as disabled when the material benefits of that role are greater than those derived from work. (Actually, the theoretical model would also include the value of psychic benefits from both roles, but no empirical specification of an economic model has ever attempted to include anything but the material benefits.) In this model, the individual implicitly compares his potential income from unearned sources, including disability benefits, with his potential income from work, which is a product of the wage he could earn and his likelihood of employment. As unemployment rises, the potential wage thus declines, so that even if disability benefits remain constant, they become relatively more valuable.[7] In fact, several correlational studies indicate that economic factors do play a strong role: people's self-definition of disability seems to be highly sensitive to local economic conditions, while levels of unemployment and other labor market characteristics apparently affect the propensity to apply for program benefits.[8]

It may well be that the popular conception (insofar as one can speak of such a conception at all) is best understood as a moral notion, rather than either a social role or an economic calculus. Disability, as one of the major categories defining the boundary between the work and need systems, is an essential part of the moral economy. Because the category represents a legitimate entitlement to social aid, people may give it meaning by "filling in" the details of circumstances which they believe ought to entitle citizens to help. Therefore, any attempt to understand the popular conception and how it corresponds to the programmatic conception must begin with an examination of popular ideas about when social aid is legitimate. Approaches that focus instead on ideas about illness or on disability benefits as one type of income are overly narrow. They have already lost sight of the context that shapes popular notions of disability—namely, a sense of justice.

If indeed popular conceptions of disability embody conceptions of justice, the question still remains, what are those ideas about justice and where do they come from? Why would popular conceptions of disability be broader than programmatic conceptions? Why should popular and programmatic conceptions be in conflict at all? We can give only some speculative answers.

Social programs—and particularly social insurance programs—seek to protect individuals against the risks of economic and technological change in order that society as a whole will have the benefits of economic growth. They do not try to prevent social change or, more specifically, prevent the causes of the conditions that drive people to need insurance benefits (youth, age, widowhood, or disability). Rather, they close barn doors after horses have left. The compassion for the individual built into social programs counterbalances the devil-take-the-hindmost attitude toward individual misfortune characteristic of both market economies and broad social movements. Thus, social programs are designed to enforce standards that promote socioeconomic change at the same time as they mitigate individual difficulties. In that sense, social programs are forward-looking, always concerned with promoting economic growth, even at the cost of individual harm. Popular moral ideas, by contrast, are backward-looking; they derive from personal and collective experience. The expectations of one generation are molded by the ideas of the previous one and predicated on rights to subsistence and norms of reciprocity. Disability as a moral concept represents the persistence of the subsistence ethic in modern society.

Whatever the explanation, the fact that the popular conception of disability is broader than the programmatic has important implications. No matter how strictly the administration of social welfare programs defines disability, no matter how tightly that definition is connected to medical conceptions of disability, the conception of disability in the general population will be constantly in flux, and will probably be influenced by changes in economic conditions as well as by any changes in either personal medical circumstances or knowledge about medicine. Redistributive programs based on disability will always need to assert a "tight" definition in the face of broader popular definitions.

Disability programs are thus always in the position of *selecting out* applicants who do not meet program criteria; rarely are they in the position of soliciting applicants or persuading people to look at themselves as disabled and therefore as potential beneficiaries. Alcoholic rehabilitation programs, to take a contrasting example, must first persuade people that they have a problem and need treatment. Disability benefit programs may need to publicize their existence, as when the new Supplemental Security Income or Black Lung Compensation programs were started, but they always have a surplus of self-defined users over formally qualified users. The sheer excess of potential applicants over potential beneficiaries creates a constant pressure on benefit-granting organizations; they must always be aware that there is a large population who would or could seek to have the definition expanded.

Individuals exert a more active pressure once they become formal applicants. The application necessarily becomes an adversarial process, even if the procedure is not formally adversarial, simply because the applicant is implicitly asking for an exemption: the very act of applying for disability benefits is a request to move from the primary work-based system into the secondary need-based system; as such, it is an attempt to go *against* the societal norm. Applicants are aware, however subtly, that they face a sort of "test" and that they must "prove" the legitimacy of their cases to the agency.

The degree to which different people consciously manipulate the presentation of their cases certainly varies enormously, but the important point is that the process leaves a great deal of scope for strategic maneuvering. The ability of people to create the appropriate picture of illness or disability for the purpose of secondary gain is well known. The most commonly cited context is military service; malingering and feigning disability for the purpose of avoiding the draft or combat is part of the folklore of military medicine. In other contexts, people simulate or exaggerate medical conditions in order to obtain the food and shelter of a hospital, or to obtain drugs.[9] It is clear that applicants are easily able to learn some of the rules and policies of medical certification, even when an organization keeps these policies officially secret, and that they are also able to "manufacture" particular clinical pictures for the purpose of certification.

Although there is little direct evidence about how applicants behave in disability determination proceedings, the prevalence of discussion in medical journals about deceptive strategies of patients indicates that physicians, at least, think the phenomenon is significant.[10] Moreover, there is no reason to suppose that disability benefit agencies are any different from other street-level bureaucracies that allocate public services. In such contexts, applicants learn through both community knowledge and personal experience the characteristics, code words, phrases, and behavior necessary to a successful application for benefits. To a large extent, the interactions of the agency personnel with its clients actually serves to teach the clients what behavior or characteristics the agency will reward.[11]

This kind of strategic behavior is not necessarily deceptive or fraudulent. It is important to distinguish between strategic presentation of one's case (doing all one can to get certified when one believes one has a legitimate claim) and cheating (deliberately presenting information one knows to be false in order to obtain a benefit). The discussion of individual pressure on the boundary through manipulation of cases is about behavior of the first kind. Cheating may, almost certainly does, take place, but its impact is small and arguably counterbalanced by the number of people kept out of disability benefit programs who legitimately belong in them. The important source of *individual* pressure on the boundary is strategic behavior in accordance with the popular moral notions about legitimate disability claims.

Those notions of legitimacy often rest on subjective information; in the final analysis, as we have seen, it is subjective experience that prevents people from working. Despite tremendous intellectual efforts by physicians, lawyers, and program administrators to transform such experiences as pain, fatigue, and shortness of breath into objective phenomena, determinations of disability are still highly dependent on the subjective reports of individuals, as well as their willingness to *tolerate* various forms of discomfort. The ability of the individual to make a choice about how much pain and discomfort to tolerate, and to control the description of his suffering, gives him a certain leverage over the agencies and a means of creating pressure on the disability definition. Given that any individual applicant has already decided he is disabled and deserving of benefits, and given the adversarial context in which he probably perceives the claim-making process, he will no doubt feel some need to manipulate his self-presentation by minimizing his ability to tolerate a particular discomfort and exaggerating his description of the symptoms.

The structure of the process of disability determination, which relies on a combination of direct contact with the applicant and a formal paper record as sources of evidence, shapes the opportunities for individuals to manipulate their self-presentation. There is an unspoken belief in the disability field that face-to-face contacts have two conflicting effects on the ability of the determination process to produce "the truth." On the one hand, such contacts give applicants more opportunity to act the part, and to convey the less tangible signs of suffering and discomfort that evoke sympathy. On the other hand, program officials and physicians have more faith in their own ability to detect deception through face-to-face contacts than through paper records.

This paradoxical attitude is manifested in several aspects of the Social Security disability determination system. In the normal or routine case (ie. without an appeal), the agency has almost no direct contact with the applicant. The applicant is expected to submit medical evidence from a physician, and that physician is the only person who formally interviews or examines the applicant. The actual eligibility decision is made by a team, which usually includes a staff physician, on the basis of the paper record submitted by the applicant and his physician. This standard approach reflects the underlying assumption of the whole program that physicians have a special vision, and that direct contact with a physician can suffice precisely because people cannot deceive their physicians.

When an applicant initially files a claim in a District Claims Office, however, he or she is unofficially interviewed by the person who receives the application;[12] the interviewer not only asks some direct questions and fills in the applicant's answers but records personal observations and impressions of the applicant's appearance, attitude, behavior, and physical condition. Though they are not apparent to the claimant, these interpretive comments become part of the first paper record of the case and the first statement, however tentative, of the likelihood of eligibility. The very fact that the official form *asks* for such information indicates the agency's belief that the face-to face contact is valuable.[13]

The determination procedure gives the applicant an opportunity to use both direct contact and paper records to manipulate the presentation of his case. He can "shop around" for different physicians, especially if he is able to pay for medical visits privately, and thus increase the number of times he gets to act out the disabled role; presumably, one can learn from practice. Even in cases where the Social Security agency requires a consultative exam, the applicant is free to reject a physician assigned by the agency. Moreover, the applicant may enter new evidence into his record at any stage of the determination process, even at the highest level of appeal.[14] So there is a fair amount of room to build in face-to-face contacts (even though the SSA does not allow a personal appearance after the initial interview) simply by visiting different physicians, and to build up the paper record by having the reports of such visits entered in the claim file.

In addition to manipulating the evidence to create a picture of eligibility, individuals can promote their cases more or less actively through the use of various procedural rights built into the determination system. All such systems provide for some form of appeal, and some allow the use of lawyers or other representatives during the process. Several studies indicate that the success rate is higher for claimants on appeal than in initial determinations, and that claimants who use legal or other representation are far more likely to win their claims than those who do not.[15]

In the American political climate of the early 1980s, with its backlash against disability beneficiaries and its campaign to prune the rolls, it is important to place this discussion in a larger context. Any description of strategic maneuvering on the part of disability applicants is likely to be taken as support for the conservative contention that the applicant universe is swarming with people who would deliberately defraud the system. On the contrary, the point of this discussion is to show that because disability is an unstable concept, there will always be structural tensions in a disability system. Pressures for expansion of the disability category come in part from individual applicants, but not because all applicants are trying to cheat the system. Individual pressures derive from the disparity between popular and programmatic definitions of disability and from the structural incentives built into any benefit program for which individuals have to be their own advocates. Moreover, even stronger pressures for expansion come from other sources.

The Pressures from Physicians

The concept of disability embodied in social welfare policy is predicated on the assumptions that most people would prefer to be in the need-based distributive system (in other words, they don't want to work) and that inability to work is highly subject to deception. As we have seen, the elaboration of the clinical concept of impairment as the basis for disability determination was the response to these problems. The clinical concept was supposed to provide a tight boundary around need-based distribution, and clinical criteria form the preliminary screen through which any applicant must pass. The so-called "vocational criteria"—age, previous work experience, education, and vocational skills—come into play only after an applicant has met clinical tests for disability.

Clinical criteria are, of course, applied by physicians, who are charged with determining impairment in individual cases and who thereby become the gatekeepers for disability programs. In that role, they can influence how strictly the intellectual concept of impairment will be applied. Yet even though the intellectual concept is designed to be restrictive, physicians as a social group have no inherent interest in making sure that disability programs are in fact restrictive. The very "softness" of clinical evidence means that judgments of impairment will indeed be subject to influence by both patients and physicians, and that structural factors in the relationships among claimants, physicians, and agency will become important.

One of the consequences of choosing a system of disability determination based on examination and reports by physicians in private practice, rather than by an agency staff of disability specialists, was that the agency became dependent on patients' personal physicians for information. And personal physicians, because they have a doctor-patient relationship, are likely to feel a stronger loyalty to the patient/applicant than would a staff physician who examined the claimant only once.

There are several reasons why the professional norms and incentives of treating physicians might push them toward more lenient decisions, favorable to the claimant, and why an organization might therefore prefer the evaluation of an independent consulting physician. First, one of the fundamental assumptions in the doctor-patient relationship is that the patient and the physician trust each other. The physician expects the patient to believe in his expertise; often this expectation includes the feeling that the patient should not seek a second opinion unless the physician explicitly makes a referral.[16] The physician assumes that the patient, as a voluntary client seeking advice, will be truthful in reporting a medical history or in describing symptoms. Professional norms incline the physician to trust the information given by the patient and to assume that the patient's primary, perhaps only, goal is to restore or maintain his health. This basic attitude of trust does not mean that the physician necessarily believes everything the patient tells him. Even in normal clinical practice, when no obvious nonmedical benefits are at stake, patients may have some distorted interpretations of their own symptoms, which the physician may want to verify through more objective tests.

For physicians who specialize in disability certification, the doctor-patient relationship is likely to differ dramatically. The consultation cannot be assumed to be a voluntary act, since the patient has been required by some agency to obtain a medical diagnosis as a prerequisite to eligibility. Therefore, the physician is prepared to be suspicious of the claim and to suspect that the patient is willing to falsify information in order to obtain some secondary gain. The contrast is expressed nicely in Dr. Roemmich's early Congressional testimony: "In medical practice, a physician *may accept at face value* the patient's statement about the severity of his shortness of breath, pain or fatigue. . . . The situation is quite different in disability evaluation. The decision we are required to make is *whether the applicant's allegation is reasonable*."[17]

Physicians who specialize in disability certification often say they "get an intuitive feeling" about patients and gear their examinations accordingly. One orthopedist, a specialist in back injuries said, "There are people you see in the office who you know intuitively are going to be a problem." Another said, "I know within a minute [whether a patient is malingering], but sometimes I get fooled." For physicians in the certifying role, trust is not something to be taken for granted. Therefore, they seek to develop specific clinical tests to distinguish malingers or "compensation patients" from the genuinely disabled.[18]

A second norm of treating physicians that inclines them toward leniency is the tendency to err in the direction of false positive diagnoses, given uncertainty. The reasoning behind this rule is straightforward: more harm can usually be caused by allowing an undiagnosed and untreated illness to run its course than by submitting a truly healthy person to extra diagnostic tests and even unnecessary treatment. The few studies of diagnostic error in which clinical judgments can be compared with confirmed diagnoses show that indeed false positive diagnoses (classifying a healthy person as sick) far outnumber false negative errors (classifying a sick person as healthy).[19]

Agencies that grant benefits on the basis of certified medical disability operate on the opposite assumption: the applicant is to be considered healthy until proven sick, and errors of treating healthy people as disabled are generally considered more harmful than the reverse. Both the harm to the agency and the harm to the individual of false positive errors are given greater significance in certification decisions than in treatment decisions. For the agency that is trying to ration scarce resources among needy people, every positive decision uses up some of those resources. Also, since these agencies are trying to rehabilitate as many people as possible and return them to productive work, they are concerned that an incorrect decision to grant disability benefits or label someone as incapacitated may undermine the individual's incentives to undergo rehabilitation.

Third, the patient's welfare is the overriding concern for the treating physician. For most aspects of medical care, doctors are taught to think in a context of unlimited resources. They are supposed to provide therapy whenever a diagnosis indicates illness; to do everything possible for each individual patient; and to treat each patient as an individual case, without regard to his "comparative worth." In the certifying role, however, physicians often face a conflicting set of norms. As employees of or consultants to an agency, they are made aware that medical and nonmedical resources are *not* unlimited. Where the physician in clinical practice makes a virtue of expending unlimited resources on each individual patient, the certifying physician is rewarded for conserving the agency's resources by imposing limits on some patients. A specialist in disability certification, because he is processing numerous applications for limited benefits, must make comparisons between patients and weigh the relative merits of different claims.

Again, Dr. Roemmich's testimony illustrates this difference in attitude:

> In medical practice . . . any errors in assessing severity of these symptoms [shortness of breath, pain, or fatigue] do not influence the basic diagnosis. These errors seldom indicate profound changes in treatment. They seldom, if ever, result in inequities to other patients. [In disability evaluation, however] if this decision—evaluating medically the reasonableness of alleged severity—is based only on the applicant's description of his sensation, a description which is highly variable, it frequently does not result in either uniform or equitable treatment in relation to decisions made on other applicants or in relation to nonapplicants who contribute to the benefit fund.[20]

Whether treating physicians are in fact more lenient than consulting physicians in justifying disability awards is a question that is very difficult to answer empirically. One can compare programs that use treating physicians as certifying agents with those that use staff or consulting physicians, but too many other factors influence the results, including the general policy of each organization on the question of leniency.[21] Also, there are some pressures on treating physicians to be strict with disability certifications. One is the desire to believe that medical treatment is effective; a finding of permanent disability is in some ways an admission of medical failure to cure or restore. Another is the general professional belief in the value of communicating a sense of hope to the patient; a determination of disability is thought to deprive the patient of belief in recovery and therefore of a will to recover.[22]

Nevertheless, there is a pervasive belief amounting to "street wisdom" among officials of disability programs that doctors indeed have enormous leeway in applying the concept of impairment and that there is a bias toward leniency among treating physicians. This belief is a major reason for the device of consultative examinations. Just as claimants may shop around for physicians likely to certify them as disabled, the programs shop for physicians likely to be more stringent. One insurance company executive explained her firm's strategy of seeking second opinions: it balances a doctor known to give a 50 percent rating with one known to give a 10 percent rating, and then takes a compromise.[23]

This belief is also expressed in administrative hearings, where examiners often have to resolve the conflicting opinions of a treating physician and a consultative physician. The Bureau of Hearings and Appeals, according to one study, has developed its own bias in favor of the consulting physician's opinion.[24] Actually, however, the courts have had to deal with the issue of a hearing examiner's bias in both directions: in some cases, an examiner has disregarded the opinion of a treating physician on the assumption that he is biased in favor of the claimant; in others, the opinion of a consulting physician on the assumption that he is biased in favor of the SSA. In Workers Compensation cases, there is the phenomenon of the "treating doctor mystique," in which more weight is given to the opinions of the treating doctor because he is assumed to have direct, firsthand knowledge of the patient.[25] Such beliefs about the biases of treating and consulting physicians are clearly pervasive, though the courts have generally taken the position that medical opinions cannot be dismissed or ignored simply because an examiner believes in a bias.[26]

The Pressures of the Legal Context

Long before the inception of the Social Security disability program, policymakers were concerned about the tendency for courts to expand the scope of disability benefit programs. Judicial expansion was a well-known phenomenon in the government's War Risk Insurance program, as well as in private commercial insurance. Presumably, the planners of all disability programs thought they were formulating clear, precise, tight operational definitions, but the Social Security planners explicitly attempted to insulate the program from the pressures of judicial expansion by taking into account the experiences of earlier programs.

Of course, the attempt failed. The most frequently cited example of the ability of the judiciary to prevail over Congressional intent is the so-called Kerner case and its aftermath.[27] The case is usually blamed for changing disability insurance from a strict medically based program to a limited unemployment compensation program.[28] The case was brought by a man who had held a variety of jobs as carpenter, mechanic, furniture repairman, and salesman, and who suffered from a cardiac condition, diabetes, and anxiety. Although he acknowledged that he was able and willing to do light sedentary work, he was unable to obtain a job. The case thus turned on his employability. The SSA denied his claim on the grounds that he *was* in fact able to engage in "substantial gainful employment." The appeals court saw the issue differently. It ruled in 1960 that "mere theoretical ability to engage in substantial gainful employment is not enough if no reasonable opportunity for this is available." The court went even further and required the SSA (actually the Secretary of Health, Education and Welfare) to "furnish information as to employment opportunities . . . or the lack of them, for persons of plaintiff's skills and limitations."[29]

Following the Kerner case, some decisions helped to reinforce the stricter Congressional interpretation of the statute, but in general the courts tended to liberalize the eligibility criteria. One major issue was whether the applicant could be expected to accept a job anywhere in the "entire national economy," as the law read, or only in some smaller geographic region surrounding his home. The courts again liberalized the statute by finding that the state was the appropriate region for determining employment opportunities.[30]

In 1967 Congress responded to this judicial attack on the boundaries of the disability program by passing amendments to clarify its intention. Leaving no doubt as to its motivation, the Committee on Ways and Means, in its accompanying report, stressed its concern with the "growing body of court interpretation of the statute which. . .could result in substantial further increases in costs in the future."[31] The amendments expanded and clarified the statutory definition of disability: a person was to be considered disabled only if, because of physical or mental impairment, "he is not only unable to do his previous work but cannot, considering his age, education, and work experience, engage in any kind of substantial gainful work *which exists in the national economy, regardless of whether such work exists in the immediate area in which he lives, or whether a specific job vacancy exists for him, or whether he would be hired if he applied for work.*"[32] But the courts have continued to construe the law liberally, so that at least one study concludes that "the Kerner doctrine. . .may have been unaffected by the 1967 amendments."[33]

The Kerner case is only one of many instances where the courts have liberalized the statutory and administrative criteria established for Social Security Disability Insurance. Congress foresaw the possibility, tried to thwart it, and parried once it became an actuality. But Social Security disability is only one of many programs that have been subject to judicial expansion.[34] This history brings to the fore two questions about the legal context of disability programs. Why do the courts have so much power over them? And why has the impact of judicial review generally been in the direction of liberalization?

The first question is somewhat easier to answer. The original conception of the program, and the one that persists, is that eligibility determinations can and will be made strictly, or at least primarily, on the basis of medical evidence and medical reasoning. Even after the Kerner case, when Congress reasserted itself in the 1967 amendments, it retreated to an elaboration of medical jargon and medical standards as the protective device to maintain tight boundaries. But as we saw in the last chapter, the clinical concept of impairment and its associated devices of medical examination, diagnostic technology, and medical reasoning could not provide unique, consistent, and incontrovertible answers to the fundamental distributive questions raised by the disability program. Thus, there is a constant need for dispute resolution, which in our society is the province of the judicial system. In fact, then, even though medical reasoning and evidence are supposed to form the basis of the program, legal concepts of evidence and legal reasoning predominate.

Because the major disputes of the disability program are resolved in a legal context, it becomes important to understand exactly how the legal context and its processes create pressures for expansion. One sort of explanation relies on the general differences in "institutional perspective" between courts and legislatures.[35] Legislatures and agencies must worry about whole programs, program budgets, and the effects of various small decisions on the program as a whole. The courts, by contrast, deal with issues on a case-by-case basis. They tend to think in a framework of absolute rights and obligations; they do not consider the impact of a decision in one case on the program as a whole; nor do they attempt to fashion compromise remedies based on an understanding of competing objectives.

The institutional explanation has some initial appeal, but it does not really explain why the courts were so very specifically expansionist in the face of clear legislative directives from Congress on the disability program. Another answer may lie in the fact that the only way the courts can take an active stance in disability issues is to *reverse* the Social Security Administration's decision. An issue will not come before the courts unless a claimant appeals a denial (if eligibility is granted at any lower level, the case never goes any further); therefore, if appellate bodies have a "natural desire" to "exercise their independence," their only option is to find for the claimant.[36] To the extent that any organization seeks to become powerful and to exercise its authority, courts will be pushed toward liberality in disability decisions.

Beyond these general precepts of organizational behavior, there are specific modes of thinking that courts apply to disability determination whose effect is systematically to expand the notion of disability. Three issues in particular are important: the question of causation; the treatment of subjective experience; and the notion of a fair determination process. The way courts treat each of these issues is markedly different from the way they are handled in either clinical judgment or administrative policymaking.

The notion of causation is important because the underlying rationale for disability programs is the lack of individual control over a condition that prevents someone from working. Hence, the reason for inability to work is a crucial element of every eligibility determination. The essence of every claim is the attempt to prove that an individual's inability to work is caused by some outside agent (or accident, event, force).

The formal demonstration of causal connection appears in two ways in disability programs. Some programs—notably Workers Compensation—are explicitly designed to compensate people for injuries *caused* by their work. (Other such programs include the Federal Employees' Compensation Act, the Railroad Retirement Act, and public employee disability programs.) They therefore require the claimant to demonstrate that his job caused his injury. Other programs are designed to provide income maintenance for people unable to work because of medical conditions, and they therefore require the claimant to show that a medical condition causes his inability to work. These are two very different kinds of causal connections; in the first case, the injury or medical condition is an effect; in the second, it is a cause.[37]

In either case, there are two possible legal procedures for the demonstration of causality. The first is to argue on a case-by-case basis, eliciting the facts in each case and demonstrating for a particular person and injury that there is a direct causal link. The second procedure, quasi-legal and quasi-political, is to create a legal presumption of causality for a *category* of cases sharing some well-defined characteristic; the test for any particular claim is then whether it fits into a category and is subject to an automatic presumption.

Under the case-by-case approach, the legal concept of causality and the standards of proof are very different from the clinical concept of cause and scientific standards of proof.[38] In general, it is much easier to "prove" causation within the legal framework than the clinical framework. In the clinical understanding, disease follows predictable patterns, and the entire diagnostic classification is based on an assumption that diseases can be grouped according to the developmental patterns they follow. What a physician is thought to mean by the "cause" of disease is the basic, underlying, or original event that set a disease pattern in motion; outside forces that influence or aggravate the course of disease are not seen as causes. Actually, this notion of cause is outmoded in academic medical circles: clinicians and epidemiologists favor a notion of multiple causation.[39] But the old concept of cause in medicine, deriving from the doctrine of specific etiology (see Chapter 3), is what remains in the popular image and what policymakers had in mind when they fashioned disability programs.

In the legal understanding (particularly in the sphere of tort law), disease or injury is viewed as an end result, and the lawyer looks for a mechanical connection between some specific event and the result. The law tries to determine whether the event had some influence on the end result—whether the event caused the result to happen even a moment sooner (even though the result might have been inevitable in the longer run), or whether the event caused the result to be even a little bit worse than it might otherwise have been. The law looks for slight differences between the "natural" course of events and the actual course of events. A satisfactory demonstration of cause is established if it can be shown that the difference between the hypothetical natural course and the actual course of a disease can be attributed to the outside force in question. Thus, where clinical reasoning might say that an injury could not be "caused" by an intermediate event, because it could not have occurred without the presence of a preexisting disorder, legal reasoning would say that the intermediate event is a cause of the injury. In programs based on compensation for occupationally caused diseases and injuries, legal reasoning will lead to much broader eligibility.

If legal and clinical reasoning differ in their concepts of causation, they also differ in their standards of proof. The legal standard for establishing cause is generally looser. It requires a demonstration that the event "probably" caused the disease, caused it "more likely than not," or caused it "with reasonable medical certainty." Sometimes the requirement is expressed as "50.1 percent probability."[40] Clinical standards of proof derive from the scientific method, which requires experimental demonstration under controlled conditions. The standard of proof is usually a demonstration that a certain result could have occurred randomly with only 5 percent probability. In other words, the scientist has to be 95 percent certain, where the lawyer has to be only a little more than 50 percent certain. Although neither the physician nor the lawyer may consciously assess causation in terms of percentages, these different professional standards probably do shape their thinking.

The second approach to causality, the creation of legal presumptions for categories, also generally works to make disability programs more liberal. To some extent, such programs all substitute a legal presumption of disability for case-by-case demonstration. The extreme of the presumptive method is represented by the "average man" approach of the Veterans Administration. A person who is found to have a disease or injury listed on the schedules is deemed disabled with no further inquiry into the effect of the impairment on that particular individual. Similarly, the SSA's Listing of Medical Impairments enables it to use a presumptive approach, despite its nominal philosophy of individual examination. And in fact, the whole underlying philosophy of categorical welfare, particularly in disability programs, virtually *requires* a presumptive approach: certain medical conditions are presumed to prevent people from working.

Since a major objective of these programs is to minimize access to the need-based distributive system, one would expect them to draw the legal presumption very narrowly. And indeed, program planners consciously attempted to do so by means of the concept of clinical impairment. However, because medical conditions and the ability to work are related only through highly variable subjective experience and through social consensus about the limits of tolerable suffering, it is nearly impossible to define very strict presumptions. As soon as policy creates a legal presumption for anything beyond a near-vegetative state, there will be the "problem of exceptions": some people with medical conditions legally presumed disabling will in fact be able and willing to work. Every physician and every disability examiner has a favorite story about a superhuman patient who overcame overwhelming physical limitations and continues to work in some productive way.

How does the categorical approach create a pressure for expansion? First, a legal presumption eliminates any need to demonstrate a causal connection. As Howards, Brehm, and Nagi point out in their study of Social Security,[41] the program has been "subtly shifted." Instead of redistributing income toward people who cannot work *because* of health conditions, it now redistributes towards those who are unemployed *and* also happen to have a serious medical condition, regardless of the causal link. The latter class of people is certainly the larger.

Second, the problem of exceptions explained above means that there will always be a reservoir of people who, although employed, are technically able to meet the medical conditions for a legal presumption of disability. Under adverse economic conditions—specifically tight job markets—many of these people are likely to perceive themselves as disabled, apply for benefits, and be found eligible.[42] Moreover, the effect of this pressure from the reserve of technically eligible claimants is one-directional. If economic conditions improve and appropriate jobs become available, the program has no means of taking away eligibility; having once granted a legal presumption of total disability on purely medical grounds, it cannot shift a person back into the labor market. (The Social Security program *can* review cases and reexamine clients to determine whether their medical condition has improved. But it cannot technically push people off the rolls because new jobs suitable for those claimants have become available.) The psychological effect on the individuals concerned is also unidirectional. Once people become accustomed to receiving disability pensions, they become dependent on that money; the prospect of returning to employment feels risky; and they may come to develop an identity as "disabled" that is hard to shed.

The problem of assessing and weighing subjective experience illustrates another important way in which legal reasoning tends to liberalize the disability definition. Because two people with objectively indistinguishable physical or mental impairments may experience, describe, and tolerate pain and discomfort differently, the clinical approach attempted to develop a concept of impairment independent of subjective experience. As a result, the Social Security Administration (and indeed all disability programs) came to rely on presumptions. And despite an avowed rejection of the "average man" concept,[43] the device of the Listings of Medical Impairment rests squarely on this approach; listed conditions are presumed to disable the average person.[44] The medical profession and administrators, then, have tended to look for population norms and to adopt the perspective of the hypothetical average person—but the courts are much more prone to adopt the perspective of the individual and to give weight to personal testimony of subjective experience.

The difference can be illustrated with excerpts from two cases. In one, the court said, "Whether or not an ordinary person would be disabled by the plaintiff's impairment is immaterial to the question of whether the plaintiff himself is disabled. The determination as to whether plaintiff is disabled must be subjective."[45] In another, the court held that "while the medical evidence may perhaps indicate that Mrs. Ber's physical symptoms were of a type which probably would have caused many people considerably less pain than Mrs. Ber suffered, it nevertheless amply supports her complaint that in her particular medical case these symptoms were accompanied by pain *so very real to her* and so intense as to disable her."[46] The willingness to consider and evaluate subjective information reflects the case-by-case approach of courts as institutions. In the area of disability compensation, the consideration of subjective information will necessarily lead to an expanded definition of eligilibility, because subjective definitions are broader than the statutory definitions.[47]

The notion of fair or due process is obviously central in judicial policymaking; and in disability hearings, it systematically produces a broader definition of disability. Implicit in both the clinical concept of impairment and the bureaucratic procedure of benefit granting agencies is a certain view of what constitutes a fair and efficient determination process. In this view, the essence of the process is to observe the applicant to determine certain objective characteristics. The process is fair if it produces accurate observations and a correct portrait of the individual. The legal view is quite different; it sees the determination process as a matter of *honoring a contract* (between insurer and insured) whose provisions are somewhat fuzzy. The role of the court is therefore to guess what people expected when they entered into the contract, what they meant by particular words and phrases, and whether there was any coercion involved.

Of course, there is no literal contract between an applicant and a public agency, but the imagery of contract is evident in much of the courts' interpretation of disputes over disability. The imagery comes, of course, from commercial insurance policies, which are in fact contracts and which preceded any public insurance programs. Since the courts first became involved in the resolution of insurance issues in the context of commercial contracts, this historical experience profoundly shapes the legal view of public insurance.

In a variety of commercial disability insurance cases during the 1920s and 1930s, courts were called upon to interpret particular language.[48] Many disability provisions included very strict phrases such as "totally hopeless," "wholly helpless" or "unable to engage in any occupation whatsoever." Generally, the courts refused to interpret these phrases literally. They reasoned that surely the parties to the contract, particularly the policyholders, never intended a strictly literal meaning, because that would have rendered the policies totally useless. Courts have recognized the unequal bargaining power of consumers and insurance companies, which puts the consumer in a position of accepting or rejecting a policy without being able to negotiate its provisions. And courts have used an implicit rule in construction of contracts that "writings are to be construed against the drafter."[49] It was in the context of a dispute over a commercial disability insurance provision that one court conjured up the image of "a person having his trunk conveyed to a busy street corner where he could make a little money selling pencils."[50] The court reasoned that neither party could possibly have intended such a severe interpretation of total disability, so that the court had no choice but to guess what the parties actually did mean.

One legal scholar suggests that the liberalizing tendency of the courts can be understood as their determination to interpret the Social Security disability program as a contract between the United States government and its citizens.[51] In their reliance on the promises of government pension programs, citizens have either tailored other savings and insurance activities to supplement the government program or forsaken other arrangements for disability pensions altogether. The courts thus give a great deal of weight to the *reasonable expectations* of individuals—the circumstances in which they would want to be covered and would expect an insurance program to cover them. There is some support for this interpretation of judicial behavior in case law. In one early Social Security disability case, the court said, "The statute must be given a reasonable interpretation. It is a remedial statute and must be construed liberally."[52]

The habit of divining "reasonable expectations" is ingrained in legal thinking. Standards of behavior in negligence law are largely determined by the concept of a hypothetical "reasonable man" who possesses "ordinary prudence" and "average intelligence." In deciding questions of negligence, courts compare the behavior of the defendant with the standard set by this reasonable man. In the context of disability determination decisions, judicial reliance on the hypothetical reasonable man combined with a judicial view of insurance programs as a kind of contract to be interpreted in accordance with public expectations leads to a sanctioning of the looser popular definition of disability.

The Pressures of the Economic Context

Now we have come full circle. We have seen several ways the disability concept is expanded. The popular conception of disability is much broader than the official definitions, and individuals have ways of acting to increase their chances of passing through the officially created boundary. Physicians are the official gatekeepers of the boundary, but they have no inherent interest in making sure that the boundary is secure. Although the medical profession obligingly developed the clinical concept of impairment as a proxy for inability to work, physicians as individuals are primarily socialized into a treating role, not a gatekeeping role. Their diagnostic technology is soft, giving them a great deal of room to maneuver on behalf of their patients if they should be so inclined. And even if they do not consciously bend the rules, their natural inclination is to be advocates of their patients. Finally, lawyers and courts approach the problems of causation, subjective experience, and fair process in such a way that they end up interpreting disability broadly, more in accord with the popular than the programmatic conception. If individuals appeal their cases, if they push against the boundaries with any energy at all, they stand a reasonable chance of getting through.

Let us look again at the mechanism for determination of disability. Individuals perceive themselves as disabled and apply for aid. Physicians examine them and determine whether they have a legitimate impairment. Administrators certify eligibility primarily on the basis of the medical criteria. If the claims are denied and the individuals appeal, courts then determine eligibility by grafting legal norms onto the statutory and administrative policy and the medical findings.

What happens to this mechanism under varying economic conditions? Specifically, what happens under economic stress, when there is high unemployment? As job opportunities tighten, individuals who previously worked in spite of some physical or mental impairment are likely to become more aware of their limitations, especially if they are laid off or have their working hours reduced so that they have less income and more difficulty making ends meet. With fewer jobs available, the real opportunities for someone with an impairment may decline. Thus, more people are likely to perceive themselves as disabled.[53] Those who do will also be more likely to apply for benefits from various disability-based welfare programs.[54] (Short-term economic fluctuations will probably have less impact on application rates than longer recessionary periods. In the short term, many unemployed people can receive unemployment compensation, and most of the disability programs impose a waiting period of several months.)[55]

What happens to administrative determinations when application rates increase? We do not really know but can make some educated guesses. Consider first the behavior of physicians. If the impairment criteria were perfectly objective, we would expect medical examination to sift out those people whose impairments are not truly incapacitating; a higher proportion of the people examined by physicians would be found to have minor impairments that do not meet program criteria. But we know that the criteria are not perfect, and there is a lot of room for slippage. Also, we can guess that unemployed persons in economic straits are likely to evoke sympathy, so there might be some slight extra pressure on physicians to diagnose more incapacitating impairments during economic recessions.

Next, consider the behavior of administrative officials, the staff of disability determination experts who work directly for benefit-granting agencies and actually make the eligibility decisions. This staff includes physicians, vocational experts, and people who specialize in disability determination. As program employees, these are the people most likely to impose a strict definition of disability, most likely to identify with the formal program goals of minimizing access to need-based benefits and conserving program resources for the most needy cases. So we might guess that as applications go up, the proportion of administrative awards will go down.[56] But we can also note here that the rate of allowances would have to decrease fairly significantly to offset the effects of the other factors identified so far—increased rate of application and possible increased medical determinations of impairment.

What will happen to the legal context of disability determination? First, we must ask whether more people will appeal their cases. Assuming an increased rate of applications and a constant rate of awards, we might expect the rate of appeals to stay the same. But even a constant rate of appeals will produce a higher absolute number, given a higher rate of applications. On the other hand, if the rate of initial denials goes up, we might expect more people to appeal their claims; this will happen even if appeals are a constant proportion of denials. In addition, it seems highly likely that a tight job market will increase the propensity to appeal; people have more at stake in a disability claim.[57]

Next, we can ask whether appeals and administrative reconsiderations are more likely to produce disability awards than did the initial decisions. They are, for a variety of reasons. Perhaps only the more severe cases are appealed. Time may worsen the medical conditions involved, so that the time between an initial decision and an appeal actually renders the claimant more severely impaired. Perhaps the legal representation more common in appealed cases helps the claimants. Whatever the reasons, the fact of a higher allowance rate on appeal means that a higher rate of appeal will produce more disability beneficiaries.[58]

Having examined the nature of legal reasoning in disability cases, we actually have some cause to expect that the rate of allowances in the legal context would go up during periods of high unemployment, independent of the other reasons for a high rate of reversal on appeal. Since courts insist on accounting for the realistic employment opportunities available to individuals, and these opportunities are realistically smaller during high unemployment, legal decisions are likely to be even more lenient during high unemployment. And since courts are also more receptive to the subjective experience of pain and discomfort as reported by individuals, to the extent that people intensify their self-reported disability during periods of high unemployment, the courts will also produce more lenient decisions.[59]

Thus, there are several mechanisms through which high unemployment can be expected to loosen the boundary around the disability category. More people will apply to programs during economic recessions, and the determination process is more likely to let them through at each of several points.

There is still another important way that the economic context will influence the disability system. Besides the additive effect of the increase in number of cases and positive decisions, the case-by-case growth may lead to more general changes: judicial expansion forces legislators and program administrators to articulate new rules that take into account the specific situations and general principles formulated in legal decisions.

The development of vocational criteria in Social Security Disability decisions provides a vivid illustration of the expansion of general rules. Vocational factors—a term generally used to mean age, education, and previous work experience—have always been part of the program. Even the Social Security Advisory Councils recommended that such personal and situational factors be considered, and various statutes incorporated into the disability definition the phrase "considering his age, education, and work experience." But vocational factors have assumed increasing importance in the program as time has passed. In the early years, most disability awards were granted on the basis of the medical listings; vocational factors were invoked only in borderline cases. Gradually, the borderline cases became so much more frequent that by 1975, over one-quarter of initial awards were granted on the basis of vocational factors.[60]

Given the complexity of defining "work" and "ability," it is not surprising that the vocational guidelines were not terribly successful in conveying clear criteria.[61] The Social Security Administration has constantly revised them, elaborating a concept of "residual functional capacity" to be applied to people who did not meet the test of strict medical impairment. Its latest vocational regulations were published in 1979, after at least three years of Congressional debate and public controversy.[62]

These newest vocational regulations rest on the same intellectual foundations as the medical listings and manifest the same concern for establishing objectively determinable criteria. The new term "exertional impairment" expresses their attempt to match the exertional capacity of individuals with the exertional requirements of jobs. All work is divided into five categories: sedentary, light, medium, heavy, and very heavy. Jobs are classified according to the maximum amount of weight lifted, the amount of weight lifted frequently, and the amounts of sitting, standing, and walking required. But the problem of determining the exertional capacity of an individual remains the same as determining impairment, residual functional capacity, or ability to work. Only the name has been changed.

The vocational regulations also follow the basic structure of disability definition by creating an automatic legal presumption of disability for certain cases. Most important is the rule that a worker over age fifty who has performed only heavy, unskilled labor and who is no longer capable of doing his previous work will automatically be deemed disabled; there is no inquiry into whether he could do lighter work. This presumption is particularly interesting because of its impact: it effectively means that the disability program will transfer more older workers from the labor force to the need-based system.[63] In a period of constantly rising unemployment, this would not be a bad strategy for a society that must find a way to mediate between its ideology of work-based distribution and its inability to provide jobs for a substantial proportion of its population.

Was a shift of older workers out of the work-based system the intended purpose of the new vocational regulations? It is impossible to prove intent, and certainly a discussion of the need to reduce the unemployment rate was never part of the formal and explicit policymaking debates. But two sorts of evidence are at least highly suggestive.

The first is the way the new vocational regulations were constructed, particularly the way the age factor was analyzed. In its first draft of the regulations in 1976, the SSA explained its reasoning:

> It must be recognized that there is a direct relationship between age and the likelihood of employment. However, the statutory definition of disability provides specifically that vocational factors must be viewed in terms of their *effect on the ability to perform jobs rather than the ability to obtain jobs*—in essence, how the progressive deteriorative changes which occur as individuals get older affect their vocational capacities to perform jobs.[64]

It then went on to say that "since no data or sources are available" on the relationship between chronological age and vocational performance, it would analyze "age-employment data" to find "a certain point where it would be realistic to *ascribe* vocational limitations based on chronological age."[65] The experience of the Social Security and Veterans Administration disability programs would also be taken into account, to determine "when age makes a difference." And finally, it noted that age fifty-five had already "gained Congressional recognition" in certain other legislation pertaining to disability.

Essentially, the agency conceded that it had no idea how age is related to specific vocational abilities, and then it proceeded to formulate such a relationship. During hearings of the Ways and Means Subcommittee on Social Security, Commissioner James Cardwell was told that the committee's medical consultant doubted whether physicians or adjudicators could make determinations of people's ability to perform at "exertional levels." He was asked how these new determinations would differ from or compare with the early determinations of medical impairment. He answered:

> As I indicated . . . considering the "state of the art," there is simply no satisfactory way to relate the effect of disease or injury to an individual's ability to work. However, since its inception, the social security disability program, in making disability determinations, has included an assessment of an individual's residual functional capacity."[66]

Like the medical criteria that are "so necessary to the program but give us the most trouble" (in Commissioner Ball's words), the vocational criteria are "impossible to specify but we do it anyway" (to paraphrase Cardwell).

One can only conclude from this bit of history that the presumption of disability for older unskilled workers was *not* the result of any careful analysis demonstrating that such workers lacked adaptability or transferability of skills. In fact, one administrative law judge, drawing on extensive testimony from vocational experts, claims that "neither advanced age nor lack of education materially affects the ability to perform [a wide range of sedentary factory jobs]."[67] Whatever the source of pressure on, or perceived need by, the Social Security Administration to produce more liberal criteria for older workers, it was certainly not from any good empirical evidence relating age to vocational ability.

The second type of evidence is comparative. The sudden expansion of disability pension programs has been a widespread phenomenon in a number of welfare states. The coincidence of expansion in several countries with a widespread and relatively long-lasting recession suggests that disability programs may play a key role in disguising unemployment in advanced industrial societies. A comparative study of eight countries concludes that "the increasing generosity and coverage of disability programs has led to a decrease in labor force participation—and labor supply—for older workers."[68] This study notes that liberalized early retirement provisions have also contributed to such a decrease, but still, "those countries which, either deliberately or inadvertently, experienced rapid growth in disability income transfers or recipients also experienced the most rapid decrease in labor supply of older workers."[69]

Studies of the relationship between disability pensions and economic factors at the subnational level reinforce this picture. In the United States, a reasonably strong relationship has been found between economic factors (especially poverty, unemployment, and the proportion of the workforce in manufacturing) and the proportion of the population on disability pensions.[70] In Sweden, pension rates for the communes are significantly correlated with communal unemployment rates, and the correlation is strongest in the upper age groups.[71] In Norway, the disability pension rate is higher in parts of the country dominated by traditional industries (fishing, agriculture, forestry), suggesting that disability pensions are used to buffer the effects of structural transformations in the economy.[72] In Italy, growth in the number of disability pensions between 1968 and 1978 was far more rapid in the high-unemployment southern region than in the relatively more prosperous north.[73]

The evidence that disability programs have the effect of disguising unemployment is striking. To conclude, however, that the *effect* of a program is its *purpose* is to make a teleological leap of faith.[74] One can certainly argue that if policy-makers wanted to design disability programs for the purpose of relieving unemployment, they could not have chosen better mechanisms. The vocational criteria of the American SSDI program are a case in point. The formal definitions used in most European welfare programs are another: in most, disability is defined in terms of earning capacity—the ability to earn some proportion of one's own prior wages, or some proportion of the average wage of a comparable healthy worker in a similar occupation in the same region.[75] The increased emphasis on earning capacity, rather than physical and mental conditions by themselves, means that the least productive workers will be drawn out of the labor market. Particularly where wages are paid on a piecework basis, or where there are wage premiums for heavy labor and work requiring physical agility, the earning capacity definition will pull out slower and weaker workers, and these will tend to be the older workers. The use of local rather than national wage scales to determine reductions in earning capacity will have the same effect, allowing the disability system to pull out the least productive workers from local economies. The mechanisms for disability programs as an economic regulatory instrument are certainly present.

The categorical welfare system and its disability component were originally conceived during a time of industrial expansion and relative labor shortage. Although there were local surpluses of agricultural labor at many times and places during industrialization, there was a relative scarcity of labor for newly emerging urban industries. A major problem of designing welfare systems was to provide humane relief without undermining the forces that would drive agricultural labor into the cities. The narrow circumscription of need-based categories served this purpose. Now, in the 1960s, 1970s, and 1980s, the fundamental economic conditions have changed; many welfare states are faced with a surplus rather than a shortage of labor. Rates of unemployment are relatively high, and the economies are incapable of accommodating the entire working age population in the labor force. Yet an ideology of work-based distribution persists and perpetuates a public ethic that "everyone should work."

In such a situation, when ideology mandates that everyone should work but society cannot provide employment for large segments of its population, the dilemma can be reconciled by *defining* a higher proportion of the population as disabled. Because disability is the most flexible of the categories of the need-based system, it is the one most readily available for use in this fashion. An expansion of the definition of disability can reduce the pressures of unemployed workers on the work-based distributive system and at the same time preserve the legitimacy of the work ideology.

6

The Political Dynamic of Disability Expansion

Despite different national systems of using disability as their basis for administration, distributive programs all share some important characteristics. All use the category to delineate boundaries between work- and need-based distribution. All rely on a clinical concept of disability and certification by physicians, though the importance of the clinical concept varies. In some, like German social insurance, medical certification is a preliminary screen; in the United States, the clinical definition is the primary restrictive mechanism of Social Security disability insurance. Disability programs everywhere are sensitive to economic conditions and are clearly related to the structure of employment in the labor market, however little we understand the connections. And finally, disability programs the world over are characterized by high rates of growth.

It is now time to return to the initial question of this book. What is the meaning of the expansion of disability programs in advanced industrial societies? Are these programs "in crisis," and if so, how? What do they tell us about the structure of the welfare state?

Rounding Up the Usual Suspects

What is happening in disability programs repeats a well-established pattern in social policy. A program grows rapidly, perhaps faster than originally estimated, or perhaps the growth rate suddenly increases. The media begin to publish reports based on data issued by the program agencies themselves, showing that the number of beneficiaries, the size of the benefits, and cost of the program are all increasing dramatically. Certain phrases become part of the common language used to describe the program: "alarming rates," "threats to financial stability," "fiscal crisis," "insolvency." Then explanations of the "crisis" are offered, along with the obvious solutions that flow from them. The explanations are always the same: the program encourages abuse because of the structure of its incentives, and the administration of the program is in need of coordination and better management to curb individual abuses.

When benefit programs are at issue, the culprit is always the program user. Analyses of these programs are usually permeated with a deep belief that the individual citizen is first and foremost a "welfare maximizer." (Here, "welfare" is meant in the general sense of well-being, happiness, or utility, rather than the current colloquial meaning of public aid.) To such a citizen, social programs represent opportunities on the economic horizon, to be compared with all other available opportunities. If the potential benefits of a social program are greater than those of other opportunities, the citizen will choose to enter the program. A corollary of this view of citizens is that there is a hidden reservoir of people just waiting to make use of any social program as soon as the rules and administrative procedures make eligibility possible.

The classical liberal doctrine from which this view of citizens is derived would put no moral judgment on such behavior; the program user is simply behaving as a "rational man," which is, after all, how everyone behaves. But inevitably, the critics of the program in crisis *do* attach a moral judgment. The explanation based on rational motivation becomes inextricably bound up with one based on laziness and fraud. It is assumed that many users of the program do not really need it, and that they are receiving benefits they do not deserve.

Thus, rapid growth in the disability insurance program is attributed primarily to an increase in *use* of the program, and the main reason for that increase is thought to be that benefits are too generous. The benefits of the disability program are compared with those of unemployment compensation or with some standard earnings level—either prior earnings or average spendable earnings.[1] The policy recommendation that flows from this interpretation is, of course, a reduction in benefits. Here the English Poor Law principle of least eligibility appears in full dress: no one should be able to obtain more through disability compensation than he could earn in the labor market.

If the reformers truly believe that the only reason for overuse of the program is excessively high benefits, then reduction of benefits is all that would be necessary to keep the excess users off the rolls. But a host of other proposals indicates that policymakers believe there is substantial fraud and abuse in addition to rationally motivated program use. Thus, in the United States there has been a move to review all Social Security Disability Insurance recipients (mandated by Congress in 1980) and to "cut back the rolls." Along with this purging of the rolls, there have been efforts to strengthen "vocational rehabilitation," to make sure that people who can work in fact do. All these reforms—reduction of benefits, review and purging of the rolls, emphasis on rehabilitation, and increase in work incentives—are exactly the reforms that logically follow, given the analysis of the problem, and they are exactly the ones that have been applied to other social welfare programs in crisis.

If, in the mythology of social policy, the culprit is always the user, the accomplice is always the "administration" of the program. When social programs grow rapidly, the growth is taken as evidence that their organization is somehow faulty, and proposals for organizational reform abound. In a sense, the two explanations always go together. The first rests on a theory of human motivation, arguing that the incentives of the program combined with natural human motivation lead to an adverse outcome for society. The second assumes that proper administration or management can control some of the bad effects of human behavior.

Typical prescriptions under the rubric of administrative reform call for "coordination," "streamlining," "reorganization," "rationalization," "better planning," and "monitoring and evaluation."[2] In the area of disability insurance, these suggestions appear with reassuring regularity. Proposals for the reform of the American Social Security Disability Insurance program include the standard litany: centralization of decision-making (in this case, transferring disability determination from the states to the federal government); better training of disability determiners; standards for the selection of claims examiners; standards and guidelines to clarify the definition of disability; and standards for various aspects of the *process* of disability determination, such as "case processing time," "accuracy," "adequacy of documentation."[3] All of these suggestions for reform come from the standard analysis of welfare programs, which sees the problem as one of designing program features to manipulate natural incentives most effectively.

The analysis of the disability category presented in this book suggests a very different interpretation of disability program expansion.

The very concept of disability is a dynamic idea fashioned to reconcile the tensions between two competing distributive principles. No definition of disability, however "standardized," can ever resolve these tensions permanently, nor can streamlined management somehow eliminate underlying conflicts. To understand the meaning of disability expansion, we need to go back to the concept of disability to see how it incorporates larger social tensions, and how the implementation of disability programs leaves room for the continued struggle over those tensions.

A Political Analysis of Expansion

The concept of disability is fundamentally the result of political conflict about distributive criteria and the appropriate recipients of social aid. Instead of seeing disability as a set of objective characteristics that render people needy, we can define it in terms of ideas and values about distribution. A political analysis must therefore begin by elucidating the dimensions of the disability concept that give it legitimacy as a distributive criterion. Three dimensions appear to be important. First, the label connotes a sense of *moral worthiness* or *desert*. The foremost element of consensus about the disability category is that its members are somehow deserving of social aid for some special reason. Second, disability connotes a significant *incapacity*. And third, disability is a phenomenon to be understood and revealed through *clinical methods*.

What gives disabled people a special moral status? It is not enough to say that, for certain public purposes, the disabled are judged more deserving than others. Two elements seem to underly this judgment: innocence and suffering. Innocence means that the condition of being disabled is beyond individual control. Society helps disabled people because they find themselves in bad circumstances through no fault of their own. As we saw in Chapter 3, the image of cause in the concept of disability is that some external agent or force prevents a person from being able to work. The imagery from infectious disease suggests an outside agent that invades the body and causes illness; and the imagery from industrial accidents suggests anonymous forces of factories and industrial life as the cause of injury. The disability concept thus eliminates motivation as a cause of inability to work. People who are unemployed because of disability have a higher moral claim because (it is assumed) they really wish to work.

Some diseases seem to be honored in social policy because they are particularly lamentable or pitiable. For example, blindness is treated well and recognized as worthy of social aid in almost every society. It is always listed as a compensable condition in social programs, without controversy, even though everyone knows that it is quite possible for blind people to work. An examination of the political concept of disability must take into account this emotional element and ask what diseases or conditions are particularly to be feared and pitied. Public fears change over time, with changes in the incidence of different diseases and injuries, changes in public knowledge, and changes in medicine's ability to alleviate the suffering caused by various physiological problems.

The claim that disability connotes deservingness may seem jolting at first, because the more common argument, especially among organizations of the disabled, is that disability is a term of stigmatization and conveys a lower social status. Much of the sociological work on disability has concentrated on the phenomenon of stigma and ways that disabled people manage a new, stigmatized identity. Even the very word "invalid," when pronounced with the accent on the second syllable, suggests the illegitimacy of the disabled status.[4]

How can this contradiction be reconciled? How can disability be at once a term of esteem and a stigma? First, judgments of social status and desert are relative. Disabled people can simultaneously be judged inferior when compared with some abstract ideal of "normal" or "healthy" people, but superior when compared with other unemployed people. Second, official policy often expresses more idealistic sentiments than citizens manifest in their behavior. While official policy elevate the disabled *as a class* to a special, higher category of citizenship, private behavior and even official practice often betray contempt for the *particular* disabled individual.

Incapacity, the second dimension of the disability concept, conveys the idea that the disabled person is less than fully capable as a human being. The actual word "incapacity" is part of the definition of eligibility in almost every program.[5] In the American Social Security program, the concept of capacity is largely mechanical; what is tested is the individual's ability to perform as a machine. The emphasis on "exertional requirements" of jobs as well as performance criteria in the definition of disability reflect the notion of physical capacity. Other programs define eligibility in terms of earning capacity, so that wages, rather than physical performance, are what is quantified.

The third dimension of disability is that it is defined through clinical methods. The clinical approach rests on two important assumptions: first, that the cause of an inability to work can be found by looking at the individual; and second, that causal factors can be separated into objective and subjective components, and that it is possible to observe and measure the objective factors, independent of the will or subjective perceptions of the individual. The clinical approach is essential to the political concept of disability because it provides the validation and thus the legitimacy of individual claims.

Once these elements of disability as a legitimating idea are set forth, the problem of expansion appears in a new light. The very concept of disability contains a powerful dynamic of *definitional expansion* that cannot be much affected by the sort of fine tuning suggested in the standard analysis. Each element of the political concept is a door through which new phenomena can enter and acquire legitimacy as types of disability for official purposes.

The criterion of desert admits new phenomena whenever it can be shown that the cause of individual incapacity or suffering is outside the realm of individual responsibility. One important way in which the disability category is expanded is the establishment of consensus that certain incapacitating conditions are *socially caused.* The argument for compensation is then analogous to that for industrial accident insurance: if injuries or diseases are caused by anonymous forces of societal development, individuals should be compensated from collective resources.

The workplace and even the general "environment" as the locus of toxic substances give rise to new forms of disease causation for which the individual cannot be held responsible. Asbestosis and its concomitant forms of lung and liver cancer are examples of diseases that have been recognized as occupationally caused; cancers due to radiation exposure are examples of diseases that have come to be seen as environmentally caused. The idea of exposure to toxic substances is the modern analogue of infection by a germ. And much like Koch's postulates, the emerging common law of compensation for occupational diseases requires a demonstration that the claimant was actually "exposed" to a particular substance.

Workers Compensation programs have begun to include some occupational diseases as compensable phenomena in the last ten years, and the end is not in sight. Similarly, there are proposals for public insurance programs to compensate people for diseases brought on by their environment (as from radiation or chemical dumps) and by household products (such as asbestos and urea-formaldehyde insulation). Unless there is a major change in the underlying political consensus that socially caused harms should be socially compensated, there will continue to be an increase in redistribution on the basis of new forms of disability.

Another significant area of expansion is in the recognition of *stress* as a causal factor of disease, injury, and disability. At least fifteen states now allow Workers Compensation benefits in cases where the disability stems from stress on the job, whether caused by a supervisor, by co-workers, or more indirectly by company policy. Needless to say, defining what constitutes stress is a tricky business, perhaps even more difficult than giving operational meaning to "impairment," and states are struggling to put solid boundaries around the idea of stress as a causal factor. Michigan has passed legislation saying stress must arise from "actual events of employment, not perceptions thereof."[6] Massachusetts, through a state supreme court decision, has said that the incapacitating mental or emotional disorder must be "causally related to a series of specific stressful work-related incidents."[7]

The disability category expands also through sheer compassion for human suffering. When a new form of suffering becomes widespread and visible, mandating compensation is something that policy-makers can do about it. In 1980, Senator Birch Bayh introduced an amendment to make people with terminal illnesses immediately eligible to receive Social Security disability payments, without the usual waiting period after application.[8] The idea is fascinating, not only for all the questions it raises about what counts as "terminal illness" but also for its illustration of the dynamic of definitional expansion.

The proposal arose in the midst of discussions of cost containment and benefit reductions. Bayh cited stories of people who died before they could collect benefits. (His own wife had died of cancer less than a year before. Conventional wisdom about health politics has it that every Congressman or -woman has a relative who recently died of some major disease, so that legislators are easy targets for lobbying on programs to aid medical research and treatment.) Despite the fact that the amendment was ruled out of order because not germane to the cost control measures, the Senate voted to adopt it. Here was a case of obvious desert—suffering of perhaps the worst kind, and certainly one that most people fear; once the idea of including it in the disability category was even suggested, the proposal seemed irresistible. (But not totally irresistible—the vote was 70–23!)

The criterion of desert forces us to ask whether there are other circumstances in which individuals find themselves through no fault, perhaps even through some virtue, of their own.[9] Why should not child-rearing, creative but unpaid endeavors, or voluntary labor count in the grand tally of moral worth? Why shouldn't contributions to one's own savings and retirement plan constitute a demonstration of fiscal responsibility equivalent to Social Security contributions? And more pointedly, why shouldn't any unemployment caused by structural factors—anything from automation to a plant-closing to the decline of an industry—generate an entitlement to aid on the same terms as that received by the disabled?

If the moral dimension of the political concept invites a stream of new problems to be included in the disability concept, the incapacity dimension invites a virtual flood. Incapacity can be judged only against some standard of full capacity or completeness, and the possibilities for broadening this standard are endless. The original programmatic concepts of disability used physical capacity as a standard of reference, but the idea of incapacity can be extended to social, emotional, and intellectual performance even within the work role.

The standard has already been broadened to include not only a capacity to perform what we normally think of as "work" but the capacity to perform a variety of other social roles as well. Most notably, there are now programs for the "learning disabled," who are judged with reference to educational performance, and the "developmentally disabled," who are judged with reference to general norms for physical, social and intellectual growth.[10] The unlimited potential for expansion buried in these concepts is illustrated by the following discussion taken from a recent essay on the definition of "developmental disability":

> Relative to their peers, the developmentally disabled are not as well equipped to interact profitably with all the environments through which children are expected to pass. As such they are potentially disabled relative to future environments; and as such, the service of "habilitation" for future environments is the treat-

> ment modality of choice rather than "rehabilitation" for those who at one time were not disabled but became so.[11]

One can only wonder who is *not* disabled in this sense. Everyone could use a little more "equipping" to interact profitably with his or her environment.

The ultimate twist in expanding the disability concept through the incapacity dimension is to attribute incapacity to those who work with the disabled. In a recent story about dyslexia, *Time* magazine labeled this reading problem as "a learning problem and a *teaching disability.*"[12] The incapacity to perform some task becomes also an incapacity of the capable to cope with the incapable.

The clinical method of definition offers still more ways of expanding the disability concept. Fundamental to clinical inquiry is the measurement of physiological processes and the comparison of the individual with population norms. Clinical methods make it possible for new types of incapacity to be translated into forms that fit official definitions of disability. Once some intangible quality (such as learning ability or adaptive ability) is put on a quantitative scale, some people are found to have more or less of it, and it comes to be understood as "capacity." From here, there is only a short step to partial incapacity and disability.

There is every prospect for a growth industry in disability evaluation. The clinical concept of impairment gives rise to a need for objective measures of subjective factors. The problem of pain has already been tackled, but there are a host of other subjective factors yet to be given clinical specification: fatigue, dizziness, shortness of breath, weakness, and anxiety, to name some of the major ones. Then the factors of age, education and work experience must be specified; the recent vocational guidelines begin this effort, but new components of these factors will surely require further elaboration. Next, psychological or personality factors should certainly be accounted for, and it is not hard to imagine the professionals in psychology and psychiatry obliging with diagnostic classifications. Furthermore, the description of jobs in terms of "functional requirements" is merely in its infancy—exertional measures are only the tip of the iceberg. Every job also has its requirements for intelligence and creativity, for sociability, anxiety tolerance, judgment. The possibilities are endless.

Finally, there is a subtle way in which epidemiological research creates pressures for expansion of the disability concept through its discovery of statistical patterns. Unlike clinical medicine, which focuses on the individual and seeks to make a determination about his or her health at a given moment, epidemiological research focuses on large populations and seeks to determine the causes of disease by finding behavioral, environmental, occupational, or demographic correlates. These correlates are then labeled "risk factors," and individuals to whom some of the risk factors for a particular disease apply are said to be "at risk." It is as though the time dimension of disease were extended backward, so that people are seen as being on the trajectory of a particular disease before they manifest any of its symptoms. People with high levels of a certain type of blood cholesterol, for example, are "at risk"—in danger of developing coronary artery disease—even though they show no signs of the disease itself. Similarly, pregnant women over age 35 are usually considered "high risk pregnancies," regardless of whether the course of the pregnancy is normal.

Since the state of being "at risk" is not usually incapacitating, this new category would not seem to have any bearing on disability programs. Although the label constitutes a prognosis, there is nothing new about this phenomenon as such; insurance companies have long required medical examinations in order to make prognoses for applicants for life insurance policies. What is new is the scale on which such prognoses are made.

As more and more diseases are studied and more risk factors identified, more people are made to bear the label of some medical prognosis as part of their identity (in much the same way that demographic characteristics become part of their public identity), and the label affects their self-image. Researchers have found that disease screening programs sometimes have the side effect of causing people to think that because they are at risk for a disease, they are also sick.[13] This suggests a dynamic by which expanded professional understanding of predisposing and causal factors may lead to an expanded popular conception of disability.

The increased identification of "at risk" populations may also work more directly to decrease employment opportunities. Employers choosing among potential employees will seek to select those with the best health prognoses. This issue becomes particularly important in the area of heart disease, which has increasingly been recognized as being "caused" by work and therefore compensable under Workers Compensation. Because the cost of Workers

Compensation to employers is related to the cost of compensating their employees, employers try to avoid hiring workers who might bring up their premiums.[14] It is not hard to imagine the process by which epidemiological research makes possible the identification of *potentially disabled* people, who are then disadvantaged in the labor market. In this way, merely being "at risk" can actually incapacitate people by preventing them from getting a job.

Who Benefits from a Flexible Disability Category?

The idea of disability provides numerous intellectual justifications for expansion of the administrative category, but the expansion itself is achieved by real political actors who take advantage of ideas as resources. Where does the impetus for expansion come from? This study does not allow us to give conclusive answers, but because we have seen that disability is a flexible category, created and adapted in different political contexts, it is worth speculating about who benefits from that flexibility and from changes in the direction of either expansion or contraction.

The disability concept was essential to the development of a workforce in early capitalism and remains indispensable as an instrument of the state in controlling labor supply. As many economic historians have pointed out, the advent of capitalism required a major transformation in the very idea of human labor.[15] In the precapitalist, mercantilist vision, a large but undifferentiated population was the source of national wealth. More workers meant both more output, especially for export, and more tax revenues. In the capitalist vision, by contrast, labor is a resource to be manipulated, like capital and land. The working population became "modifiable and manipulable human material whose yield could be steadily enlarged through improvements in use and organization."[16]

Transformation of the labor force did not just happen; it required state policies to close off alternatives to wage labor, such as begging, and other policies to mold the workforce into a more skilled and specialized collection of people. The distinction between the ablebodied and nonablebodied was only part of a larger process of differentiation in which various skills and abilities were recognized and applied in assigning people to jobs. The map of disabilities used by social programs implicitly matched individual capabilities to the physical and mental requirements of available work. Nowhere is the connection between disability definition and labor force requirements more explicit than in the American Social Security "vocational grid," with its matching of individual characteristics to the exertional requirements of jobs, and in the notion of "residual work capacity.

The search for objective measurement of work capacity is not necessarily coercive. These methods are used to help redesign machines and work environments that produce fewer injuries, and to identify remaining abilities that a handicapped person can parlay into broader skills and greater independence. (For example, paraplegics who still have muscle control above the neck are taught to use their mouths to operate levers and switches that control wheelchairs and other appliances.) But these methods are also used to detect malingering and to find remaining work capacity in disability claimants.

When identification of residual work capacity "proves" that a handicapped person can still do some jobs, and when that proof becomes the basis for denial of benefits, the technology of disability evaluation certainly can have a coercive effect. Particularly in fragmented systems like the American one, where disability evaluation is not connected with actual job-finding services, the determination of residual working ability is likely to leave the individual in a no-man's-land: he or she is "found" able to work but not "found" a job. Most important, the air of objectivity surrounding disability evaluation helps legitimize government decisions not to provide social aid and creates a sense of ultimate correctness, beyond which there can be no appeal.

Disability evaluation is thus an instrument of the state (as the purveyor and arbiter of public programs) and of employers—an instrument not in the sense of a single tool to be wielded by a monolithic actor, but rather in the sense of an organization or system whose overall pattern of decision-making shapes the labor force by pushing some people into it and allowing others out. Policy decisions of legislative, administrative, and judicial bodies profoundly influence the way the system works. But at the same time, disability evaluation is not an instrument over which the state has exclusive control. Applicants' decisions to apply for benefits and to appeal their cases, as well as physicians' and lawyers' efforts to advocate the cases of their clients, create tugs and pulls on the system.

In addition to shaping the internal composition of the labor force, disability programs can have the effect of absorbing and disguising unemployment and thus controlling the total supply of labor. By making policy decisions to define disability more liberally for older workers, states are able to retire older workers from the labor force more quickly than otherwise. When people go on disability pensions instead of unemployment insurance, they are no longer part of the labor force and therefore not counted in the unemployment rate. In times of high unemployment, flexible disability categories provide a holding tank where otherwise unemployed people can be "hidden." But while the disabled are statistically invisible in the unemployment figures, they are a fiscal presence: they still cost money from the public treasury. The "hide now, pay later" aspect of disability programs may explain the cycle of expansion and contraction in the United States and Europe.

Employers also benefit from a flexible disability category. A standard Marxist argument about welfare programs holds that they are used by employers and the state to absorb excess labor in times of high unemployment when the unemployed show signs of political unrest; in times of labor shortage, welfare programs are contracted, pushing people back into jobs and restoring the disciplinary effect of low welfare benefits on the wage demands of the employed. The disability category could certainly be used this way in theory, but one does not even need to postulate inhumane motives to explain why employers benefit from a flexible category. Assuming competitive markets and some pressure to make his workforce more productive, the *most compassionate* employer would find it far easier to let go an older worker by pushing him into a disability program than by discharging him onto the unemployment rolls.

Since employers do not pay direct premiums for Social Security disability programs, as they do for industrial accident insurance, they do not perceive any direct costs when they shift their less productive workers into these social insurance schemes. The existence of disability programs might even be a valuable bargaining resource for an employer who is trying to prune his workforce of older, weaker, slower, less productive workers. One can easily imagine an employer trying to convince a worker to retire by hinting that a disability pension could be arranged and that unemployment would be a dismal alternative:

> I know you prefer to continue working, but you just can't keep up to speed any longer. I'd really hate to let you go, because at your

age, it won't be easy to find another job. But if you'll agree to see the company doctor, I think he'd probably find your arthritis is the cause of your inability to keep up. And we would help you file for a Social Security disability pension—how about it?

Legislators have a strong interest in flexibility, too. They face conflicting pressures with respect to welfare programs: on the one hand, they get specific requests for help from individual constituents who want to obtain disability benefits;[17] on the other, they incur general resistance to expansion from their constituency-at-large, which has a diffuse interest in keeping government spending and taxes low. Flexible standards allow legislators to satisfy both constituencies. They can press simultaneously for eligibility of specific constituents and for wholesale trimming of the rolls, and agencies can respond to both demands at the same time. They can find definitional openings to justify eligibility for the particular case, and use other definitional ambiguities to eliminate large classes of recipients.

Legislators, at least in the United States, have always had a deep ambivalence about disability programs. As one scholar notes, "Congress has continuously believed the [Social Security] program to be both essential to a basic system of income security *and* an open invitation to drop out of the work force."[18] A system of seemingly firm, objective standards (such as the SSA's Listing of Medical Impairments or the VA's Disability Rating Schedule) combined with a high degree of discretion on the part of disability determiners helps legislators resolve their ambiguity. Strict standards provide symbolic reassurance to the side that worries about abuse and to the general public concerned with fiscal restraint; discretionary eligibility mechanisms satisfy the compassionate side by allowing legislators to help particular constituents.

The agencies responsible for determining eligibility also have a large stake in keeping the definitions flexible. For one thing, if these administrative agencies know they are going to have to respond to legislative changes of mood, they will want criteria fluid enough to enable decisions to swing with the political wind. Second, ambiguity serves the same function for determination agencies as it does for legislatures; it allows the agency to *appear* to satisfy consituencies that make conflicting demands. Third, the knowledge base of the disability and rehabilitation field is changing rapidly. Whereas heart attacks were seen as permanently and totally disabling a decade ago, the new therapeutic approach is to return heart patients to exercise and work extremely quickly. Given the rapid accumulation of scientific information, it is prudent policy for an agency to use imprecise language that can accommodate changes in clinical wisdom. Last but not least, administrative agencies are staffed by people who regard themselves as professionals and who place a high value on their autonomy. Their professional identity is tied to their ability to use discretion and judgment in decision-making. The more precisely disability is formally defined, the more mechanical and uncreative the determiner's task becomes.

Service agencies for the disabled, especially rehabilitation agencies, also benefit from definitional flexibility. The paradox of social service agencies is that while they nominally seek to reduce the number of problem cases who need their services, they are rewarded in the political and budgetary worlds by demonstrating that problem cases abound. A rehabilitation agency, for example, needs clients in order to survive and grow. If it is successful in rehabilitating many people, it depletes the supply of potential clients and can obtain more clients only by expanding the types of problems it treats and the definition of the handicaps it purports to serve. If, on the other hand, an agency is unable to rehabilitate many of its clients, its most effective strategy in the political arena is to publicize the large number of disabled people who need its services. It can deflect attention from the ineffectiveness its services by dramatizing the size of the needy population instead. Thus, whether or not an agency is successful in its nominal mission of rehabilitation, it always has an interest in making the disability problem bigger. Definitional expansion is part of the strategy for agency survival.

Agencies that serve the disabled may also create disability in a more direct sense. Robert Scott's classic study of blindness agencies showed that much of the behavior of blind men is taught to them by agencies rather than being a necessary result of sightlessness. Docility, acquiescence, dependence, helplessness, melancholy, and asceticism, for example, are all part of the stereotypical image of blind people, and blind people may be socialized by acquaintances and professional blindness workers to adopt these roles.[19]

The legal definition of blindness (corrected vision in the better eye is less than 10 percent of normal vision) is an arbitrary line through a range of visual acuity. Although a 90 percent loss of vision is serious, people with only 10 or even 5 percent vision can still see enough to perform many daily activities. Only a small fraction of the legally blind have no vision at all.[20] Yet once people are pronounced legally blind, they are referred, if not pressured, by eye doctors and acquaintances to agencies for the blind and are treated as if they couldn't see at all. They are taught braille, even when special lenses might enable them to read; they are taught to use canes and guide dogs, even when they can see well enough to move around; and they are trained in jobs for the blind, even when their remaining sight is enough to do other jobs.[21] In these ways, rehabilitation agencies actually make people more incapacitated than they are.

Such agency behavior might lead to expansion of cash transfer programs in three ways. First, people who are socialized by the agencies to think of themselves as more handicapped, rather than less, are more likely to define themselves as disabled and apply for benefits. Second, to the extent that socialization and training actually reduces the independence and performance of the handicapped, these clients do in fact come to need more social aid. And third, when rehabilitation agencies participate in or are responsible for disability determination for public programs, their general organizational bias toward expanding the definition of disability will inevitably lead them to apply those broader definitions. There is a certain irony, then, in the willingness of American Congressmen to place their faith in state vocational rehabilitation agencies as the guardians of strict eligibility criteria.

Finally, there are interest groups who benefit from disability expansion and indeed devote themselves to creating official recognition of particular disabilities. Disease and injury provide a focal point for citizens' organizations. Many groups have crystallized around specific diseases or disabilities,[22] and having realized that disability provides one legitimate way to receive aid from the state, they use standard pressure-group tactics to obtain statutory recognition of new categories of disability. Once a particular disease or condition obtains such recognition, an individual is automatically entitled to aid if he can prove he has it. These statutory presumptions eliminate the need for each affected individual to demonstrate either incapacity or work-related cause.

A well-known example of interest group success is the federal compensation program for black-lung disease, which affects coal miners. Less well-known are the "heart laws" obtained by many public employee groups to govern their state and municipal pension programs. These laws create an automatic presumption that any heart disease suffered by certain public employees was caused by their work. Courts have tended to expand the effect of the laws by allowing the presumption to hold even when the claimant suffers an acute onset of the problem while off duty or years after retirement.[23] Interest groups have expanded the scope of the presumption by lobbying for its application to more and more employee groups; from its original application to policemen and firemen with frontline or street jobs, it has been broadened to include sheriffs, investigators, safety officers, highway patrolmen, prison officers, and even fish and game wardens. These groups have also been able to obtain presumptions for other types of diseases and conditions such as pneumonia, tuberculosis, hernia, and back problems.

Although disease- and injury-based interest groups have been part of the political scene for a long time, recent years have seen the development of a new type of group that appeals to the disabled as a general category rather than to specific conditions. Examples are the Citizens for Independent Living and the Coalition of Citizens with Disabilities in the United States, and the Union of the Physically Impaired Against Segregation in England. Unlike the disease-specific interest groups, which seek either legal recognition or public funds for research and treatment or "their" disease, the general disability organizations lobby for the extension of rights, privileges and protections for the disabled as a class. Their main focus has been on access to buildings, public transportation, educational programs, and jobs. In the United States, their main victory is a provision in the Rehabilitation Act of 1973 that prohibits programs or institutions receiving federal aid from discriminating against "otherwise qualified" handicapped people.[24]

The general disability groups typically do not define "disabled" in their platforms. It is likely that to do so would bring to the surface some conflicting interests that are masked by the general term. For example, in a 1975 controversy over proposed federal regulations on job rights for the "handicapped," groups representing the blind, deaf, and physically impaired opposed the rules because they did not want to be lumped together with alcoholics, drug addicts, and the mentally ill.[25] Nevertheless, even though the general-interest groups probably do not expand the definition of disability *per se*, by expanding privileges and rights for all the disabled, they give impetus to other disability- and disease-specific groups to seek legal recognition of their problems as disabilities.

The conventional analysis of disability expansion sees the program recipient as the prime beneficiary and presumably the instigator of program expansion. But there is a strong case that indeed much more powerful organizational interests benefit from flexibility and even expansion of the category: the state, employers, legislators, disability program agencies, and rehabilitation agencies all benefit from having a disability category they can manipulate. Thus, reforms aimed at curbing the use of programs by individuals would hardly seem to be an effective solution to the disability expansion problem. One has to question whether anyone other than budget officers and taxpayers—two notably diffuse constituencies—has any real interest in restraining the growth of the disability phenomenon. If disability expansion is really a problem, one is hard put to say *whose* problem it is.

Disability Expansion and the Crisis of the Welfare State

Disability programs are said to be exploding, but they are only the latest symptom for harbingers of crisis. Similar warnings have been issued about public welfare expenditures, public health insurance programs, and old age pensions. The titles of recent books on the welfare state proclaim its impending doom: *The Fiscal Crisis of the State*, *Welfare States in Crisis*, *Contradictions of the Welfare State*.[26] What does it mean to say that the welfare state is in crisis, and what does the study of disability programs teach us about the nature of crisis?

The term "crisis" is often used simply to mean very rapid growth; a significant increase in a program's growth rate is taken as a sign of loss of control by the agencies in charge. Journalistic and academic discussions use images of ravenous appetite and suggest that the expanding program will compete all too successfully with other programs for scarce public resources. In this sense of "crisis," disability programs surely qualify. But if "crisis" is simply a label for "quickening" or "expansion," it is merely a rhetorical device and does not give us much insight.

Assertions of crisis are sometimes meant to imply a total breakdown or collapse of the system. Breakdown theories almost always point out trends, such as increasing expenditures or growth of political unrest, and suggest that what has heretofore been a linear or even exponential trend will suddenly behave differently. Predictions that the American Social Security system will collapse are of this nature.[27] The chief image here is a threshold beyond which a system undergoes structural transformation. But rarely do these theories specify the location of the threshold, the factor that will push the system over the brink, or the nature of the predicted collapse.

Marxist interpretations of crisis are also breakdown theories and rely on analyses of trends, but their distinctive feature is the idea of internal contradiction. In these theories, the very structure of the (capitalist) state embodies two principles that cannot coexist in the long run. To use Claus Offe's definition, "A *contradiction* is the tendency inherent within a specific mode of production to destroy those very pre-conditions on which its survival depends."[28] According to Offe, the difference between a contradiction and a crisis is that in the former, "the self-destructive tendencies . . . and their destructive and revolutionary potential can well be controlled and kept latent through various adaptive mechanisms of the system, at least temporarily."[29] Theories of contradiction, including Offe's, usually imply that a breakdown is imminent or inevitable, but it is worth distinguishing the idea of an ongoing incompatibility or tension from the idea of complete collapse or structural transformation. Many theorists who accept the idea of contradiction are concerned to explain why two seemingly incompatible phenomena can coexist as long as they do, without breakdown.[30]

There are basically two versions of the contradiction theory of crisis, the economic and the political, though the distinction is more a matter of emphasis than of separate explanatory factors. The economic version, sometimes called "fiscal crisis,"[31] holds that the state must constantly expand its expenditures, but its revenues cannot expand fast enough. The state must provide for economic growth (or capital accumulation, which fuels growth) and for the welfare of its citizens. Money for both functions must come from the surplus product—the extra value added to raw materials by human labor. In fact, the surplus product must be divided three ways: some must be reinvested to produce more profit; some must be returned to workers in the form of higher wages; and some must go to the state in the form of taxes. In a sense, three animals are feeding out of the same trough, and all three must be satisfied if the system is to keep going. In this version, the breakdown occurs when the economy can no longer be productive enough to sustain all three feedings, or (to leave the farm reluctantly and return to academia), when there is a decline in labor productivity and a falling rate of profit.[32] The rate of profit might fall either because the workers demand and get too much (the welfare state has gradually redistributed more of the total product away from capital and toward labor),[33] or because business revolts against the state's excess taking and refuses to reinvest.[34]

The political version puts more emphasis on support for existing economic and political arrangements. In democratic capitalism, the workers' consent to the right of government to rule and to the system of private ownership of property is essential. Legal rights to social aid are the central element of both consent and contradiction. On the one hand, the state garners a great deal of political loyalty through its welfare spending; social welfare entitlements reduce class conflict by reducing workers' motives to demand higher wages. On the other hand, workers and the poor eventually come to demand these entitlements as "rights to subsistence," and they are less willing to tolerate either low wages or low welfare benefits and spending.[35] The breakdown in the political version is signaled by an erosion of political support.

What contradiction theories of crisis have in common is the idea that there are two parts of society, each of which operates with its own logic, and these two sorts of logic are mutually incompatible or destructive. The economic version of contradiction emphasizes the scarcity or finiteness of resources, out of which several competing functions must be funded. The political version emphasizes the organization of society around competing sets of rights or distributive principles: market power versus political power, rights in property versus rights in persons, or—as I have drawn it—work versus need.

Even granting that these tensions exist, there is still the question of whether the two parts can coexist indefinitely. One answer is that there must eventually be a breakdown because there is no actor or agency sufficiently unaffected by the contradiction to be able to step outside the system to counteract its self-destructive tendencies.[36] In this view, the system is on a collision course, and no one from inside can stop it.

The interpretation of disability as a concept that mediates the boundary between two conflicting distributive principles offers a very different answer to the question of coexistence. The focus on the boundary *between* two systems, rather than on their *internal* logic and operations, reveals the way the boundary is socially constructed. It is not fixed, either by objective characteristics of individuals or by objective requirements of the economy. It is something society creates and constantly redesigns. To view disability in historical and cross-national contexts is to see that societies have different options for resolving the contradiction between work and need, and that they can adapt and adjust any choice over the course of time.

Theories of crisis that postulate inevitable breakdown make the same mistake as do bureaucratic concepts of disability. The bureaucratic notion assumes that given a certain physical constitution, a person can or cannot do a certain task. In fact, humans are nearly infinitely adaptable. That is why the disability literature is replete with anecdotes of people who climb steel girders with their arms or do fine penmanship with their toes. Breakdown theories of crisis make similarly erroneous assumptions about state and society. The existence of conflicts or contradictory tendencies does not mean that the state must devour its own tail or collapse in total paralysis. States, too, can learn to walk with crutches and braces. And while it is not the most elegant form of locomotion we can imagine, hobbling has accomplished much of what we consider worthwhile in the history of civilization. Social theory would do well to borrow an analogy from the rehabilitation field and see the state as disabled rather than incapacitated.

But if there is no imminent or even inevitable breakdown, there is still a social truth to the sense of crisis about public disability programs that pervades policy circles and media reports. Given all the ways in which major social and political institutions benefit from flexibility and expansion of the disability category, it is hard to believe that expansion itself is the source of panic. More likely, the sense of crisis is better accounted for by a decline in flexibility.

There are several reasons why the disability category has lost flexibility. First, as programs mature, the standards of eligibility get more and more detailed through adjudication and rulemaking and the sheer creation of precedent. Less and less is left to the discretion of gatekeepers. Each time a legislative or administrative body seeks to revise definitions and standards, there is pressure to make them more precise. To make a standard more vague seems a violation of fairness, and indeed courts sometimes overturn statutes and regulations for being too vague.

Second, standards of disability work in large measure by the device of legal presumptions for entire categories of people, injuries, or causes. Once a legal presumption is created, it is hard to eliminate. A presumption comes to be viewed as an entitlement, virtually creating a political constituency of people who stand to gain from being eligible. These groups are identifiable people, each of whom will incur a great loss if the presumption is removed, and each of whom therefore has a strong motivation to work for its continuation. Moreover, these groups comprise people who already suffer some condition historically deemed pitiable and worthy of compensation; they can call upon public sympathy in their struggle to preserve the presumption. The disability category thus grows by incorporation of large classes, but can be cut back only through case-by-case examination of individuals.

Third, once people are categorized as disabled, they become socialized to the role. The degree to which different people accept the image of themselves as dependent and unable to work, of course, varies. But the longer people do not work, the less likely it is that they will return to work. Dependence creates dependence. There is even a psychiatric term for people who are pathologically dependent on social aid—"compensation neurosis." Programs tend to make their own clients, Pygmalion-like.

Fourth, the labeling of a condition as disabling by both the medical profession and state bureaucracies educates the public to believe the condition is actually disabling. Popular wisdom about health in any given era is in large part the trickle-down of professional wisdom from an earlier era.[37] The general public went on believing in and requesting antibiotics for colds and sore throats long after the leading edge of the medical profession abandoned the practice of prescribing them. Once a condition such as heart attack or "Agent Orange syndrome" is officially accepted as disabling, people with that condition may be induced to think of themselves as disabled, even after science has found effective treatment methods.

All of these are ways that the state as well as employers, determination agencies, and rehabilitation agencies loses flexibility as programs mature. But there is no reason to think that a system which has lost flexibility must collapse entirely. It can continue to adapt, even if some options, particularly contraction, are not open or are more difficult to accomplish.

In the face of decreased flexibility of the disability category, what options does the state have? Disability programs are at bottom a social mechanism for compensating people in need. There are basically two ways society can compensate people it deems needy: it can impose liability, which means identifying someone as responsible for the need and shifting the costs to that party; or it can set up public insurance or welfare programs that diffuse the costs to society at large.

Welfare states have chosen to rely heavily on the insurance/welfare option. To compensate via insurance is to "normalize" the problem, to assert that in a large population a certain number of cases are expected to happen in the normal course of things. We insure against events we believe cannot be prevented—fire, flood, death. We impose liability, by contrast, for those harms we believe *can* be prevented by the exercise of proper care. The choice to move from employer liability systems to industrial accident insurance, however fortunate for the injured worker in the short run, was also symbolically and politically a denial of responsibility on the part of employers to prevent occupational injury.

The most important option for the state may be to abandon the no-fault insurance model of compensation—if not entirely, then at least in such a fashion as to raise questions of responsibility and prevention. The physical conditions of work that contribute to injury are eminently changeable. The presence of toxic substances in the workplace and the exposure of workers to them is within the control of human beings; this is not a case of machines gone amok or anonymous industrial forces. Toxic substances in the environment—pesticides, defoliants, chemical weapons, waste products—are all put there by identifiable human agents. Society can choose to reattribute responsibility to employers through liability rules; it can place more responsibility on workers through requirements for individual protective devices and personal exposure monitoring; it can place pressure on manufacturers to do more careful testing of products and substances; and government itself can take a greater role in funding, promoting and performing research.

The crisis of disability programs is in part the result of an impossible concept—the concept of categories as a sure means of separating the needy from the non-needy. The categorical resolution itself rests on an atomistic view of society in which people are seen to exist as individual, self-sufficient entities. In that view, it is possible to create categories which describe the objective characteristics and circumstances that render people dependent. If one starts from the opposite assumption—that people exist only as social beings, inherently dependent and inextricably bound to familial, communal, and economic structures—the very idea of self-sufficiency on which the categories are predicated becomes absurd. Then it is clear why the keepers of the categories will have to elaborate ever more situations in which people are legitimately needy, until the categories become so large as to engulf the whole. The notions of developmental disabilities and environmentally-caused diseases would seem to come dangerously close.

The crisis of disability programs is also in part a crisis of faith in fundamental social and political structures. In its emotional tenor, public discussion of the disability problem is strangely reminiscent of sixteenth century European discussions of the vagrancy problem. Vagrants in the sixteenth century, besides constituting a problem of public order and fiscal strain, must have presented a foreboding of what all citizens might become—individuals detached from family and community, detached from the land, and detached from a source of subsistence and security. In a similar way, the disabled in the twentieth century affect us at some far deeper level than our concern with the fiscal integrity of public programs or the sapping of productivity of the labor force. They are a foreboding of what we all might become, through assaults on our environments, homes, and workplaces and through the scientific imperative to detect more and more diseases at earlier and earlier stages, until we are all at risk of disability from the moment we are born, and even before. The disability problem forces us to contemplate ourselves as less than whole.

Epilogue

Old Will . . . looks for all the world like Uncle Tom, with grizzled hair and whiskers, and walks with a cane. The cane is a badge of his independence, indicating that he is frail and cannot or will not stoop to labor. But he was a hard worker in his day and made money on cotton and at share-cropping of all sorts. When I am his age, if I have no other subsistence, I think that I too shall walk with a cane and accept a livelihood as my right, after years of toiling.

Marjorie Kinnan Rawlings, *Cross Creek*

Notes

Introduction

1. Daniel Price, "Income Replacement During Sickness, 1948–78," *Social Security Bulletin* 44, no. 5 (1981): 18–32. Five states (California, New York, New Jersey, Rhode Island and Hawaii) and Puerto Rico have compulsory temporary disability insurance programs; and the Railroad Retirement Act provides this coverage. Despite the paucity of public programs for temporary disability insurance in the United States, the patchwork of public and private programs provides protection for about 65 percent of the workforce; in states without compulsory temporary disability insurance, fewer than half the workers in private industry have short-term sickness protection. These figures are for 1978.

2. In 1969, medical disqualifications constituted only 44% of all draft deferments and exemptions, but by 1972, only three years later, they accounted for 87% (calculated from table 542, U.S. Bureau of the Census, *Statistical Abstract of the United States: 1977*, [Washington, D.C., 1977], p. 339).

3. Two British courts have accepted PMS (premenstrual syndrome) as a disease that can mitigate responsibility for criminal actions, and an American criminal court is considering a similar situation (*Hastings Center Report* 12, no. 4, [Aug. 1982], p. 2). See also Michael Wheeler and André Mayer, *The Crocodile Man* (Boston: Houghton Mifflin, 1982), for a discussion of the introduction of organic brain damage as evidence in a criminal trial based on the insanity defense.

4. Many states have statutes with such requirements. In Massachusetts, ch. 164 sec. 124(a) of the General Laws requires gas and electric companies to continue service, despite non-payment, if a doctor certifies by letter that the customer has a "serious illness." Although this statute has not been read to include disabilities (chronic but stable conditions), if a doctor is willing to certify someone as having a serious illness, his or her letter is sufficient evidence for a presumption of illness. And since there is no limit on how long the utility company must provide service to a sick person, the situation could continue indefinitely. (Katherine Hearn, Director of Consumer Division, Massachusetts Department of Public Utilities, personal communication with author, April, 1984.)

5. H.R. 92-708, Conference Rept. to Accompany H.R. 10947, 92d Cong., 1st sess. (1971), p. 49.

6. Mia Bracke-Defever, "Rehabilitation Policy in Belgium," in Gary Albrecht, ed., *Cross National Rehabilitation Policies: A Sociological Perspective* (London: Sage Publications, 1981), pp. 205–22; citation from p. 211.

7. See Public Law 94–142. Also, Richard Weatherly, *Reforming Special Education: Policy Implementation from State Level to Street Level* (Cambridge, Mass.: Massachusetts Institute of Technology Press, 1979).

8. For Sweden, see V. Halberstadt and R. H. Haveman, "Public Policies for Disabled Workers," Madison, Wis.: Institute for Research on Poverty, 1981, pp. 92–93.

9. Published literature is available for the United States, Netherlands, Federal Republic of Germany, Great Britain, Italy, Belgium, France, Sweden, Denmark, Norway, and Finland. Sources include Jonathan Sunshine, "Disability: A Comprehensive Overview of Programs, Issues and Options for Change," Working Papers of the President's Commission on Pension Policy, January, 1981; Mordecai Lando and Aaron Krute, "Disability Insurance: Programs, Issues and Research," *Social Security Bulletin* 39, no. 10 (1976); Mordecai Lando, Malcolm Coate, and Ruth Kraus, "Disability Benefit Applications and the Economy," *Social Security Bulletin* 42, no. 10 (1979): 3–10; Lois Copeland, "Defining Disability: A Cross Country Department of Health, Education and Welfare, Social Security Administration, Office of Research and Statistics, HEW Publication No. (SSA) 77–11853, Washington, D.C., 1977; Lois Copeland, "International Trends in Disability Program Growth," *Social Security Bulletin* 44, no. 10 (1981): 25–36, 61; Hans Emanuel, "Factors in the Growth of the Number of Disability Beneficiaries in the Netherlands," *International Social Security Review* 33, no. 1 (1980): 41–60; H. Berglind, "Pension or Work? A Growing Dilemma in the Nordic Welfare States," *Acta Sociologica* 21, spec. supp. (1978): 181–91; Richard Mörschel and Uwe Rehfeld, "Untersuchungen der Rentenzugänge im Zeitablauf," Part I, *Deutsche Rentenversicherung* no. 4 (1981): 234–53;Victor Halberstadt and Robert H. Haveman, "Public Policies for Disabled Workers," Madison Wisconsin, Institute for Research on Poverty, 1981; Richard V. Burkhauser and Robert Haveman, *Disability and Work: The Economics of American Public Policy* (Baltimore: Johns Hopkins University Press, 1982); Robert Haveman, Victor Halberstadt, and Richard V. Burkhauser, *Public Policy Toward Disabled Workers: Cross-National Analyses of Economic Impacts* (Ithaca: Cornell Univ. Press, 1984).

10. Sunshine, "Disability," Table 2.

11. Burkhauser and Haveman, *Disability and Work*, p. 37.

12. I took the estimate of total spending on the disabled for 1977 from Burkhauser and Haveman, *Disability and Work*, p. 37. They warn, rightly, that these estimates are necessarily crude and should be taken with caution. Nevertheless, they do give an idea of the order of magnitude. For my estimate of the proportion of all social welfare expenditures accounted for by disability programs, I used the figure for total welfare expenditures of $362 billion estimated by Alma McMillan, "Social Expenditures under Public Programs, Fiscal Year 1977," *Social Security Bulletin* 42, no. 6 (1979): 3–12.

13. For example, some studies measure from beginning to end of the

decade, 1960–1970; others measure from the mid-to-late sixties to the mid-to-late seventies.

14. Berglind, "Pension or Work?" p. 17; Jonathan Sunshine "Disability Payments Stabilizing After Era of Accelerated Growth," *Monthly Labor Review* vol. 104, no. 5 (1981): 17–20; Emanuel, "Factors," p. 42; Mörschel and Rehfeld, "Untersuchungen," pp. 246–47. Copeland's figures ("International Trends," p. 30) show peaks in the "gross disability incidence rate" (number of disability benefits/pensions awarded per 1,000 insured workers) for Belgium and Finland in 1973.

15. Copeland, "International Trends," p. 33; Jon Evind Kohlberg, "Conceptions of Social Disability," in G. Albrecht, ed., *Cross National Rehabilitation*, pp. 97–108; and P. Taylor, "Sickness Absence: facts and misconceptions," *Journal of the Royal College of Physicians* vol. 8, no. 4 (1974): 315–33.

16. Emanuel, "Factors," p. 56; Lando, Coate, and Kraus, "Disability Benefit Applications," p. 6; Sunshine, "Disability Payments," p. 19; Halberstadt and Haveman, *Public Policies*, pp. 102–5; Lando and Krute, "Disability Insurance," pp. 12–13; Burkhauser and Haveman, *Disability and Work*, pp. 55–56.

17. Lando and Krute, "Disability Insurance," pp. 8–9; Lando, Coate, and Kraus, "Disability Benefit Applications," p. 6; Copeland, "International Trends," p. 31, and pp. 35–36.

18. See Emanuel, "Factors"; Copeland, "Defining Disability"; and Haveman, Halberstadt and Haveman, *Public Policy*.

19. Copeland, "Defining Disability," p. 16.

20. Lando, Coate, and Kraus, "Disability Benefit Applications"; Mörschel and Rehfeld, "Untersuchungen"; Jon Evind Kohlberg, "Limits to Welfare," *Acta Sociologica* 21, spec. supp. (1978): 113–123; Berglind, "Pension or Work?"; Emanuel, "Factors," pp. 51–52; Monroe Berkowitz, William G. Johnson, and Edward H. Murphy, *Public Policy Toward Disability* (New York: Prager, 1976); Burkhauser and Haveman, *Disability and Work*, p. 47; Haveman, Halberstadt and Burkhauser, *Public Policy*, 1984, Ch. 5.

21. See Copeland, "International Trends," p. 35; Burkhauser and Haveman, *Disability and Work*, p. 47; Max Horlick, "Impact of an Aging Population on Social Security: The Foreign Experience," in *Social Security in a Changing World*, (Washington, D.C.: Social Security Administration, Office of Research and Statistics, 1979).

22. Berglind, "Pension or Work?"; Mörschel and Rehfeld, "Untersuchungen"; Sunshine, "Disability Payments," p. 19.

23. U.S. Congress, House Committee on Ways and Means, Subcommittee on Social Security, 94th Cong. 2d sess., hearings, 17, 21, 24 May and 4, 11 June 1976, *Disability Insurance Program*, p. 40 (cited hereafter Ways and Means *Disability Insurance* Program, 1976); Haveman, Halberstadt, and Burkhauser, *Public Policy*; Health Insurance Association of America, "Compensation Systems Available to Disabled Persons in the United States," (Wash., D.C. Health Insurance Assn. of America, 1979).

24. Ways and Means, *Disability Insurance Program*, pp. 42–43; and Copeland, "International Trends," p. 35, citing a Finnish study of public awareness.

25. See references in note 16, above.

26. Berglind, "Pension or Work?"; Kohlberg, "Limits to Welfare"; Georges Midre, "Market Forces and Social Policy" (paper presented to Tenth World Congress of Sociology, Mexico City, Aug. 1982); Haveman, Halberstadt, and Burkhauser, *Public Policy*, ch. 5.

Chapter 1

1. The phrase is, of course, Mancur Olson's, from *The Logic of Collective Action* (Cambridge, Mass.: Harvard Univ. Press, 1971).

2. See T. R. Malthus, "A Summary View of the Principle of Population," in Anthony Flew, ed., *Malthus: An Essay on the Principle of Population* (Hammondsworth: Penguin, 1970), p. 245.

3. Claus Offe, for example (in *Contradictions of the Welfare State* [Cambridge, Mass.: MIT Press, 1984], ch. 4), argues that the "commodification of labor" under capitalism creates the instrumental view of work; the material motivation for work is not a natural characteristic of man but an outlook to which he is socialized in capitalist society. Nevertheless, Offe still believes that the need-based welfare system undermines the "normative syndrome of possessive individualism" whereby citizens hold themselves responsible for their economic position. State-provided welfare transfers reveal to the citizen that his economic position is in fact collectively determined.

4. Marxist theories would hold, in contrast to my argument, that it is precisely private control of capital that creates the distributive dilemma. In those theories, both the narrow instrumental view of work and the logic of collective action are artifacts of capitalism, not inevitable characteristics of individuals and groups. Welfare policy (need-based distribution) is the major instrument by which the state constitutes the working class; only because the state looks after certain aspects of housing, health care, and family care can workers become sellers of labor power. But I would argue, first, that welfare policy, in the sense of need-based redistribution, exists in noncapitalist societies. (For examples, see James C. Scott, *The Moral Economy of the Peasant: Rebellion and Subsistence in Southeast Asia* [New Haven, Conn.: Yale Univ. Press, 1976]). Second, even in those societies, there are clear rules/norms for drawing boundaries between work- and need-based distribution. And third, noncapitalist societies may *resolve* the distributive dilemma differently from capitalist societies, but they still face the dilemma.

5. E. P. Thompson, "The Moral Economy of the English Crowd in the Eighteenth Century," *Past and Present* 50 (1971): 76–136.

6. James C. Scott, "*The Moral Economy*," (1976).

7. This is Hugh Heclo's interpretation in his *Modern Social Politics in Britain and Sweden* (New Haven, Conn.: Yale Univ. Press, 1974).

8. For example, in Germany, private "sickness funds" that provided income to workers during temporary illness were allowed to become providers of health under the National Health Insurance scheme when it was adopted in 1883. For the German case, see essays in W. J. Mommsen, ed., *The Emergence of the Welfare State in Britain and Germany* (London: Croom Helm, 1981). For a general treatment of voluntary organizations, see Ralph Kramer, *Voluntary Agencies in the Welfare State* (Berkeley, Cal.: Univ. of California Press, 1981).

9. See Christopher Hill, "The Puritans and the Poor," *Past and Present* 2 (Nov. 1952): 32–50; John Garraty, *Unemployment in History* (New York: Harper and Row, 1972), p. 26.

10. See Carol Stack, *All Our Kin* (New York: Harper and Row, 1974); Marcel Mauss, *The Gift* (New York: W. W. Norton, 1967).

11. Phillipe Aries, *Centuries of Childhood* (New York: A. Knopf, 1962).

12. V. Finkelstein, "Research Requirements," in W. T. Singleton and L. M. Debney, eds., *Occupational Disability: The Approaches of Government, Industry and the Universities* (Ridgewood, N.J.: Bogden, 1982), pp. 279–87; quotation from p. 286. For a statement of this position from the American side, see Frank Bowe, *Handicapping America* (New York: Harper and Row, 1978).

13. The first two cases are anecdotes from friends; the last is from MIT's weekly newspaper, *Tech Talk*, 26 no. 24 (Feb. 3, 1982), p. 4.

Chapter 2

1. A comprehensive reference on vagrancy in Europe is C. J. Ribton-Turner, *A History of Vagrants and Vagrancy and Beggars and Begging* (1887; reprint, Montclair, N.J.: Patterson Smith, 1972). It is a minutely detailed chronological treatise on begging in England, with several chapters on other European countries, all based on a wealth of reports by local officials; heads of benevolent societies, charitable organizations; societies for the suppression of vagrancy; social reformers; and convicted or reformed vagrants who provided confessional material in the vein of criminals gone straight. Other sources for this section include E. M. Leonard, *The Early History of English Poor Relief* (Cambridge: Cambridge Univ. Press, 1900); Karl de Schweinitz, *England's Road to Social Security* (Philadelphia: Univ. of Pennsylvania Press, 1943); Garraty, *Unemployment*; Derek Fraser, *Evolution of the British Welfare State* (New York: Harper and Row, 1973).

2. This brief excursion through a major field of historical scholarship does not pretend to offer anything more than a glimpse. The reader interested in pursuing the subject would do well to start with the debate between Beier and Pound and then pursue some of the many references cited

there: see A. L. Beier, "Vagrants and the Social Order in Elizabethan England," *Past and Present* 64 (Aug., 1974): 3–29; J. F. Pound and A. L. Beier, "Debate" *Past and Present* 71 (May 1976): 126–34. Differences in local patterns of migration and vagrancy and the causes of local variations are examined in P. Clark and P. Slack, *Crisis and Order in English Towns, 1500–1700: Essays in Urban History* (London: Routledge and Kegan Paul 1972), and *English Towns in Transition, 1500–1700* (London: Oxford Univ. Press 1976). In general, Clark and Slack tend to emphasize structural factors in local economies as forces that exert more or less "pull" on vagrants seeking a means of subsistence.

3. Joan Thirsk, *Economic and Policy Projects* (Oxford: Clarendon Press, 1978), p. 159; Garraty, p. 31.

4. Thirsk, *Projects*, pp. 161–64.

5. Garraty, *Unemployment*, pp. 33–34.

6. Leonard, *Early History*, pp. 14–15.

7. Ibid., p. 16; Thirsk, *Projects*, pp. 129–60.

8. Ribton-Turner, *Vagrants*, pp. 163–64; Garraty, *Unemployment*, p. 35.

9. Ribton-Turner, *Vagrants*, pp. 27–32, 64–65, and passim.

10. Mr. John Daughtry, Stipalfields Benevolent Society, 1814, quoted in Ibid., p. 223; emphasis in original.

11. Thomas Harman, *Caueat or Warening for Common Cursetors*, 1566, cited in Leonard, *Early History*, pp. 11–12; Martin Luther, *Liber Vagatorum*, 1528: for an English translation of his twenty-eight classes, see Ribton-Turner, *Vagrants*, pp. 544–46; Giacinto Nobili, under the pseudonym Rafaele Frianoro, *Il vagabondo overo sferza de bianti e vagobondi*, 1627: for his thirty four classes, see Ribton-Turner, *Vagrants*, pp. 557–60; the corporations in France are described in Ribton-Turner, *Vagrants*, pp. 518–21.)

12. See Ribton-Turner, *Vagrants*; Beier, "Vagrants," pp. 3–29.

13. Ribton-Turner, *Vagrants*, pp. 204–5.

14. From a statute of 1530, 22 Henry 7, ch. 12.

15. George Rosen, *Madness in Society* (Chicago: Univ. of Chicago Press, 1968) pp. 94–95.

16. Ribton-Turner, *Vagrants*, p. 520.

17. Ibid., pp. 223, 233–34; Benjamin Thompson, Count of Rumford, *Essays, Political, Economical, Philosophical* (London, 1796), cited in de-Schweinitz, *England's Road*, pp. 94–95; Jacques Donzelot, *The Policing of Families* (New York: Pantheon, 1979), p. 59.

18. See especially Beier, "Vagrants," pp. 8, 11–14, and more generally, the Beier/Pound debate and the works of Clark and Slack (see n. 2).

19. Beier, "Vagrants," p. 17.

20. Ibid., p. 13.

21. 23 Edward 3, Statute of Laborers, 1349, cited in de Schweinitz, *England's Road*, p. 1

22. Ibid., p. 6; also Leonard, *Early History*, pp. 64–65.

23. Leonard, *Early History*, pp. 3–6; de Schweinitz, *England's Road*, p. 7.

24. My interpretation of the law of 1388 differs considerably from that of William Chambliss in his "Sociological Interpretation of the Law of Vagrancy," *Social Problems* 12, no. 1 (Summer 1964): 67–77. Chambliss argues that in the period from 1349 (the first Statute of Laborers) to 1503, the substance of vagrancy law did not change, the law was not enforced, and it was not an effective control mechanism. He sees the statute of 1388, therefore, as merely a minor change in the statutory punishment of beggars, from a fifteen day prison term to a stint in the stocks. As is clear from my text, I think that important steps in the evolution of both the definition of the vagrancy category and administration of policy were already happening in the fourteenth century.

25. de Schweinitz, *England's Road*, p. 8.

26. 22 Henry 8, ch. 12, An Act Concerning Punishment of Beggars and Vagabonds, 1531; see de Schweinitz, *England's Road*, p. 21, and Leonard, *Early History*, pp. 53–54.

27. de Schweinitz, *England's Road*, pp. 22–23; Leonard, *Early History*, pp. 54–56; Ribton-Turner, *Vagrants*, pp. 81–83.

28. 5 Elizabeth, ch. 3, cited in de Schweinitz, *England's Road*, p. 87.

29. 8 & 9 William 3, ch. 30, 1697, cited in de Schweinitz, *England's Road*, p. 87; see also Ribton-Turner, *Vagrants*, pp. 173–76.

30. Chambliss, "Interpretation," p. 73.

31. The Law of Settlement of 1662 is generally considered a milestone in the development of Poor Law policy. It established local residency requirements for eligibility and limited the mobility of laborers. But residency requirements, though they controlled eligibility, were significant because they solidified local administration, not because they further articulated the principles of categorical welfare.

32. Sidney Webb and Beatrice Webb, *English Poor Law Policy*, vol. 10 of *English Local Government* (London: Longman's Green, 1910; reprint, London: Frank Cass, 1963); de Schweinitz, *England's Road*, pp. 131–34; Fraser, *Evolution*, pp. 30–34, 48–50.

33. 9 George 1, ch. 7, cited in de Schweinitz, *England's Road*, p. 60.

34. Derek Fraser, "The English Poor Law and the Origins of the British Welfare State," in Mommsen, ed., *Emergence of the Welfare State*, pp. 9–31; my figures are derived from tables on pp. 21–22.

35. Report from His Majesty's Commissioners for Inquiring into the Administration and Practical Operation of the Poor Laws, 1834, edition of 1905, p. 228 cited in de Schweinitz, *England's Road*, p. 123.

36. Quotation is from "Report of Her Majesty's Commissioners, p. 307, cited in Webbs, *Poor Law Policy*, pp. 9–10.

37. Webbs, *Poor Law Policy*, p. 2.

38. The term "disability" was not common in English policy; it was apparently used only by one particular inspector of the Poor Law Board (Mr. Longley, appointed in 1872) to mean "the aged" (Ibid., p. 229).

39. This description of the internal organization of sick wards in local poorhouses is compiled from Ruth G. Hodgkinson, *The Origins of the National Health Service: The Medical Services of the New Poor Law* (Berkeley: Univ. of California Press, 1967), pp. 147–60; Webbs, *Poor Law Policy*, p. 136.

40. Hodgkinson, *Origins*, pp. 13–17.

41. Outdoor Relief Prohibitory Order, 1844; cited in Webbs, *Poor Law Policy*, pp. 32–33.

42. Hodgkinson, *Origins*, p. 17. Note the interesting similarity to the Medicaid "spenddown" provisions, wherein a poor person is required to exhaust all savings in order to become eligible for Medicaid.

43. Mr. Longley in the Third Annual Report of the Local Government Board, 1873–74, p. 142, cited in Webbs, *Poor Law Policy*, p. 150.

44. Ibid., pp. 150–51, 207–10.

45. Ibid., p. 117; Fraser, *Evolution*, pp. 81–87.

46. Webbs, *Poor Law Policy*, p. 218; Hodgkinson, *Origins*, pp. 150–53.

47. Statement of Mr. Gathorne Hardy, President of the Poor Law Board, 1867, cited in Webbs, *Poor Law Policy*, p. 121.

48. Hodgkinson, *Origins*, p. 6 (quotation of Charles Mott).

49. Seventh Annual Report of the Poor Law Commissioners, cited in Ibid., p. 60.

50. Fraser, "Poor Law," pp. 12–18.

51. Hodgkinson, *Origins*, chs. 1, 3.

52. Ibid., pp. 19–22.

53. Sources for this section on insanity as a category in English social policy are Andrew Scull, *Museums of Madness* (London: Allen Lane/Penguin, 1979), which is by far the most interesting; Hodgkinson, *Origins*, ch. 4; Michel Foucault, *Madness and Civilization* (New York: Random House, 1965).

54. Webbs, *Poor Law Policy*, p. 49.

55. See Scull, *Museums*, pp. 234–38, for a fuller discussion of the definition of insanity. The interpretation of "professional imperialism" is his; I find he makes a plausible case.

56. Ibid., pp. 234–36, for all quotations.

57. Foucault, *Madness*, ch. 2, esp. pp. 39–44; Scull, *Museums*, pp. 250–53; the quotation is Scull's.

58. See Hodgkinson, *Origins*, pp. 178–80. For a description of similar treatment of the insane in colonial America, see Albert Deutsch, "The Mentally Ill in Colonial America," *Social Service Review* 10 (Dec. 1936): 606–22, esp. 614–17.

59. Webbs, *Poor Law Policy*, p. 49.

60. Ibid., p. 125.

61. Ibid., p. 125.

62. In 1871, with the general crackdown against outdoor relief and the strengthening of deterrence in the workhouses, authorities were allowed to detain the ablebodied pauper under some conditions; see Ibid., p. 244.

63. Ibid., p. 80. Two other groups could be detained—orphaned children and vagrants—but only for four hours.

64. Hodgkinson, *Origins*, pp. 183–84.

65. Scull's *Museums* analyzes and documents this struggle and the ultimate victory of the medical profession in laying claim to the treatment of insanity as part of its domain.

66. Foucault, *Madness*, p. 116; Deutsch, "Mentally Ill," p. 607.

67. Webbs, *Poor Law Policy*, pp. 223–34, citing the Lunacy Act of 1885; 53 Victoria, ch. 5.

68. Webbs, *Poor Law Policy*, pp. 50, 127–28, 227–28.

69. Webbs, *Poor Law Policy*, pp. 18 and 50.

70. Webbs, *Poor Law Policy*, p. 51.

71. Special Report of Poor Law Commissioners on the Further Amendment of the Poor Law, 1839, p. 47, cited in ibid., p. 53.

72. de Schweinitz, *England's Road*, pp. 140–41, 156.

73. Ibid., p. 156, citing First Annual Report of Local Government Board, 1871–72, p. 64.

74. Webbs, *Poor Law Policy*, pp. 150, 229–30.

75. de Schweinitz, *England's Road*, pp. 156–57; Webbs, *Poor Law Policy*, pp. 150–51.

76. Circular of 11 July 1896, cited in Webbs, *Poor Law Policy*, p. 231.

77. de Schweinitz, *England's Road*, pp. 160–61.

78. Sidney Webb and Beatrice Webb, *English Poor Law History, Part II: The Last Hundred Years*, 2 vols., (London: Longmans Green, 1929), 1:1042–43.

79. See Karl Polanyi, *The Great Transformation* (Boston: Beacon Press, 1944), esp. chs. 6, 7; de Schweinitz, *England's Road*, ch. 8.

80. Marc Blaug, "The Myth of the Old Poor Law and the Making of the New," *Journal of Economic History* 23 (June 1963): 151–84.

81. See especially Fraser, *Evolution*, pp. 33–41.

82. Thirsk (*Projects*) has explored the use of "projects" from about 1540 to 1700 as a means of employing the poor and thus providing for their subsistence and enhancing the national economy. These projects were new agricultural and manufacturing ventures, such as woad growing and knitted stocking production, which produced goods primarily for domestic consumption. Although such ventures were financed primarily with private capital, they were protected by the state with special privileges, especially patent rights; they were thus not strictly private-sector solutions to the problem of unemployment. In this connection, the workhouse might be

seen as another form of project in which financing was mostly public. Even here, the boundary between public and private was not hard and fast, however, as some workhouses contracted out their inmates to local employers.

83. See Garraty, *Unemployment*, pp. 111–18, for a discussion of the work of Denis Poulot in France, and Charles Booth in England, both of whom developed eight-part classifications of the unemployed.

84. Juan Luis Vives, *De subventione pauperum*, 1526, trans. Margaret Sherwood, cited in de Schweinitz, *England's Road*, p. 32.

85. Garraty, *Unemployment*, p. 51.

86. For the U.S., see Edward D. Berkowitz, "The American Disability System in Historical Perspective," in E. Berkowitz, ed. *Disability Policies and Government Programs* (New York: Praeger, 1979), pp. 23–24; I. S. Falk, *Security Against Sickness* (New York: Doubleday, 1936); and Roy Lubove, *The Struggle for Social Security* (Cambridge, Mass.: Harvard Univ. Press, 1968). For Britain, see de Schweinitz, *England's Road*, pp. 204–9. For Japan, see Howard Leichter, *A Comparative Approach to Policy Analysis* (Cambridge: Cambridge Univ. Press, 1979). These sources all indicate that policymakers either studied German documents or visited Germany to observe its insurance system. Another study suggests that the timing of social insurance legislation in different countries is better explained by a model of diffusion based on geographic, cultural and political proximity than by a model of domestic socioeconomic and political factors as predisposing conditions. See David Collier and Richard Messick, "Prerequisites versus Diffusion: Testing Alternative Explanations of Social Security Adoption," *American Political Science Review* 69 (1975): 1299–1315.

87. Ralf Dahrendorf, *Society and Democracy in Germany* (Garden City, N.J.: Doubleday, 1969), pp. 36–37.

88. Gustav Friedrich von Schmoller, *Die Soziale Frage: Klassenbildung, Arbeiterfrage, Klassenkampf* (Munich: Duncker and Humboldt, 1918), p. 414.

89. See. H. Rothfels, "Bismark's Social Policy and the Problem of State Socialism in Germany," *Sociological Review* 30, nos. 1, 3 (Jan. 1938); William Dawson, *Social Insurance in Germany, 1883–1911* (London: Scribner's, 1912).

90. Dawson, *Social Insurance*, p. 111.

91. Ibid.; Gaston V. Rimlinger, "Welfare Policy and Economic Development: A Comparative Historical Perspective," *Journal of Economic History* 26 (1966): 556–71.

92. Dawson, *Social Insurance*, p. 113.

93. Ibid., p. 112.

94. Florian Tennstedt, *Berufsunfähigkeit im Sozialrecht* (Frankfurt: Europaische Verlagsanstalt, 1972), p. 25. I rely heavily on Tennstedt's narrative and analysis in the following account.

95. Ibid.; emphasis added. I have used the terms "disabled" and

"disabled person" to translate the German *erwerbsunfahig* and *der Erwerbsunfahiger*.

96. Ibid., p. 28.

97. Hermann Molkenbuhr, quoted in Ibid.

98. Reichstag-Drucksache, 7. Legisl.-Per., IV. Session 1888/89, Nr. 10, s. 40, cited in Tennstedt, *Berufsunfähigkeit*, p. 26.

99. Rimlinger, *Welfare Policy*, pp. 117–19.

100. Tennstedt, *Berufsunfähigkeit*, esp. 124–34.

101. Rimlinger, *Welfare Policy*, pp. 117–19; Dawson, *Social Insurance*, pp. 124–25.

102. Called the Federal Insurance Office after 1946.

103. Tennstedt, *Berufsunfähigkeit*, p. 29.

104. *Invalidensversicherungsgesetz*, 13 July, 1899, cited in Ibid., p. 30; emphasis added.

105. Ibid.

106. RVA Revisionsentscheidung, 31 Oct., 1900, cited in Ibid., p. 31.

107. Ibid., pp. 32–35.

108. Erlass des Ministers. . ., 22 Dec., 1905, cited in ibid., p. 33.

109. Ibid., pp. 39–40.

110. Ibid., pp. 52–53.

111. Ibid., p. 50.

112. Ibid., p. 60.

113. Ibid., pp. 64–67. The name "transferability cross" was not Dersch's term; it only later came into common usage, but the concept had been fully articulated by Dersch and was in use by 1926.

114. Badischen LVA, 23 Dec. 1932, cited in Tennstedt, *Berufsunfähigkeit*, p. 43.

115. Ibid., p. 68.

116. See William Safran, *Veto Group Politics: The Case of Health Insurance Reform in West Germany* (San Francisco: Chandler, 1967) for an account of this reform.

117. Tennstedt, *Berufsunfähigkeit*, pp. 73–85.

118. Kurt Jantz and Hans Zweng, Kommentar zu den Gestzen zur Neuregelung des Rechts des Rentenversicherung der Arbeiter und der Rentenversicherung der Angestellten, Stuttgart, 1957, Anmerkung I 2a zu 1246 RVO; cited in Tennstedt, *Berufsunfähigkeit*, p. 78.

119. Ibid., p. 80.

120. The phrase used by the court was *wesentlich geringeres Ansehen geniessen in den Augen der Umwelt* (Ibid., p. 84).

121. Werner Weber, "Die Eigentumsgarantie (Art. 14GG) in der Rechtsprechung des Bundessozialgerichts," in *Rechtsschutz im Sozialrecht*, Köln and Berlin, 1965; cited in Ibid., p. 97.

122. For the general "welfare laggard" thesis see, e.g., Harold Wilensky, *The Welfare State and Equality* (Berkeley: Univ. of California Press, 1975);

and Phillips Cutright, "Political Structure Economic Development, and National Social Security Programs," *American Journal of Sociology* 70 (1965): 537–55. In 1972, the United States spent 5.75% of its GNP on social security; by contrast, Belgium, France, Germany, Luxembourg, Norway, Netherlands and Italy all spent in excess of 10%. The United Kingdom (5.40%), Switzerland (5.64%) and Denmark (3.45%) were the only European countries spending proportionately *less* than the U.S. Alan Peacock and Martin Ricketts, "The Growth of the Public Sector and Inflation," in Fred Hirsch and John Goldthorpe, eds., *The Political Economy of Inflation* (Cambridge, Mass.: Harvard Univ. Press, 1978), pp. 122–123.

123. In addition to the documents and articles cited in this chapter, I have relied heavily on two comprehensive histories of the disability insurance component of the Social Security program: George J. Goldsborough, Jr., William G. Tinsley and Arnold C. Sternberg, *The Social Security Administration: An Interdisciplinary Study of Disability Evaluation*, Part 1, *The Administrative Determination of Disability*, and Part 2, *The Judicial Concept of Disability Under the Social Security Act* (Washington, D.C.: George Washington University, 1963); and Martha Derthick, *Policymaking for Social Security* (Washington, D.C.: Brookings, 1979). The interpretation of the significance of the boundary issue is my own.

124. Derthick, "*Policymaking*" p. 23–27.

125. Ibid., pp. 24–25.

126. Ibid., ch. 4.

127. Ibid., ch. 15.

128. Edwin E. Witte. *The Development of the Social Security Act* (Madison: Univ. of Wisconsin Press, 1962).

129. Final Report of the Advisory Council on Social Security, 10 Dec. 1938; Senate Finance Comm., 76th Cong., 1st sess. 1939.

130. Proposed Changes in the Social Security Act, Report of the Social Security Board to the President and to the Congress of the United States, 30 Dec. 1938, H.R. Doc. 110, 76th Cong., 1st sess., 1939.

131. Ibid., pp. 7–8; cited in Goldsborough et al. "*SSA*," pt. 1, p. 42.

132. Edward Berkowitz, "Rehabilitation: The Federal Government's Response to Disability, 1935–1954," Ph.D. diss., Northwestern University, 1976), p. 49.

133. *Permanent and Total Disability Insurance*, a Report to Senate Committee on Finance from Advisory Council on Social Security, 80th Cong., 2d sess., 1948, S. Doc. 1621 (cited hereafter as 1948 Advisory Council Report).

134. See R. J. Myers, "Disability Benefit Provisions Under the Social Security Act—An Early Report," *Journal of the American Society of Charter Life Underwriters*, 16, no. 1 (Winter 1962): 5–12, and *Expansionism in Social Insurance* (London: Institute of Economic Affairs, 1970).

135. The House Ways and Means Committee said in a 1949 report: "Your committee, in considering appropriate definitions for a social insur-

ance disability program, has studied the precedents of commercial insurance policies and Government life insurance for veterans" (House Committee on Ways and Means, House Report No. 1300, on H.R. 6000, 81st Cong., 1st sess., 1949, p. 29). There was also a major report available in 1949: Dan Mays McGill, *An Analysis of Government Life Insurance* (Philadelphia: Huebner Foundation, Univ. of Pennsylvania Press, 1949).

136. *Social Security Amendments of 1955*, Hearings before Senate Committee on Finance, 84th Cong., 2d sess., on H.R. 7225; Part 2, pp. 446–47.

137. The definition of the professional man's clause is from John H. Miller, "History and Present Status of Non-cancellable Accident and Health Insurance," *Proceedings of the Casualty Actuarial Society* 21 (1934–35), p. 251. See also Bruce D. Mudgett, *The Total Disability Provision in American Life Insurance Contracts* (Philadelphia: American Academy of Political and Social Sciences, 1915), p. 48. Both cited in Goldsborough et al., "*SSA*," pt. 1, p. 472.

138. Goldsborough, et al., "*SSA*," pt. 1, p. 473.

139. See Douglas Anderson, *Regulatory Politics and Electric Utilities* (Boston, Mass.: Auburn House 1981). His interpretation of the state utility regulation makes the same argument for electric utilities.

140. Kenneth W. Herrick, *Total Disability Provisions in Life Insurance Contracts* (Philadelphia: Huebner Foundation, Univ. of Pennsylvania, 1956), 23; cited in Goldsborough et al., "*SSA*," pt. 1, p. 474.

141. Goldsborough et al., "*SSA*," pt. 1, pp. 480–81.

142. Marshall v. Metropolitan Life Insurance Company, 164 So. 441 (1935), cited in Goldsborough et al., "*SSA*," pt. 1, p. 482.

143. Goldsborough et al., "*SSA*," pt. 1, pp. 474, 468.

144. Ibid., pp. 291–92.

145. Regulation No. 11 of the Bureau of War Risk Insurance, 9 March 1918, cited in Goldsborough et al., "*SSA*," pt. 1, p. 320.

146. Goldsborough et al., "*SSA*," pt. 1, pp. 324–27.

147. E. Berkowitz, "Rehabilitation," pp. 47, 52–53.

148. Ibid., p. 53.

149. 1948 Advisory Council Report, pp. 18–19; Berkowitz, "American Disability System," p. 55.

150. See also Gerald S. Parker, "Quality in Disability Insurance," *Journal of the American Society of Chartered Life Underwriters* 16, no. 1 (Winter 1962): 38–56; Parker argues that the occupational disability clause was particularly abused during the Depression.

151. 1948 Advisory Council Report, pp. 2, 12.

152. Dan Mays McGill, *Government Life Insurance*, p. 103, cited in Goldsborough et al., "*SSA*," pt. 1, p. 323–24.

153. Social Security Administration, Bureau of Old Age and Survivors, 1954 Report, cited in Goldsborough et al., "*SSA*," pt. 2, ch. 1, p. 5.

154. Martha Derthick, *Policymaking*, p. 314. Derthick finds this interpretation of trickery too strong (personal correspondence with author, Au-

gust 1983). As she points out, the Eisenhower Administration eventually came around to support the freeze, and after 1954 the Democrats had a majority in Congress, so trickery wasn't necessary. Nevertheless, I think many statements of the political actors show that they saw themselves as either tricking or being tricked.

155. Quoted in testimony of Dr. R. L. Sensenich, Senate Finance Committee, hearings on H.R. 6000, 81st Cong., 2d sess., 1949, Sen. Rept. 1669 (hereafter cited as Senate Finance Committee 1949), p. 1314. See also Derthick, *Policymaking*, pp. 301–3; Berkowitz, "Rehabilitation," p. 228; E. Berkowitz, "American Disability System," pp. 55–57, 60–65; and Irving Howards, Henry P. Brehm and Saad Z. Nagi, *Disability: From Social Problem to Federal Program* (New York: Praeger, 1980), p. 60.

156. E. Berkowitz, "Rehabilitation," p. 227.

157. H.R. 1698, 83rd Cong., 2d sess., 1954, pp. 23–24; Derthick, *Policymaking*, p. 302.

158. Interview with Wilbur J. Cohen by David G. McComb for the Lyndon Baines Johnson Library, 1968; cited in Derthick, *Policymaking*, p. 26. Wilbur Cohen served for many years in the Social Security Administration, first as special assistant to its head (Arthur Altmeyer) and then as head of the Division of Research and Statistics. He resigned his position in 1956, presumably not wanting to work for a Republican administration whose views on Social Security he could not uphold, but he continued to champion development of the program from his academic post in Ann Arbor. Thus, he was an insider when the disability freeze was passed and an outsider when cash benefits were added.

159. Derthick, *Policymaking*, p. 305.

160. 1948 Advisory Council Report, p. 6; emphasis added.

161. The 1938 Advisory Council defined a disabled person as one "who is afflicted with a physical impairment which continuously renders it impossible for the disabled person to engage in any gainful employment and which is founded upon conditions which render it reasonably certain that the person will continue to be disabled throughout the remainder of his life" (E. Berkowitz, "Rehabilitation," p. 49).

162. 1948 Advisory Council Report, p. 5.

163. Ibid., p. 8.

164. Senate Finance Committee 1949, Part 2, p. 508; emphasis added.

165. Statement of Dr. Leo Price in Senate Finance Committee hearings on H.R. 7225 (Social Security Amendments of 1955), p. 517, 84th Cong. 2d sess., 1956 (cited hereafter as Senate Finance Hearings 1956).

166. Dr. Alan Emanual, Ibid., p. 821.

167. In hundreds of pages of testimony, the physicians quoted above were the only ones who believed that medical determination was possible.

168. Dr. Cyrus Anderson, Senate Finance Hearings 1956, p. 358.

169. Dr. Lewis B. Flinn, Senate Finance Hearings 1955, p. 786.

170. Statement of Dr. R. B. Robbins, a former vice president of the

AMA and former president of the American Academy of General Practice, Senate Finance Hearings 1956, p. 354. Other expressions of the reservoir theory are to be found in the testimony of Dr. Philip S. Hench, a rheumatism specialist (p. 395) and Dr. Gerald D. Dorman (pp. 815–16), Senate Finance Hearings 1956.

171. Dr. Robert S. Green, president of National Medical Veterans Society, Senate Finance Hearings 1956, p. 360.

172. Interchange between Senator Alben Barkley and Dr. J. W. Chambers, Senate Finance Hearings 1955, pp. 365–66, 369.

173. Senator Barkley, Senate Finance Hearings 1956, p. 783.

174. Interchange between Senator Russell B. Long and Dr. Lewis B. Flinn, Senate Finance Hearings 1956, pp. 792–96.

175. Senator Barkley, Senate Finance Hearings 1956, p. 801.

176. Report of House Ways and Means Committee on Social Security Amendments of 1954 (H.R. 9366), 83rd Cong. 2d sess., H. Report 1698 (1954) p. 23; emphasis added.

177. U.S. Department of Health, Education and Welfare, Social Security Administration, Bureau of Old Age Survivors Insurance, OASI-29f, October 1958, p. 1; emphasis added. Cited in Goldsborough, et al., "*SSA*," pt. 1, p. 93.

178. Goldsborough, et al., "*SSA*," pt. 1, pp. 47–49.

179. House Ways and Means Committee, Subcommittee on the Administration of Social Security Laws, Hearings on Social Security Amendments of 1960 ("Harrison Subcommittee Report"), 11 March 1960, 86th Cong. 2d sess.; cited in Goldsborough, et al., "*SSA*," pt. 1, p. 152.

180. See Howards, Brehm, and Nagi, *Disability*; Berkowitz, Johnson, and Murphy, *Public Policy*.

181. Goldsborough, et al., "*SSA*," pt. 1, p. 48 (the quotation is from Goldsborough, not the Bureau).

182. Administration of the SSDI program, House Ways and Means Committee, Subcommittee on the Administration of the Social Security Laws, 86th Cong., 1st sess. (1959), p. 28, cited in Goldsborough, et al., "*SSA*," pt. 1, pp. 88–89.

183. "Harrison Subcommittee Report," 1960, cited in House Ways and Means Committee staff report on the Disability Insurance Program, July 1974, p. 45.)

184. See House Ways and Means Committee, Staff Report, *Disability Insurance Program* July 1974, p. 46 (cited hereafter as Ways and Means, *Disability Insurance Program* 1974) for a summary. Judicial expansion of the definition of disability is discussed in more detail in ch. 5.

185. Social Security Act, sec. 223(d)(2)(A) (1967).

186. Ways and Means, *Disability Insurance Program* 1974, p. 117.

187. House Ways and Means Committee, Rept. on H.R. 12080 (H.R. No. 544), 90th Cong., 2d sess. 1967, p. 30.

188. Social Security Act, sec. 223 (d)(3) (1967).

189. Mathews v. Eldrige, 44 U.S.L.W. 4224 (24 Feb. 1976). Quotation is from p. 4232 and the phrase "routine, standard, and unbiased" is in turn a quotation from Richardson v. Perales 307 U.S. 269 (1971).

190. This debate is the focus of E. Berkowitz's 1976 dissertation (see n. 132).

191. See testimony of Dr. R. L. Sensenich, Senate Finance Committee 1949, pp. 1315–16. Sensenich testified on behalf of the Board of Trustees of the AMA. The same argument was repeated ad infinitum by physicians in later testimony.

Chapter 3

1. J. K. Crellin, "The Dawn of the Germ Theory: Particles, Infection and Biology," in F. L. N. Poynter, ed., *Medicine and Society in the 1860s* (London: Wellcome Institute of the History of Medicine, 1968), pp. 57–76.

2. See Stanley Reiser, *Medicine and the Reign of Technology* (Cambridge: Cambridge Univ. Press, 1978), pp. 82–90.

3. Robert Koch, "The Etiology of Tuberculosis," in *Recent Essays by Various Authors on Bacteria in Relation to Disease*, ed. W. Watson Cheyne (London: New Sydenham Society, 1886), pp. 70–73; cited in Reiser, *Medicine*, p. 85.

4. See René Dubos, *Mirage of Health* (New York: Harper and Row, 1959), pp. 151–57.

5. Ibid., pp. 71–76.

6. See Asa Briggs, "Cholera and Society in the Nineteenth Century," *Past and Present* 19 (1961): 76–96; Charles Rosenberg, *The Cholera Years* (Chicago: Univ. of Chicago Press, 1962).

7. Rosenberg, *Cholera Years*, p. 120.

8. Briggs, "Cholera and Society," p. 85.

9. Ibid., pp. 77–78, 87–90; Crellin; "Germ Theory"; Phyllis Allen Richmond, "American Attitudes toward the Germ Theory of Disease," *Journal of the History of Medicine* 9 (1954): 428–54; Paul Starr, *The Social Transformation of American Medicine* (New York: Basic Books, 1982), pp. 189–97.

10. For this description of Stiles and the history of hookworm (though not for my interpretation of its political meaning), I rely on Mark Sullivan, *Our Times* vol. 3 (New York: Scribner, 1930), pp. 290–32; and John Ettling, *The Germ of Laziness: Rockefeller Philanthropy and Public Health in the New South* (Cambridge, Mass.: Harvard Univ. Press, 1981).

11. Reiser, *Medicine*, p. 89.

12. Hodgkinson, *Origins*, pp. 15–16.

13. Ibid., pp. 28–31, 61.

14. Diseases Prevention Act, 1883, 46 and 47 Victoria, Ch. 35.

15. Fraser, *Evolution*, pp. 82–87.

16. Reiser, *Medicine*, p. 89; Richmond, "American Attitudes," p. 452; and Dubos, *Mirage*, pp. 151–65.

17. Phillips Cutright, "Political Structure, Economic Development, and National Social Security Programs," *American Journal of Sociology* 70 (1965): 532–50.

18. For Germany, see Gaston V. Rimlinger, *Welfare Policy and Industrialization in Europe, America and Russia* (New York: Wiley, 1971), ch. 4. For Britain, see David G. Hanes, *The First British Workmen's Compensation Act, 1897* (New Haven, Conn.: Yale Univ. Press, 1968). For the United States, see Lawrence Friedman and Jack Ladinsky, "Social Change and the Law of Industrial Accidents," *Columbia Law Review* 67 (1967): 50–82; Lubove, *Struggle*, ch. 3; James Weinstein, *The Corporate Ideal and the Liberal State: 1900–1918* (Boston: Beacon Press, 1968).

19. In English and American common law, three of the most significant hurdles were the "fellow servant rule" (the employer was not liable if a fellow employee of the plaintiff was even partially responsible for the injury); "assumption of risk" (in dangerous occupations, the plaintiff was assumed to have taken the risk of accident knowingly and voluntarily, and therefore the employer could not be held liable); and "contributory negligence" (if the worker's negligence was at all a contributing factor to the accident, the employer was not held liable).

20. Ferd C. Schwedtman and James A. Emery, *Accident Prevention and Relief* (New York: Published for the National Association of Manufacturers 1911), p. 6. Schwedtman was president of the National Association of Manufacturers, probably the strongest proponent of insurance in the United States.

21. Tiller v. Atlantic Coast Line Railroad, 318 U.S. 54, 58–59 (1943), cited in Friedman and Ladinsky, "Industrial Accidents," p. 58.

22. See esp. Lubove, *Struggle*, ch. 3.

23. See Friedman and Ladinsky, "Industrial Accidents"; Weinstein, *Corporate Ideal*, chs. 1–2.

24. Alexis De Tocqueville, "Memoir on Pauperism," delivered to Royal Academic Society of Cherbourg, 1835; in Seymour Drescher, ed. and trans., *Tocqueville and Beaumont on Social Reform* (New York: Harper and Row, 1968), pp. 1–27. Reprinted in *Public Interest* 70 (Winter 1983): 102–20; quotation is from pp. 111–12.

25. de Schweinitz, *England's Road*, pp. 7–8.

26. A. L. Beier, "Vagrants," p. 14.

27. Vives, *De subventione pauperum*, p. 31.

28. Baron [Kaspar] von Voght, *Account of the Management of the Poor in Hamburg between the Years 1777 and 1794* (1796), cited in de Schweinitz, *England's Road*, p. 92; emphasis in original.

29. Cited in Donzelot, *Policing*, pp. 68–69.

30. This description is taken from ibid., pp. 121–24, which in turn is based on three French treatises about welfare eligibility: "L'Enquete sociale," *Revue philanthropique* (1920), pp. 363ff; *Services auxiliares des tribunaux pour enfants*, (1931); and Rene Luaire, *Le role de l'initiative privée dans l'assistance publique* (1934).

31. Donzelot, *Policing*, p. 124.

32. "*Report from His Majesty's Commissioners*," p. 271, cited in de Schweinitz, *England's Road*, p. 123; emphasis in original.

33. Webbs, *Poor Law Policy*, p. 157; de Schweinitz, *England's Road*, p. 135.

34. Webbs, *Poor Law Policy*, p. 160; the quotation is from Mr. Longly. Note the assumption that each applicant makes a rational calculus, doing a cost-benefit analysis on the decision to seek relief!

35. Heclo, *Modern Social Politics*, pp. 79–81.

36. For a review of this history, see Joseph A. Page and Mary-Win O'Brien, *Bitter Wages* (New York: Grossman, 1973). For an early refutation of the "workers are careless" argument, see Crystal Eastman, *Work Accidents and the Law* (New York: Russell Sage Foundation, 1910).

37. The following account of the development of diagnostic technique in the nineteenth century is based primarily on Stanley Reiser, *Medicine*.

38. René Laënnec, *Diseases of the Chest* (1819), xvii, cited in Reiser, *Medicine*, p. 31.

39. Ibid.

40. Ibid., p. 38; emphasis added.

41. Ibid., pp. 25, 30.

42. Lester King, *Medical Thinking* (Princeton, N.J.: Princeton Univ. Press, 1982), pp. 82–83.

43. Hasket Derby, "The Relations of the Ophthalmoscope to Legal Medicine," *Boston Medical and Surgical Journal* 66 (1862): 525–27, cited in Reiser, *Medicine*, p. 47.

44. Reiser, *Medicine*, p. 93.

45. See Ibid., pp. 59–62.

46. The song is "Turning Japanese," by David Fenton, published by Glenwood Music Corporation, ASCAP, 1979. Recorded by The Vapors, on the album "New Clear Days," (Liberty Records, Hollywood, California, 1980.)

47. 1948 Advisory Council Report, p. 8.

48. Ernest Tarboureich, *La cité future: Essai d'une Utopie Scientifique* (Paris: P. V. Stock, 1902).

49. This distinction originated in the AMA Guides (see n. 57). It occurs so frequently in the medical and legal literature on disability evaluation that any citations can only be illustrative. See, for example, Henry Kessler, *Disability—Determination and Evaluation* (Philadelphia: Lea and Febiger, 1970), p. 184; "Report of the Committee on Stress, Strain and Heart Disease of the American Heart Association," *Circulation* 55 (May 1977): 825; Gary Epler, Fay Saber, and Edward Gaensler, "Determination of Severe Impairment (Disability) in Interstitial Lung Disease," *American Review of Respiratory Disease* 121 (1980), p. 647. The distinction has now been enshrined in common law: see Smith v. Industrial Commission, 460 P. 2d 1198 (Ariz. 1976),

where the Arizona Supreme Court adopted the definitions of "permanent impairment" and "permanent disability" found in the AMA Guides.

50. In the literature, the terms "anatomical," "biological," and "pathological" are often used, but I will use the word "physiological" to encompass them all.

51. See Lawrence D. Haber, "Identifying the Disabled: Concepts and Methods in the Measurement of Disability," *Social Security Bulletin* 30 (Dec. 1967): 17–35; Saad Nagi, *Disability and Rehabilitation: Legal, Clinical and Self-Concepts and Measurement* (Columbus: Ohio State Univ. Press, 1969); Earl D. McBride, *Disability Evaluation* (Philadelphia: Lippincott, 1963); Kessler, *Disability*, 1970.

52. Such surveys are done by the National Center for Health Statistics, which conducts the Health Interview Survey and provides annual data on the proportion of the population experiencing so-called "bed-disability days." Since 1966, the Social Security Administration has been conducting a disability survey that provides estimates of the proportion of people who are severely and moderately disabled. Again, these studies are based on answers to interview questions in which people are asked simply to classify themselves as severely, moderately, or not at all disabled.

53. See Marvin Sussman, ed., *Sociology and Rehabilitation* (Washington, D.C: American Sociological Association, 1966), p. 68.

54. Berkowitz, "American Disability System," pp. 44–45.

55. Saad Nagi makes a similar distinction between "impairment schedules" and "standards," both of which are based on the concept of impairment. See his testimony, "Criteria and Decisionmaking Structure for Disability Evaluation: Policy and Program Issues and Options," in Ways and Means, *Disability Insurance Program* 1976, p. 318. The SSA guidelines for disability determination are administrative regulations No. 4, Subpart P, 20 Code of Federal Regulations 404; No. 16, Subpart I, 20 Code of Federal Regulations 416. These are published as a separate booklet, called "Rules for Determining Disability and Blindness," U.S. Dept. of Health and Human Services, Social Security Administration, Office of Operational Policy and Procedures, Washington, D.C. June 1981 SSA Pub. No. 64–014.

56. Kessler, *Disability*, pp. 184–94.

57. American Medical Association, Committee on Medical Rating of Physical Impairments, "Guides to the Evaluation of Permanent Impairment," *Journal of the American Medical Association*: "The Extremities and Back," 15 Feb. 1958; "The Visual System," 27 Sept. 1958; "The Cardiovascular System," 5 March 1960; "Ear, Nose, Throat and Related Structures," 19 Aug. 1961; "The Central Nervous System," 6 July 1963; "The Digestive System," 13 April 1964; "The Peripheral Spinal Nerves," 13 July 1964; "The Respiratory System," 22 Nov. 1965; "The Endocrine System," 10 Oct. 1966; "Mental Illness," 19 Dec. 1966; "The Reproductive and Urinary System," 13 Nov. 1967; "The Skin," 5 Jan. 1970; "The Hematopoietic System,"

24 Aug. 1970 (cited hereafter as AMA Guides with specific title). The committee is often called the "McKeown Committee," after its head, Dr. Raymond M. McKeown.

58. Kessler, *Disability*, 1970, pp. 41–45 and Preface. Kessler's original scheme for disability evaluation of work accidents is *Accidental Injuries* (Philadelphia: Lea and Febiger, 1931).

59. Kessler, 1970, p. 44 (emphasis added).

60. William Roemmich, "Memorandum," Ways and Means, *Disability Insurance Program* 1976, pp. 161–62.

61. Dr. R. L. Sensenich's, testimony for the AMA Board of Trustees, U.S. Congress, Senate Finance Committee 1949, pp. 1317–18.

62. Senate Finance Hearings 1956, pp. 355–59.

63. Kessler, *Disability*, pp. 208–9.

64. AMA Guides, "The Cardiovascular System," p. 1049.

65. Ibid.

66. Ibid., p. 1050.

67. Apparently, the committee began with an integer scale, then reduced it to a categorical scale but maintained the integer scale labels. The reliance on categories may be a reflection of the fact that clinicians do not think in terms of continua but rather in terms of discrete pathological entities. I am indebted to Keith Lind, J.D. (personal communication) for this point.

68. AMA Guides, "The Cardiovascular System," p. 1052.

69. Ibid., p. 1060.

70. Ibid., p. 1050. The principle for combination was originally developed by Kessler, *Accidental Injuries*, in his evaluation scheme.

71. Kessler, *Disability*, p. 183.

72. Ibid., pp. 227–28. This quotation is from his critique of the Veterans Administration disability rating schedule, but the context and remainder of his book make it clear that he means these comments to apply to all such rating schedules.

73. See for example, Terra Ziporyn, "Disability Evaluation: A Fledgling Science," *Journal of the American Medical Association* 250, no. 7 (19 Aug. 1983): 873–74, 879–80, which describes the work of several research institutes and organizations dedicated to the objective determination of disability.

74. See Michael Lipsky, *Street Level Bureaucracy* (New York: Russell Sage Foundation, 1981).

Chapter 4

1. Goldsborough, et al., "SSA," pt. 1, p. 95; Dr. Herbert Blumenfeld, Chief Medical Consultant, Office of Disability, Social Security Administration, interview with author Dec. 1983, Baltimore, Md. The Medical Advisory Committee was effectively disbanded in 1969 as part of a general

move by the Nixon administration to eliminate advisory committees and strengthen the control of elected officials over policymaking. Although the committee was never officially dissolved, the administration never approved new nominations, so it just languished without members.

2. Ways and Means, *Disability Insurance Program*, 1976, p. 168; this bit of information is from SSA's Draft Regulations on Nonmedical Factors, 1976.

3. See Reiser, *Medicine*, p. 1, for a nineteenth-century change in this meaning; Michel Foucault, *The Birth of the Clinic*; Alvan Weinstein, *Clinical Judgment* (Baltimore: Williams and Wilkins, 1967), pp. 131–32, for modern usage; King, *Medical Thinking*, pp. 73–89, for a view that rejects the subjective/objective distinction.

4. Ways and Means, *Disability Insurance Program* 1976, pp. 156–57. Roemmich's statement appears in a memorandum he wrote to the committee at its request.

5. Code of Federal Regulations 404.1510(a), 22 June 1961, cited in Goldsborough, et al., "SSA," pt. 2, ch. 8, p. 6; emphasis added.

6. Report and Recommendations of the Medical Advisory Committee on the Administration of the OASI Disability Provisions, Dept. of Health, Education and Welfare, Social Security Administration (Baltimore, Md., Nov. 1960), p. 13, cited in Goldsborough, et al., "*SSA*," pt. 1, p. 101; see also the testimony of William Roemmich in Ways and Means, *Disability Insurance Program* 1976, p. 162.

7. Code of Federal Regulations, Title 20, Chapter 3, Part 404. The Harrison Subcommittee Report (p. 17) asserted that fairness required that claimants and their representatives should know the standards used to make determinations, and urged the Social Security Administration to make its standards public. Goldsborough et al. ("*SSA*," pt. 1, pp. 104–5) surveyed 300 lawyers about this practice of secrecy. "Only 33" indicated that "the absence of published medical standards greatly hindered or impeded their ability to properly represent their clients." However, since only 100 responses were received, the complaint was evidently fairly serious.

8. This information is from Goldsborough, et al., "*SSA*," pt. 1, pp. 103–4; they compared the published regulations and the manual and found quantitative requirements for presumptions of disability in the latter only, for musculoskeletal system, vision and hearing, and the respiratory system.

9. Code of Federal Regulations 404.1517.

10. Goldsborough, et al., "*SSA*," pt. 1, pp. 93–94, reported in 1963 that of 300 physicians employed by state agencies, 95% were in private practice and worked only part time for the agencies; of the 102 physicians employed by the federal SSA Disability Division, 85% were in private practice or teaching. In 1984, about 80% of the physicians employed by the state disability determination agencies were part-time employees (1,060 part-time and 193 full-time), and about 90% of those employed by the Medical Consultant Staff of the Social Security Administration were part-time (113 part-time, 11 full-time). 1984 figures are from Ms. Ann Dowling, Office of

Disability, Professional Relations Staff, Social Security Administration, Baltimore, Md. (personal correspondence, May 1984).

11. General Accounting Office, "Controls over Medical Examinations Necessary for the Social Security Administration to Better Determine Disability," HRD 79–119, Washington, D.C., 9 Oct. 1979, p. 9.

12. Ibid., p. 6. The report gave no actual data on denial rates.

13. Mr. Sandy Crank, testimony before the House of Representatives, Committee on Ways and Means, Subcommittee on Social Security and Subcommittee on Oversight, 97th Cong., 1st Sess., Sept. 18, 1981, "Volume Providers of Medical Examinations for the Social Security Disability Program," Serial 97–27, p. 60 (Cited hereafter as Ways and Means, Volume Providers, 1981). Mr. Crank gave the following figures as evidence:

Fiscal Year	Denial Rate	Consultative Exam Rate
1980	64.5	34.6
1979	61.9	33.2
1978	59.0	31.3
1977	54.8	28.0
1976	52.2	23.4

Obviously, the simultaneity of two trends does not mean one necessarily causes the other. More likely, the increases in both the consultative exams and denial rate during the same period were the result of organizational policy to be more stringent.

14. James B. Cardwell, Commissioner of Social Security, information submitted to Ways and Means, *Disability Insurance Program* 1976, p. 297.

15. The figure for 1975 is from GAO, "Controls over Medical Examinations," p. 6; the 1980 figure is from the Crank testimony cited in n. 13. Figures for 1961 through 1973 are given in Ways and Means, *Disability Insurance Program* 1974, pp. 154–62.

16. See testimony of heads of the Pennsylvania and Tennesee disability determination units, Ways and Means, Volume Providers 1981.

17. General Accounting Office, "The Social Security Administration Should Provide More Management and Leadership in Determining Who Is Eligible for Disability Benefits," HRD-76–105, Washington, D.C., 17 Aug. 1976.

18. See General Accounting Office, "The Social Security Administration Needs to Improve Its Disability Claims Process," HRD 78–40, Washington, D.C., 16 Feb. 1978, and "A Plan for Improving the Disability Determination Process by Bringing It under Complete Federal Management and Control Should Be Developed," HRD 78–146, Washington, D.C., 31 Aug. 1978.

19. GAO, "Controls over Medical Examinations."

20. See testimony of Sandy Crank, in Ways and Means, Volume Pro-

viders 1981, pp. 9–12. The Social Security Administration's standards appear in the same volume (pp. 78–79).

21. See Exhibit 2 attached to the testimony of Herbert Brown, Director of Disability Determination in Nashville, Tenn., in Ways and Means, Volume Providers 1981.

22. 1948 Advisory Council Report, pp. 4–5.

23. "Disability benefits should be withheld if a disabled person refuses without reasonable cause to accept rehabilitation services" (1948 Advisory Council Report, p. 8).

24. H.R. 1698, 83rd Cong. 2d sess. (1954), pp. 23–24; cited in Ways and Means, *Disability Insurance Program* 1974, p. 111.

25. This is the thrust of Edward Berkowitz's interpretation of the legislative history of disability insurance "American Disability System," esp. 55–66.

26. *Congressional Record*, 102, Part 10, 84th Cong., 2d sess. July 1956, pp. 13039–40.

27. Ibid., p. 13039.

28. Code of Federal Regulations, 404.1530.

29. Lance Liebman, "The Definition of Disability in Social Security and Supplemental Security Income: Drawing the Bounds of Social Welfare Estates," *Harvard Law Review* 89 (March, 1976), p. 862 (emphasis added). Dr. Herbert Blumenfeld, current Chief Medical Consultant, says the program has never enforced the treatment requirements; the Medical Staff "made a decision not to take adverse action on the basis of 'willful failure to follow' prescribed treatment." He sees the treatment requirements as a symbolic "stick" (interview with author, Dec. 1983, Baltimore, Md.).

30. Code of Federal Regulations 404.1509.

31. Code of Federal Regulations 404.1588. Reexamination is used much more commonly in temporary disability programs, which pay cash benefits in lieu of wages during short periods of sickness, and use several mechanisms to reduce malingering. One is the "home visit," reminiscent of Gerando's home investigations (ch. 2), in which an official visits sick people to find out whether they are really at home, in bed, sick. Officials in some systems (including the Swedish and French sickness insurance programs) simply visit a random sample of claimants; in others (for example, in the United Kingdom) they visit those whose claims are suspicious, either because the symptoms are trivial or because claims have been made frequently (Copeland, "Defining Disability," p. 13). In West Germany, beneficiaries may be required to undergo a reexamination by a staff doctor. In the Chinese welfare system, workers on sick leave are often visited by teams of coworkers, called "comfort missions," whose explicit purpose is to encourage sick people to go back to work. (John Dixon, *The Chinese Welfare System* [New York: Praeger, 1981], pp. 283–84).

Presumably, such methods are unnecessary in the case of *permanent disability*, because the certification process has determined a definitive, objective impairment. But that presumption may be changing with recent publicity about abuses. Particularly in public employee pension programs, there have been numerous revelations of workers certified as disabled showing up as winners in athletic tournaments or holding down jobs involving physical labor. See, e.g., Tom Nicholson, "The Great Postal Sting," *Newsweek*, 27 Feb. 1978, pp. 65, 69; Tom Ashbrook, "Disabling Injuries: A Question of Proof," Boston *Globe*, 23 April 1983, pp. 1, 18. The latter article is one of a series that appeared in the *Globe* in April and May 1983, investigating the pension system for state and municipal employees.

32. See William Roemmich's testimony in Ways and Means, *Disability Insurance Program* 1976, pp. 155–60.

33. Memorandum from the Director, BOASI, to SSA Commission, 17 Jan. 1955, cited in Goldsborough, et al., "*SSA*," pt. 1, p. 95; emphasis added.

34. William Roemmich, testimony in Ways and Means, *Disability Insurance Program*, 1976, p. 156. "Sets" emphasized in original; other emphasis added.

35. See Harold Sackman, *Delphi Critique: Expert Opinion, Forecasting and Group Process* (Lexington, Mass.: Lexington Books, 1975); and Harold A. Linstone and Murray Turoff, eds., *The Delphi Method: Techniques and Applications* (Reading, Mass.: Addison-Wesley, 1975).

36. The review of studies of diagnostic error presented in this section is based on Reiser, *Medicine*, pp. 183–95; and the specific studies cited are described therein.

37. Cited in Ibid., p. 185.

38. Cited in Ibid., p. 186, n. 25.

39. Ibid., pp. 188–90.

40. Cited in Ibid., p. 190.

41. Lorrin Koran, "The Reliability of Clinical Methods, Data and Judgments," *New England Journal of Medicine* 293 (1975): 700.

42. See William Roemmich, memorandum in Ways and Means, *Disability Insurance Program* 1976, pp. 155–60.

43. Reiser, *Medicine*, p. 183.

44. Dr. Gary Epler, statement at Conference on "Medical Determinations in Workers' Compensation" sponsored by American Society of Law and Medicine, December 3–4, 1981, author's notes, Cambridge, Mass. (Cited hereafter as "ASLM Conference").

45. A. L. Cochrane, P. J. Chapman, and P. D. Oldham, "Observers' Error in Taking Medical Histories," *Lancet* 1 (1951): 1007–9, cited in Reiser, *Medicine*, p. 191.

46. Coates, J. E., "Assessment of Disablement due to Impaired Respiratory Function." *Bulletin Physiopathologique Respiratoire* (Nancy, France) 11 (1975): 210–17; G. Epler, F. Saber, and E. Gaensler, "Determination of Severe Impairment [Disability] in Interstitial Lung Disease," *American Review of Respiratory Disease* 121 (1980): 647–59.

47. Veterans Administration, Schedule for Rating Disability, Sept. 1975;

cited in Epler, Saber, and Gaensler, "Severe Impairment," p. 652.

48. Gary Epler, "Evaluation of Pulmonary Disability," American College of Chest Physicians, Continuing Education Series, vol. 3 (Park Ridge, Ill., n.d.).

49. Ibid.

50. Statement of Dr. Edward Gaensler, at "ASLM conference," author's notes.

51. See Social Security Regulations: Rules for Determining Disability and Blindness, Department of Health and Human Services, Social Security Administration, Office of Operational Policy and Procedures, June 1981, p. 58.

52. In the Forced Expiratory Volume (FEV_1) test, a patient inhales and then exhales (but with maximum effort), and the volume of air exhaled in one second is measured. In Forced Vital Capacity (FVC), the patient inhales and exhales, and the total volume exhaled as well as time for complete exhalation, are measured. In the Maximal Voluntary Ventilation (MVV) test, the patient takes several breaths and the maximal volume per minute is measured. Single Breath Diffusing Capacity, a measure of the diffusion of oxygen to the blood, has the person inhale and exhale carbon dioxide, and measures the difference in the volume inhaled and exhaled. All of these measures are "effort dependent," and to some extent, "technician dependent," in the sense that the ability of the technician to encourage the patient to make a maximum effort influences the test results. Pulmonary specialists have developed machines to measure lung capacity without being sensitive to patient effort, such as the body plethysmograph (a full body chamber), but the SSA regulations still use the standard older effort dependent pulmonary function tests as criteria for disability.

53. See Epler, Saber, and Gaensler, "Severe Impairment," pp. 24–25, for excellent discussion.

54. Nagi, *Disability and Rehabilitation*, Table 31, p. 115.

55. GAO, "Management and Leadership."

56. Sal Gallicchio and Barry Bye, "Consistency of Initial Disability Decision among and within States," Dept. of Health, Education and Welfare, Social Security Administration, SSA Publication No. 13–11869, Staff Paper No. 39, March 1981.

57. See both the GAO report and SSA report, cited in nn. 56, 57; see also Commissioner James B. Cardwell's statement in Ways and Means, *Disability Insurance Program* 1976, pp. 296–98.

58. William Roemmich, "Determination, Evaluation, and Rating of Disabilities under the Social Security System," *Industrial Medicine and Surgery* 30, no. 2 (Feb. 1961), p. 62.

59. See Goldsborough, et al., "*SSA*," pt. 2, ch. 8, p. 16.

60. Roscoe N. Gray, *Attorney's Textbook of Medicine* (New York, M. Bender, 1963) cited in Goldsborough, et al., "*SSA*," pt. 2, p. 11.

61. Cyril M. MacBryde, *Signs and Symptoms* (Philadelphia: Lippincott,

1952), pp. 10–11; cited in Goldsborough, et al., "*SSA*," pt. 2, ch. 8, p. 11.

62. See Donald L. Newman, "Specific Tests," an unpublished list of sixteen tests for lower back injury distributed at "ASLM Conference"; Hugo Keim, and W. H. Kirkaldy-Willis, "Low Back Pain," *CIBA Clinical Symposia* 32, no. 6 (1980); and Jack Bleich, *Back Pain Malingering: Legal and Medical Aspects* (Atlanta: American Health Consultants, Inc., 1983), p. 12.

63. Willard I. Nesson and Packard Thurber, Jr., *The Evaluation of Subjective Complaints in Relation to Disability Claims*, cited in Goldsborough, et al., "*SSA*," pt. 2, ch. 8, p. 16.

64. Boyce Rensberger, "Heat 'Pictures' of Pain Expected to Aid Sufferers, Detect Fakers," *New York Times*, Oct. 21, 1980, p. C3.

65. Ziporyn, "Disability Evaluation."

66. Lewis V. Flemming, 176 F. Supp. 872, ca. 1960; cited in Goldsborough, et al., "*SSA*," pt. 2, ch. 8, p. 25.

67. Sampson v. Flemming, 189 F. Supp. 725 (D. Kan. 1960), cited in Goldsborough, et al., "*SSA*," pt. 2, ch. 6, pp. 23–24; emphasis added.

68. Cantrell v. Ribicoff, 206 F. Supp. 436 (1962) cited in Goldsborough, et al., "*SSA*," ch. 8, p. 33

69. Page v. Calebrezzi, 311 F.2nd 757 (1963), cited in Goldsborough, et al., "*SSA*," pt. 2, ch. 8, p. 34.

70. Theberge v. United States, 87 F.2d. 697 (1937), cited in Goldsborough, et al., "*SSA*," pt. 2. ch. 8, p. 20.

71. Butler v. Flemming, 288 F.2d 591. (1961), cited in Goldsborough, et al., "*SSA*," pt. 2, ch. 8, p. 29.

Chapter 5

1. See Katheryn Allen, "First Findings of the 1972 Survey of the Disabled: General Characteristics," *Social Security Bulletin* 39, no. 10 (Oct. 1976): 18–37. This survey asks respondents whether they have a limitation in the amount or kind of work they can do resulting from a chronic health condition lasting three months or longer; it does not ask respondents whether they think they meet programmatic criteria—i.e., inability to work at all due to a medical condition expected to last longer than twelve months.

2. Lando and Krute, "Disability Insurance," p. 6.

3. Daniel Price, "Three Aspects of the Relationship of Workmen's Compensation to Other Public Income-Maintenance Programs" in National Commission on State Workmen's Compensation Laws, *Supplemental Studies*, (Washington, D.C.: Government Printing Office, 1973), p. 310. For discussion of the various public surveys of the disabled, including the National Health Interview Survey, the Survey of Disabled Adults, and the Census, see Rita S. Gallin and Charles W. Given, "The Concept and Classification of Disability in Health Interview Surveys," *Inquiry* 13, no. 4 (Dec. 1976): 395–407; Berkowitz, Johnson, and Murphy, *Public Policy*, pp. 7–23.

4. Hannelore Dohrner, "Chronisch Kranke und Behinderte Patienten einer Chirurgischen Universtitätsklinik," Dissertation for Doctor of Philosophy, University of Hamburg, 1982, pp. 190–91.

5. See Lawrence Haber and Richard T. Smith, "Disability and Deviance: Normative Adaptations of Role Behavior," *American Sociological Review* 36 (Feb. 1971): 87–97, for a review and critique of this literature.

6. See David Mechanic, "Response Factors in Illness: The Study of Illness Behavior," *Social Psychiatry* 1 (1966): 11–20; M. J. Lefcowitz, "Poverty and Health: A Re-examination," *Inquiry* 10 (1973): 3–13; Earl Koos, *The Health of Regionville* (New York: Columbia University Press, 1954); Andrew Twaddle, "Health Decisions and Sick Role Variations," *Journal of Health and Social Behavior* 10 (1969): 105–15; Irving Zola, "Culture and Symptoms; an analysis of Patients' Presenting Complaints," *American Sociological Review* 31 (1966): 615–630; and Marek Zborowski, "Cultural Components in Response to Pain," *Journal of Social Issues* 8 (1952): 16–30.

7. For this approach, see Berkowitz, Johnson, and Murphy, *Public Policy*; Lando, Coate, and Kraus, "Disability Benefit Applications," pp. 3–10; and Burkhauser and Haveman, *Disability and Work.*

8. Howards, Brehm, and Nagi, *Disability*, ch. 4; Lando, Coate, and Kraus, "Disability Benefit Applications"; Lando and Krute, "Disability Insurance," pp. 12–13; J. Hambor, "Unemployment and Disability: An Econometric Analysis with Time Series Data," Staff Paper No. 20 (Washington, D.C.: Social Security Administration, Office of Research and Statistics, 1975).

9. For further references, see Deborah A. Stone, "Physicians as Gatekeepers," *Public Policy* 27, no. 3 (1979): 227–54; Judith Lorber, "Deviance as Performance," in Eliot Freidson and Judith Lorber, eds., *Medical Men and Their Work* (Chicago: Aldine, 1972), pp. 414–24.

10. For direct evidence of patient behavior, see Coates, "Assessment," pp. 210–17, documenting the fact that patients seeking disability compensation report more severe levels of dyspnea than other patients; W. K. Morgan, "Clinical Significance of Pulmonary Function Tests: Disability or Disinclination?" *Chest* 75, no. 6 (June 1975): 712–15; articles on detecting "true" pain, cited in ch. 4; and articles in medical journals, e.g., Fred Darvill, "Why I've Stopped Certifying Disability Claims," *Medical Economics* 54 (8 Aug. 1977): 224–26, and I. Rose, "Could That Patient Be Trying to Drive You Crazy?" *Medical Economics* 54 (7 Feb. 1977): 259–68.

11. On this point, see esp. Lipsky, *Street Level Bureaucracy*, pp. 164–65.

12. Goldsborough, et al., "SSA," pt. 1, pp. 168–71.

13. Agency procedure allows only an inference about official beliefs with regard to direct contact, but a survey of administrative law judges provides a more explicit statement: 92% of them said that their ability to judge pain and general credibility through face-to-face evaluations is a very important element of the hearing process. House Committee on Ways and Means,

Subcommittee on Social Security, 96th Cong., 1st sess., *Social Security Administrative Law Judges: Survey and Issue Paper*, 1979, p. 46.

14. In 1982, there was some discussion in Congress of limiting the right of applicants to introduce new medical evidence on appeal (*Congressional Quarterly*, 22 May 1982, p. 1178).

15. The best study on the effect of representation is William D. Popkin, "The Effect of Representation in Nonadversary Proceedings—A Study of Three Disability Programs," *Cornell Law Review* 62 (1977): pp. 989–1048. See also Frank Bloch, "Representation and Advocacy at Non-adversary Hearings," *Washington University Law Quarterly* 59, no. 2 (1981): 367–69; Jerry Mashaw, "The Management Side of Due Process," *Cornell Law Review* 59 (1974): 772–824, who disputes whether representation on appeal does much good (see p. 782, n. 26); see also, "Growth Industry: Disability Claim Cases under Social Security are a Boon to Lawyers," *Wall Street Journal*, Jan. 14, 1982, p. 1. The higher rate of awards on appeal, at least in Social Security, does not necessarily indicate that decisions at the appeal level are somehow more lenient; it may only indicate that those cases which are appealed are also the strongest cases. Nevertheless, the point here is that there is some payoff to aggressive self-promotion, and individual decisions to appeal denials constitute another form of pressure on the system.

16. See "Principles of Medical Ethics," *Judicial Opinions and Reports* (Chicago: American Medical Association, 1971), sec. I, subsecs. 7–9.

17. Dr. William Roemmich, testimony, in *Administration of Social Security Disability Insurance Program*, Hearings before the Subcommittee on the Administration of the Social Security Laws of House Committee on Ways and Means, 86th Cong., 1st. sess., 1959, p. 354, cited in Goldsborough, et al., "*SSA*," pt. 2, ch. 8, p. 10; emphasis added.

18. Both quotations are from speeches given at the Conference on "Medical Determinations in Workers' Compensation," sponsored by the American Society of Law and Medicine, Cambridge, Mass., December 3–4, 1981. For systems of distinguishing malingers in cases of low back pain, see Keim and Kirkaldy-Willis, "Low Back Pain," pp. 26–28; R. N. DeJong, *The Neurological Examination*, 4th ed. (Hagarstown, MD: Harper and Row, 1979; and Jack Bleich, "Back Pain Malingering: Legal and Medical Aspects" (American Health Consultants, 67 Peachtree Drive, Atlanta, Ga. 30309, 1983). For malingering in cases of respiratory disability, see Morgan, "Clinical Significance," pp. 712–25. For a general discussion of distinguishing true pain from faked pain in disability cases, see ch. 4.

19. See Thomas Scheff, "Decision Rules and Types of Error, and Their Consequences in Medical Diagnosis," *Behavioral Science* 8 (1963): 97–107; and Paul M. Gertman, "Physicians as Guiders of Health Services Use," in *Consumer Incentives for Health Care*, ed. Selma J. Mushkin (New York: Prodist, 1974), pp. 362–82.

20. Dr. William Roemmich, testimony in Ways and Means *Administra-*

tion of Social Security Disability Insurance Program 1959, 354; cited in Goldsborough, et al., "*SSA*," pt. 2, ch. 8, p. 10.

21. See Stone, "Gatekeepers," pp. 245–50.

22. It has often been suggested that the norms of psychiatrists and psychologists with respect to false positive and false negative errors are more like those of benefit-granting agencies: the professional attitude toward psychological disabilities is that it is therapeutically harmful for a patient to be labeled as sick. A whole school of "combat psychiatry" was built on this notion. See Arlene Kaplan Daniels, "Military Psychiatry: The Emergence of a Subspecialty," in Freidson and Lorber, eds., *Medical Men*, pp. 145–162. And, as one disability rights advocate has said, "Psychiatrists are astonishingly insensitive to the therapeutic benefits of having an income" (William Simon, personal communication, Sept. 1983).

23. Interview with author, Boston, Mass., Dec. 1981; (the interviewee requested anonymity).

24. In one case, the examiner dismissed the treating physician's opinion with the loaded comment: "It is appreciated that the opinions may have been honestly made in the light of the existing doctor-patient relationship." (Talley v. Flemming, 195 F. Supp. 264, cited in Goldsborough, et al., "*SSA*," pt. 1, p. 133; the general bias is identified by Goldsborough, et al., "*SSA*," pt. 1, pp. 132–33.

25. Gerald Haas, Lowell Reed, Jr., and Irvin Stander, "Presenting Medical Evidence in Workmen's Compensation Heart Cases," *Philadelphia Medicine* (Journal of the Philadelphia County Medical Society) 78, no. 6 (June 1982).

26. See Goldsborough et al., "*SSA*," pt. 2, ch. 7, pp. 7–18 for discussion of individual cases.

27. Kerner v. Flemming, 283 F.2d 916 (2d Cir. 1960).

28. This interpretation is made by Goldsborough, et al., "*SSA*;" pt. 2, ch. 1, p. 8. S. Rockman, *Judicial Review of Benefit Determinations in the Social Security and Veterans' Administration*, Report to the Committee on Grants and Benefits, Administrative Conference of the United States (Washington, D.C.: Government Printing Office, 1970), p. 37; Robert Dixon, *Social Security Disability and Mass Justice* (New York: Praeger, 1973), pp. 95–96. It is generally followed by subsequent studies of disability insurance, including Berkowitz, Johnson, and Murphy, *Public Policy*; Howards, Brehm, and Nagi, *Disability*.

29. Kerner v. Flemming, 283 F.2d 916 (2d Cir. 1960), 922.

30. Hall v. Celebrezze, 314 F.2d. 718 (4th Cir. 1967).

31. House Ways and Means Committee, Rept. on H.R. 12080, 90th Cong., 2d sess., H.R. 544, 1967, p. 28.

32. Social Security Act, sec. 223(d)(2)(a), emphasis added; cited in Ways and Means, *Disability Insurance Program*, 1974, p. 117.

33. Berkowitz, Johnson, and Murphy, *Public Policy*, p. 56.

34. See Rockman, *Judicial Review*, p. 27.

35. See esp. Donald Horowitz, *The Courts and Social Policy* (Washington, D.C.: Brookings, 1977), ch. 2, for the most comprehensive exposition of this approach. This is also Liebman's explanation ("Definition of Disability," pp. 845–46) for the high rate of reversals of Social Security decisions.

36. Ibid., p. 846.

37. The legal phrases are as follows: for Worker's Compensation, a claimant needs to show that injury "arises in the course of or out of employment"; for SSA, a claimant needs to show that he cannot work "by reason of physical or mental impairment."

38. For this discussion, I draw primarily on Douglas Danner and Elliot Segall, "Medical Causation: A Source of Professional Misunderstanding," *American Journal of Law and Medicine* 3 (1977): 303–8; William Prosser, *Handbook of The Law of Torts*, 4th ed. (St. Paul: West Publishing Co., 1970), ch. 7.

39. See, e.g., Lester B. Lave and Eugene P. Sleskin, "Epidemiology, Causality, and Public Policy," *American Scientist* vol. 57 (1979): 178–186; King, *Medical Thinking*, chs. 9, 10.

40. In general, the standard of proof in civil law, of which negligence is a part, is "a preponderance of the evidence." In criminal law the standard is "beyond a reasonable doubt."

41. Howards, Brehm, and Nagi, *Disability*, pp. 86–87.

42. This point is made very persuasively in Ibid., pp. 113–14, though in a different context.

43. See Goldsborough, et al., "SSA," pt. 1, pp. 144–148.

44. The SSA's decision to use the average man approach is stated most clearly in its 1967 *Disability Insurance Manual:* "It is ordinarily justifiable to conclude that an individual who is not working and has [a listed] impairment is unable to work by reason of his medical impairments. Thus, where an individual's impairment or a combination of impairments equals or exceeds the level of severity described in the listing, inability to engage in any substantial gainful activity should be found on a basis of the medical facts, in the absence of evidence to the contrary, e.g., the actual performance of substantial gainful activity" (paragraph 321c, cited in Berkowitz, Johnson, and Murphy, *Public Policy*, p. 59). Herbert Blumenfeld, the current Chief Medical Consultant for Social Security, notes that "of course the listings are an average man concept, but since they only *allow* [eligibility], who would complain?" (interview with author December 1983, Baltimore, Md.).

45. Randall v. Flemming, 192 F. Supp. 111, W.D. Mich. (1969), p. 128.

46. Ber v. Calebrezze, 332 F.2d. 293, 296 (2d Cir. 1964), cited in Liebman, p. 844, emphasis added.

47. One could also see the courts' predilection to accept subjective information as a reflection of its statutory construction function: Congress said it wanted individualized determinations, and the courts are holding Congress to its word. Early in the history of the Social Security program, the court

expressed its view that "the Act is concerned not with a standard man of ordinary and customary abilities, but with the particular person who may claim its benefits and the effect of the impairment upon that person, with whatever abilities or inabilities he has" (Dunn v. Folsom, 166 F. Supp. 44, (1958), cited in Goldsborough, et al., "*SSA*," pt. 2, ch. 1, p. 3. However, the courts clearly did not feel bound by strict statutory construction when confronted with the issues raised by Kerner and the 1967 amendments, so this explanation loses persuasiveness, even though the courts sometimes justified their reasoning in terms of the statute. Also, the courts' insistence on consideration of individual experience and rejection of the average man approach was evident long before the Social Security program; this legal philosophy was quite clear and explicit in several cases involving War Risk Insurance, beginning as early as 1923 (see Goldsborough, et al., "*SSA*," pt. 1, pp. 322–23). It would seem that judicial willingness to consider subjective experience is better explained by the legal propensity to deal with the specific facts of each case than by the courts' role in statutory construction.

48. In this paragraph, I draw on Goldsborough, et al., "*SSA*," pt. 1, pp. 478–83.

49. Goldsborough, et al., "*SSA*," pt. 1, p. 481. The stance of courts portrayed here has been true for commercial insurance disputes in general, not simply disability insurance. See Geary D. Cortes, "Jarchow v. Transamerica Title Insurance Co.: A Trend Toward Strict Liability for Emotional Distress in the Insurance Industry, " *California Western Law Review* 12 (1976): 591–613. Courts assume that people buy insurance to protect themselves against risk of loss, not for commercial gain, and they are thereby seeking "peace of mind and security." Recognizing the disparity of bargaining power and the inability of most consumers to understand the technical language of policies, the courts have looked to the "reasonable expectation of the public when enforcing insurance contracts" (Cortes, "Strict Liability," p. 23.

50. Cited earlier in ch. 2; the case was Marshall v. Metropolitan Life Ins. Co., 164 So. 441 (1935).

51. Liebman, "Definition of Disability," pp. 838–39, 846–47.

52. Klimaszewski v. Flemming, 176 F. Supp. 927, E.D. Pa., (1959); other cases in which the court focused on its interpretation of the intentions of Congress to be remedial include: Yendes v. Flemming (Mich. 1961), cited in Goldsborough, et al., "*SSA*," pt. 2, ch. 1, p. 6 ("As . . . the Social Security Act is remedial in nature, it should not be given a strict construction. . . . The courts should construe that act liberally in favor of the party claiming its benefits . . ."); Hockenbury v. Ribicoff, 199 F. Supp. 666 E.D. Pa. (1961) (rejects notion that a person is not entitled to benefits unless he is "a hopeless mental and physical wreck," on grounds that such was not "the purpose of the Act nor the intention of Congress.")

53. Howards, Brehm, and Nagi, *Disability*, pp. 68–75.

54. Ibid., pp. 75–80; Lando, Coate, and Kraus, "Disability Benefit Ap-

plications"; Mordecai Lando, "Demographic Characteristics of Disability Applicants: Relationship to Allowances," *Social Security Bulletin* 39 (May 1976): 15–23; Emanuel, "Factors."

55. Janice D. Halpern, "The Social Security Disability Insurance Program: Reasons for Its Growth and Prospects for the Future," *New England Economic Review* (Boston: Federal Reserve Bank, May/June 1979), p. 39.

56. There is some empirical support for this proposition in the Social Security program. Lando and Krute ("Disability Insurance," p. 7) found that as the rate of applications increased, the proportion of initial allowances decreased.

57. Commissioner Cardwell noted in testimony during 1976 that in the previous ten years, as the rate of initial denials on Social Security disability claims went up slightly, there was a 400% increase in requests for reconsideration (an administrative procedure) and a 500% increase in the number of hearings (Ways and Means, *Disability Insurance Program* 1976, p. 276).

58. Lando and Krute ("Disability Insurance," p. 7) found that during the period 1969 to 1974, when the program was growing rapidly, the biggest relative increase in allowances came at the administrative hearing and appeals levels, rather than at the level of initial determinations. For the Social Security Disability insurance program during 1979, 57% of all OASDI disability decisions and 53% of all concurrent OASDI and SSI disability cases brought to hearing were reversed by the administrative law judge. Over 40% of all OASDI and SSI cases brought to federal district courts were remanded to the agency for further administrative proceedings; fewer than 10% were reversed outright. U.S. Dept. of HEW, Social Security Administration, Office of Hearings and Appeals, OHA Fact Sheet for Fiscal Year 1979, published 1980, cited in Frank Bloch, "Representation and Advocacy," p. 351.

59. This seems to be the import of the Lando and Krute findings cited in n. 58.

60. See Dixon, *Mass Justice*, pp. 53–59; also Ways and Means *Disability Insurance Program* 1976, p. 22, chart 7.

Basis for Disability Allowance		
	1960	1975
Meets listings	70%	28.7%
Equals listings	20%	44.9%
Vocational factors	10%	26.2%

The exactitude of these figures has been disputed, but not the general trend.

61. See Dixon, *Mass Justice*, pp. 58–61.

62. Code of Federal Regulations 401 and 1381.

63. Alan Goldhammer, "The Effect of New Vocational Regulations on

Social Security and Supplemental Security Income Disability Claims," *Administrative Law Review* 32 (Summer 1980): 501–10. The author, an administrative law judge presiding over disability claims, asserts that the new regulations will probably lead to findings of disability in claimants who would not previously have been found disabled.

64. Dept. of HEW, Social Security Administration, Rules for Adjudicating Disability Claims in Which Vocational Factors Must Be Considered, 1976. Reprinted in Ways and Means, *Disability Insurance Program*, 1976, pp. 166–265, quotation is from pp. 184–85; emphasis added.

65. Ibid., p. 185; emphasis added.

66. James B. Cardwell, written replies included with his testimony of May 21, 1976, *Disability Insurance Program* 1976, p. 290.

67. Goldhammer, "Vocational Regulations," p. 507.

68. Halberstadt and Haveman, "Public Policies," p. 107. See also Haveman, Halberstadt, and Burkhauser, *Public Policy*, ch. 5.

69. Halberstadt and Haveman, "Public Policies," p. 109. Israel is an exception to this pattern, but apparently for reasons that are quite consistent with the theory that disability programs were used to disguise unemployment of older workers during the recession of the 1970s.

70. Howards, Brehm, and Nagi, *Disability*, ch. 4.

71. Berglind, "Pension or Work?" p. 191.

72. Georges Midré, "Market Forces," p. 11.

73. Haveman, Halberstadt, and Burkhauser, *Public Policy*, ch. 5.

74. See Herbert Simon, *The Sciences of the Artificial* (Cambridge, Mass.: MIT Press, 1969) for a defense of this kind of reasoning. Simon argues that sometimes the assumption that a system behaves as if it had some purpose can help us predict the behavior of the system, regardless of whether it really has a purpose in the sense of conscious intention.

75. See Lois Copeland, "Defining Disability," pp. 15–17.

Chapter 6

1. For examples of this type of analysis, see Lando and Krute, "Disability Insurance," p. 10; Halpern, "Disability Insurance Program," pp. 36–39; Emanuel, "Factors," pp. 41–60.

2. For a description of exactly the same verbal campaign in the area of health care reform in the 1960s, see Robert Alford, *Health Care Politics* (Chicago: Univ. of Chicago Press, 1976).

3. See several reports of the General Accounting Office, Washington, D.C.: "The Social Security Administration Should Provide More Management and Leadership in Determining Who Is Eligible for Social Security Benefits" (17 Aug. 1976); "The Social Security Administration Needs to Improve Its Disability Claims Process" (16 Feb. 1978); "A Plan for Improving the Disability Determination Process by Bringing It Under Complete Fed-

eral Management Should be Developed" (31 Aug. 1978); "Controls Over Medical Examinations Necessary for the Social Security Administration to Better Determine Disability" (9 Oct. 1979). James W. Singer, "It Isn't Easy to Cure Ailments of Disability Program," *National Journal*, 6 May 1978.

4. Irving K. Zola, *Missing Pieces* (Philadelphia: Temple Univ. Press, 1982). This book is also excellent for conveying some of the myriad ways that disabled people are stigmatized.

5. Copeland, "Defining Disability."

6. "Paying for Stress on the Job," *Dun's Business Month*, Jan. 1982, p. 72.

7. "Stress Induced Illness Ruled a Job Disability," *Boston Globe*, 5 May 1979, p. 1.

8. *Congressional Quarterly*, 9 Feb. 1980, p. 347.

9. This is the essence of Liebman's analysis ("Definition of Disability," p. 866) of the Supplemental Security Income program, in which he argues that the boundaries of SSI reflect a moral judgment. He concludes that if the purpose of SSI (and by implication, similar programs) is to create a category of moral worth, to define a social group of people who cannot work for legitimate reasons, then the medical definition of inability to work used by SSI is too narrow; "the bounds of the categories must be tested against a larger scheme of shared values."

10. Congress defined children with a "learning disability" as those "who have a disorder in one or more of the basic psychological processes involved in understanding or in using language, written or spoken" (Public Law 91-230, 1970). The term "developmental disability" has had several definitions. It was first a euphemism for "mental retardation" in much the same way as "physically challenged" is used as a nonstigmatizing term for "handicapped." The Congressional definition includes disabilities attributable also to cerebral palsy, epilepsy, or "other substantially handicapping chronic neurological conditions either closely related to mental retardation or requiring similar treatment" (Developmental Disabilities Services and Bill of Rights Act, 1975; Arnold Capute, "Developmental Disabilities: An Overview," *Dental Clinics of North America* 18 [July 1974]: 557–77).

11. John J. Dempsey, "Defining, Classifying, and Serving Handicapped Children," in E. Berkowitz, ed., *Disability Policies*, p. 77.

12. Ellie McGrath, "Don't Call It a Disease", *Time*, 6 Sept. 1982, p. 58; emphasis added.

13. See J. V. Warren and Janet Wolter, "Symptoms and Diseases Induced by the Physician," *General Practitioner* 9 (1954): 77–84; M. L. Hampton et al. "Sickle Cell 'Nondisease,': A Potentially Serious Public Health Problem," *American Journal of Diseases of Childhood* 128 (1974): 58–61; Abraham Bergman and S. F. Stamm, "The Morbidity of Cardiac Non-disease in School Children," *New England Journal of Medicine* 276 (1977): 1008–1013; and R. Brian Haynes, et al., "Increased Absenteeism

from Work After Detection and Labeling of Hypertensive Patients," *New England Journal of Medicine* 299 (1978): 741–744.

14. In order to mitigate this problem, most states have "second" or "subsequent injury laws." Where an employee has already been injured and compensated once, these laws limit the liability of a second employer to the costs of the "extra" disability caused by a subsequent injury. This policy has led to very complicated rules for the apportionment of costs and to voluminous litigation about apportionment. One study estimated that within thirty days of a state court's ruling *not* to allow apportionment of costs, "between seven and eight thousand one-eyed, one-legged, one-armed and one-handed men were displaced" (U.S. Bureau of Labor Statistics Bulletin no. 536 (1931), p. 272, cited in *Equity Eroded: The Disintegration of Workers' Compensation Policies* (Berkeley, Calif.: Institute for Local Self-Government, 1977), p. 27.

15. See esp. Polanyi, *Transformation*; E. P. Thompson, *The Making of the English Working Class* (New York: Random House, 1963).

16. Scull, *Museums*, p. 38.

17. Senator Edward Kennedy's office estimated that he received one to two calls a day of this nature before the Social Security Disability Insurance crackdown in 1980, and fifty to sixty calls a week in 1982 (Alan Lupo, "Shame: Death by Regulation and other Social Security Tragedies," Boston *Phoenix*, 26 Jan. 1982, p. 6). And the Social Security Administration has several hundred employees who devote their time to answering Congressional inquiries on behalf of constituents (Jerry L. Mashaw, *Bureaucratic Justice: Managing Social Security Disablity Claims* [New Haven: Yale Univ. Press, 1983], p. 71.)

18. Mashaw, *Bureaucratic Justice*, p. 20.

19. Robert A. Scott, *The Making of Blind Men* (New York: Russell Sage Foundation, 1969).

20. Ibid., p. 72.

21. Ibid., p. 74.

22. The list of disease-specific political interest groups bears out these general observations. It includes the American Cancer Society, American Diabetes Association, American Foundation for the Blind, National Federation for the Blind, National Society for the Prevention of Blindness, American Hearing Society, American Heart Association, Arthritis and Rheumatism Foundation, Muscular Dystrophy Association, National Multiple Sclerosis Society, National Paraplegia Foundation, National Tuberculosis Association, and United Cerebral Palsy Association.

23. For a fascinating analysis of the heart legislation and its judicial expansion in California, see Institute for Local Self-Government, *Equity Eroded*.

24. The provision is in Section 504 of the Rehabilitation Act of 1973. A comprehensive analysis of the implementation of this section primarily as a civil rights measure can be found in Richard Scotch, "Section 504: The Crea-

tion of Civil Rights for the Disabled," Ph.D. diss., Harvard Univ., 1982.

25. Lawrence Mosher, "Job Rights for Drunks, Addicts?" *National Observer*, 15 Jan. 1977.

26. See James O'Connor, *The Fiscal Crisis of the State* (New York: Saint Martin's, 1973); Organization for Economic Cooperation and Development, *Welfare States in Crisis* (Paris: OECD, 1981); Offe, *Contradictions.*

27. See N. Keyfitz, "Why Social Security is in Trouble," *Public Interest* No. 58 (1980): 102–19; Caroll Estes, "Social Security: The Social Construction of a Crisis," *Milbank Memorial Fund Quarterly/Health and Society* vol. 61, no. 3 (1983): 445–61; and John F. Myles, "Conflict, Crisis, and The Future of Old Age Security," *Milbank Memorial Fund Quarterly/Health and Society* vol. 61, no. 3 (1983): 462–72.

28. Offe, *Contradictions*, p. 131.

29. Ibid., p. 132.

30. See e.g., Ibid., ch. 8; Adam Przeworski, "Material Bases of Consent: Economics and Politics in a Hegemonic System," in Morris Zeitlin, ed., *Political Power and Social Theory*, vol. I (Greenwich, Conn.: JAI Press, 1980), pp. 21–66.

31. The pioneering author of this version is O'Connor, *Fiscal Crisis.*

32. Samuel Bowles and Herbert Gintis, "The Crisis of Liberal Democratic Capitalism: The Case of the United States," *Politics and Society* 11, no. 1 (1982): 51–93.

33. Ibid., p. 75 and Table 6. Bowles and Gintis argue that the post–World War II welfare state is predicated on an "accord" between capital and labor whose chief result has been a redistribution of the total social product toward labor. All of the increase for labor is attributable to a growth in *social expenditures* (what they call "citizen wages" or what I would call "need-based redistribution") rather than wages. Such expenditures grew from 8 percent of total output in 1948 to 19 percent in 1978.

34. Fred Block, "The Ruling Class Does Not Rule: Notes on the Marxist Theory of the State," *Socialist Revolutions* 7 (May/June 1977): 6–28.

35. Frances Fox Piven and Richard Cloward, *The New Class War: Reagan's Attack on the Welfare State and Its Consequences* (New York: Pantheon, 1982); Offe, *Contradictions*, p. 127.

36. Offe, *Contradictions*, p. 132.

37. Rarely, the opposite is true: the medical profession adopts as its norm the conventional wisdom of a lay group. The influence of the women's self-help movement, particularly on medical practices in pregnancy and birth, has been very strong.

Index